SURVIVAL
AND
REGENERATION

SURVIVAL
AND
REGENERATION

DETROIT'S AMERICAN INDIAN COMMUNITY

EDMUND JEFFERSON DANZIGER. JR

WAYNE STATE UNIVERSITY PRESS   DETROIT

Library of Congress Cataloging-in-Publication Data

Danziger, Edmund Jefferson, 1938–
  Survival and regeneration : Detroit's American Indian community /
Edmund Jefferson Danziger, Jr.
    p. cm. — (Great Lakes books)
  Includes bibliographical references and index.
  ISBN 978-0-8143-4332-6 (alk. paper); ISBN 978-0-8143-4333-3 (ebook)
  1. Indians of North America—Michigan—Detroit Region—Urban
residence. 2. Indians of North America—Michigan—Detroit Region—
Social conditions. 3. Indians of North America—Michigan—Detroit
Region—Economic conditions. I. Title. II. Series.
E78.M6D36 1991
305.897'077434—dc20   90-29857

Book design by Mary Primeau

NATIONAL ENDOWMENT FOR THE
Humanities

THE
ANDREW W.
MELLON
FOUNDATION

The publication of this volume in a freely accessible digital format has been
made possible by a major grant from the National Endowment for the
Humanities and the Mellon Foundation through their Humanities Open
Book Program.

http://wsupress.wayne.edu/

FOR MY CHILDREN,
JOHN DAVID AND ANNE ELIZABETH,
AND FOR MY BROTHER DOUG'S FAMILY

⟩⟩⟩ CONTENTS ⟨⟨⟨

⟫⟫ ABBREVIATIONS ⟨⟨

AID   Associated Indians of Detroit

AIS   American Indian Services

BIA   Bureau of Indian Affairs

CETA   Comprehensive Employment and Training Act

DAIC   Detroit American Indian Center

DIECC Detroit Indian Educational and Cultural Center

GED   General Educational Development (a high school equivalency certificate)

HEW   United States Department of Health, Education and Welfare

LEA   Local Educational Agency

MESC Michigan Employment Security Commission

NAIA   North American Indian Association of Detroit

NIAAA National Institute on Alcohol Abuse and Alcoholism

PI   Personal interview with the author

SEMI   South Eastern Michigan Indians

SH   Self-help group therapy for Indian alcoholics

WIRC   Walpole Island Research Centre

>>> PREFACE <<<

Interviews can be nerve-racking, especially when much is at stake. While driving north to Detroit on a spring morning in 1977, I was worried about an appointment with Dean George. Several times he had delayed our meeting. I persisted because the fate of my project—writing a history of Detroit's native American community—was in the balance. Somehow I had to penetrate the well-founded cynicism of George and other urban Indians if I were to get firsthand knowledge of their experiences. The key was Dean George: a respected elder, past president of the North American Indian Association of Detroit, and former director of the Detroit American Indian Center. When I arrived at his home, we met in the kitchen and over coffee talked history. He listened patiently as I expressed belief in the relevance of my study for the people of Detroit and southeastern Michigan. George remained noncommittal; but a conference was arranged with several staff members of the downtown Indian center. For two hours I described my plan, outwardly calm but inwardly apprehensive that the promising proposal would be thwarted. The listeners, who were less than effusive, nevertheless gave tacit permission for weekly visits to see what I could learn from native peoples who frequented the center. New life was breathed into the project.

For years I had been concerned about the paucity of scholarship on urban Indians. Most studies—articles and dissertations by geographers, sociologists, and anthropologists—lacked the historical dimension. Furthermore, the American Indian Policy Review Commission reported to Congress in 1977 that 45 percent of the nation's Indians, perhaps half a million, lived off the reservations. For most of this century they were "invisible" despite their pressing economic and social needs and their historic importance, neglected by Washington as well as by scholars. The Review Commission observed that one of the greatest obstacles faced by native peoples in their "drive for self-determination and a place in this Nation is the American public's ignorance ... of the status of the American Indian in our society today." For Indian leaders and government officials at all levels to comprehend fully the present condition of urban native Americans, histories of these groups must be available.

Detroit's Indian community has been one of the most important. Its population was large—5,207 in 1970. In that year the census documented that native socioeconomic levels were shockingly low and generally typical of conditions found among other Indians in such cities as Chicago, Denver, and Albuquerque. Yet there were no in-depth historical studies of any of them. Thus I was determined to write a history for Detroit.

From the start I sought answers to three fundamental questions:

1. How did twentieth-century federal Indian policy foster out-migration from Great Lakes reservations to Detroit?
2. Among rural Indians who cut themselves off from the Bureau of Indian Affairs programs and moved to the Motor City during the past ninety years to find a better life, how many became victims of cultural disorientation, poor health, and poverty—and why?
3. More recently, how have Indian-organized and Indian-staffed programs, financed largely by federal self-determination grants, solved these and other pressing problems?

Authentic answers could not be found simply by consulting reference books, government records, newspapers and magazines, or legal documents. Only by listening to Indians could I get close to the bone of individual experience and explore sensitive subjects with the people involved. Only by allowing Indians to speak for themselves could I learn how native peoples viewed their past and envisioned their future needs and aspirations.

Permission to gather information at the Detroit American Indian Center beginning in 1977 sparked a lengthy and rewarding journey of discovery. My procedure was to tell the Indians who I was, my reason for being in Detroit, and what I wished from them. Then I frequented the center and other Indian gathering places—becoming, over time, a participant-observer, a marginal native. I met hundreds of Detroit Indians during the ensuing decade. Several friendly informants patiently submitted to extensive discussions over a period of years. These Indians opened to me their personal lives as well as those of family and friends—in Detroit and on their home reservations. They also shared critical historical documents from their files and those of several Indian centers. This cooperation enabled me to capture something of the heritage of Detroit's colorful and important Indian community.

I say "something," of the heritage for good reason. It was impossible, within a reasonable length of time, to meet, count, and interview most of Detroit's Indians. Native Americans were the city's most "invisible" minority group—so mobile and dispersed throughout the metropolitan area that not even the Indian organizations knew where they all lived. Among those with whom I did establish contact, many were too suspicious to communicate or reluctant to discuss certain subjects. Even those willing to talk shunned the tape recorder and notebook. Moreover, humanistic and ethical considerations demanded that informants—still alive and vulnerable—be shielded from the consequences of revealing embarrassing and incriminating data. Sources for contemporary studies, besides being incomplete and somewhat restricted, were still "hot." In handling them the scholar risked "burning" himself and his subjects. How much more comfortable it would have been to wait fifty or a hundred years for the twentieth-century Detroit Indian story to "cool off" a little. But if cautious scholars hung back, much evidence—the memories of native people—would be lost. Nor was waiting the answer for urban Indians, who needed and wanted to know their history during the post-World War II period.

The history presented in this volume is at base a success story. Indian migration to Detroit from rural reservations in Michigan and elsewhere began about the turn of the century and greatly increased during the fifties and sixties, thanks to an aggressive federal relocation program and the lack of job opportunities on the reservations. The Chippewa, Cherokee, Iroquois, and Sioux nations contributed the largest number to Detroit's burgeoning native community. Cut off from the Bureau of Indian Affairs services, many newcomers had difficulty establishing

13

themselves successfully in the city and experienced feelings of insecurity and powerlessness. By 1970 they were a minority of minorities in the Motor City, plagued with persistent health-care needs, cramped and unhealthy living conditions, little control over the education of their children, and high unemployment. Amid these crises, several forceful and farsighted native American leaders emerged and drafted grant proposals, hoping to secure assistance from Washington. (There had been a dramatic policy shift toward Indian self-determination under the Nixon administration. A host of federal programs encouraged and helped Indians to strike out on their own while retaining cultural ties.) Government help, rather than domination, triggered a "great awakening" among native American Detroiters. A half dozen Indian centers sprang up to minister to the community's wide-ranging needs, providing job and health programs and places where natives could gather socially. By 1980 this self-determination initiative had only begun its assault on intractable community problems. Nevertheless, significant progress had been made. Compared with reservation relatives, Detroit Indians enjoyed better housing, higher educational achievement, less unemployment, and greater average family incomes.

It is hoped that this book will help non-Indian city planners, teachers, social workers, and citizens understand better their Indian neighbors: why they moved to the city, what they endured during the painful adjustment process, how many of them triumphed while preserving their Indian identity, and what some of their hopes for the future are. Perhaps, too, Indians as well as non-Indians will be reminded of how much they share—not simply as fellow Detroiters but as human beings.

An ambitious project of long duration can be sustained only by time, money, and much cooperation and understanding. I am grateful for a research fellowship from the National Endowment for the Humanities and a research leave from Bowling Green State University. Bowling Green's history department and the William T. Jerome Library staff also gave noteworthy support. My colleague, Prof. Lawrence J. Friedman, and Margaret Christy Danziger, my wife, reviewed a rough draft of the manuscript and made excellent suggestions for strengthening it. Judy Gilbert, a secretary of the history department, typed the final version with great care and concern. As always my children, stalwart and loving, encouraged Dad's research despite his many absences from home.

Most deserving of thanks are the Great Lakes native peoples, who never failed to impress me with their warmth, generosity, deep sense of history, and pride in their heritage. I have quoted them at length hoping to illustrate these qualities. Special assistance was provided by several Indian center directors and program heads: Dean George; Harry Command (American Indian Services); Dean Jacobs (Walpole Island Research Centre); Judy Mays (Detroit Indian Educational and Cultural Center); Bill Memberto and Chris Bell (Indian Health Center); Fred Boyd (Native American Strategic Services); and Rose Silvey, Irene Lowry, Frank Alberts, Louise Morales (Detroit American Indian Center). May this book be worthy of their trust.

⟩⟩⟩ PROLOGUE ⟨⟨⟨
Survival and Regeneration

The fourth Friday in September is Michigan Indian Day, a state holiday. Delegations from communities across the state and the province of Ontario gather for refreshments at the Detroit American Indian Center; then they join hundreds of local native residents for the march south along Woodward Avenue toward the Detroit River. A mounted-police escort clears automobile traffic in their path. First come honored Indian veterans—of World War II, Korea, Vietnam—followed by the Oneida marching band and by scenic floats and decorated cars that represent Indian groups. The cavalcade extends for three city blocks. Eventually it draws up at a designated park where a minipowwow is staged. Native American speakers and state officials also commemorate the occasion. Afternoon passersby, interrupted by the parade or drawn by the rhythmic drum beats, marvel at the presence of so many exuberant Indians: outfitted in colorful traditional garb, proud yet hospitable, and seemingly united.[1] One curbside native American was particularly impressed: "The pride I myself felt as our youth and veterans passed by on Woodward caught me off guard and I was actually overwhelmed, it filled my heart as well as my eyes with a great amount of joy and respect for all. As I paused and reflected on many things once again my thoughts were reaffirmed. I am very proud to be a NATIVE AMERICAN!!!"[2]

16

The importance of Detroit's American Indian community is not limited to an annual parade and riverside festival. In 1980 federal census takers recorded 12,487 native persons in the metropolitan area, an impressive figure, even though Indian leaders claimed their people had been grossly undercounted.[3] Many had obtained a good education, a suburban home, and meaningful, sustaining work. Theirs was a success story. Other Detroit Indians, less fortunate, became trapped below the poverty level in inner-city ghettos. Yet special assistance was provided for them in the 1970s by native-run organizations like the Detroit American Indian Center, which had a large staff and an average annual budget of $700,000.[4]

I

Natives were hardly newcomers to the area. "Indians have always been in Detroit," insisted Winona Arriaga, a Chippewa woman, to a surprised television talk show host during a February 1979 interview for a series on the city's newest immigrant groups.[5] Historical documents verified this. When the La Salle expedition pushed up the Detroit River in 1679, it sighted a large Indian village.[6] Twenty-two years later the French established a command post (Fort Pontchartrain) at this strategic riverside location. Indian groups came in to trade; some even built homes nearby so that by 1736 the outpost's natives exceeded five hundred Hurons, Ottawas, and Potawatomis. Even after the withdrawal of the French in the 1760s, the large Indian population in what is today southeastern Michigan was powerful enough to manipulate Britain and the United States into bestowing bountiful provisions and presents. This balance-of-power diplomacy ended with the War of 1812, whereupon white frontier pressure forced the tribes to cede holdings in Michigan's Lower Peninsula and fall back to a few northern reservations. Some warriors and their families found refuge with Canadian cousins. Thus the *Detroit Free Press* could comment by April 1853:

> INDIANS.— We noticed four aborigines yesterday, on seeing whom we could not but reflect on the great changes that have taken place in our city in fifteen years. In 1838, a person, by merely glancing through almost any street, could see parties of these children of the forest scattered throughout its entire length. Many were the Indian dances that took place, about that

time, near Woodworth's Hotel, on the corner of Brush and Woodbridge streets; and horrible were the grimaces and discordant the yells, of the dusky-featured performers, as they hopped and writhed with the utmost agility, destitute, as they were, of nearly every article of clothing. Now, it is comparatively rarely that one of them is to be seen. They are almost all gone, and in a short time, their former existence among us will we know only through the medium of tradition. Farewell, "Injuns" "Nitchees," a long farewell!

Not until the twentieth century did native Americans return in substantial numbers. This time, rather than bringing furs and other forest products to trade, they came as skilled and unskilled laborers searching for work, which did not exist in their destitute home communities.

II

Michigan cession treaties did more than arrange for tribal emigration beyond the Mississippi and the establishment of reservations for the Chippewas and Ottawas left behind; they provided for a cultural transformation of the Chippewas and Ottawas through a program of technical assistance and education. Civilization of the Indian, it was hoped, would improve his economic and social situation, restore peace to the troubled Northwest frontier after the War of 1812, and free the Bureau of Indian Affairs (BIA) of a financial burden.

Meanwhile, for thousands of Canadian Indians, especially those just east of Michigan, the advent of Europeans was equally momentous. Both groups benefited at first; then transactions became woefully lopsided. Dependence on the fur trade undermined the economic self-sufficiency of many tribes, once so fiercely independent. During the seventeenth and eighteenth centuries, European imperialists pushed Indian allies into a series of bloody colonial wars for dominance in North America and caused, as one historian observed, a "breaking down of the old [Indian] social order, of the systems of law, government, and religion on which their societies rested." In the nineteenth century the expansion westward of many white farmers forced Indian cessions of vast land holdings. Ultimately they were confined to 226 reserves across Canada, where aggressive agents employed many of the same methods used by the BIA in Michigan to destroy traditional Indian cultures.[7]

A tragic result of this assault became obvious on both sides of the border by the mid-twentieth century. Native peoples were unemployed, ill-housed, undereducated, politically enfeebled, and patronized by innumerable federal functionaries. "The opportunity to live in decency and dignity is based on a sound economic system," proclaimed the authors of a study of Michigan's Isabella Indian reservation. "When there is economic instability, personal tragedy is the result.... For the Tribal Council to solve major social problems, it must first be able to rely on a stable economy within the Indian community." Yet 34.7 percent of the Chippewas actively seeking work were unemployed. Two-thirds of the Isabella households had an annual income of eight thousand dollars or less, and only 61 percent of their moneys derived from salaries, wages, self-employment, rents, and dividends; the rest came from pensions, unemployment compensation, and public assistance programs.[8] At Keweenaw Bay in the Upper Peninsula, 1970 statistics likewise demonstrated that economic deprivation was the major problem facing tribal officials. Compared with a statewide unemployment rate of less than 7 percent, the figure for adult Chippewas was three times as high. Seventy-eight percent of Keweenaw Bay Indian families had incomes of five thousand dollars or less, though for Michigan residents generally it was only 15 percent.[9]

On the Canadian Indian reserve of Walpole Island, located on the St. Clair River delta twenty miles south of Sarnia, Ontario, poverty among its eighteen hundred residents was equally pronounced—and tragic. By the 1970s farming no longer furnished a significant economic base, and there was a chronic lack of jobs on the reserve. An unemployment rate of 60 percent plagued the predominantly unskilled Indian workers. Reserve housing stock, mirroring its owners' financial plight, was short more than eighty homes. This sometimes forced two or three families to share a building. Poor sanitation precipitated serious health problems, especially among the children. Moreover, too many quit school after grade ten and thus deprived themselves of job opportunities.[10] Hence, just as in Michigan, the vicious reservation poverty cycle continued.

To escape the welfare rolls of rural communities like Walpole Island, more and more Indians moved to cities for employment and a better life. When Lewis Meriam's investigators asked about the reasons for urban relocations in the United States in the 1920s, they "almost invariably met with the answer, in one form or another, from every migrated Indian man questioned: 'No way to make a living on the reservation.' The alternative was starvation or pauperism."[11] O. D. and Marjorie Armstrong visited reserves throughout the Far West during the summer of 1954, and everywhere saw "the tragedy of ... underdevelopment for men and women anxious to work." When the Armstrongs asked some Chicago Indians why they had left their traditional homeland, the response of Charley Gray Fox was typical: "Me—I'm tired of little jobs around Rosebud. I want a regular pay check!"[12] Native Americans in the cities were also a major concern of Congress's American Indian Policy Review Commission. Aware of the lack of job opportunities in rural areas and of the many migrants to cities who were in the prime employment ages of twenty to forty, the commission concluded in 1977 that "increasing numbers of Indians are moving from rural Indian communities and reservations [in the United States] primarily to seek employment."[13]

The same generalizations applied across the border to reserves like Walpole Island. By 1977, when one-third of Canada's registered (status) Indians lived off the reserves and mainly in large cities of more than 100,000, a report of Canada's National Indian Brotherhood remarked: "Observers of Indian migration all agree that the primary factor in migration is the push factor of no employment in most Indian communities." As in the states, the largest emigration clearly took place among the prime employment ages (twenty-five to forty-five).[14] A survey team on Walpole Island discovered in 1965 that 43 percent of the male population between sixteen and sixty-five years of age had left the reserve. Thirteen years later, 26 percent of the total band members still did not reside on the island.[15]

Indian immigration to urban areas became a trend of increasing significance. The United States census for 1910 noted 12,000 off-reservation tribesmen. During the next decade this rose by 3,000 persons. The twenties saw their numbers more than double—to 33,000—and the influential Meriam Report of 1928, a nationwide survey of Indian conditions, devoted a lengthy section to "Migrated Indians" living in such cities as Los Angeles, Phoenix, Albuquerque and Santa Fe, Minneapolis, and Milwaukee. The expansion of native American urban populations from 1930 to 1960 (146,000) was a little more than four-fold. Another dramatic increase occurred in the sixties; the proportion of all Indians living in cities climbed from 30 to 45 percent.[16]

Researchers offered two convincing explanations for this shift of 500,000 native Americans from rural to urban areas. Indirectly, the United States government promoted an exodus by neglecting reservation economic development—hence the lack of local job opportunities. Washington also was directly responsible through activities that encouraged out-migration.

The BIA's Relocation Program originated in 1948 as an off-reservation job placement service for needy Navajos, seventeen thousand of whom soon found employment with the help of federal officers in Denver, Los Angeles, and Salt Lake City.[17] During the early fifties the government extended relocation services to other destitute tribes; their rural reservations, observed a 1954 congressional report, "could not support the present population at anything approaching a reasonably adequate American standard of living. Past studies indicate that the resources of many reservations, when fully developed, could support no more than 60 percent of the current population, and the Indian population is increasing rapidly."[18] By 1972, when the Relocation Program was drastically modified, the BIA had colonized about 160,000 Indians, both individuals and families, who voluntarily moved to selected urban areas. Bureau officials screened native applicants for relocation. When necessary the bureau subsidized transportation to the place of employment. During the first year of adjustment, relocation field offices also provided low-cost temporary housing, housewares, counseling, and vocational and job-placement services.[19]

The 160,000 Relocation Program volunteers represented just one-third of those who left impoverished reservations, the rest having settled in cities without federal assistance, yet Washington was sharply censured over the years for mishandling these clients. The American Indian Policy Review Commission's 1977 *Final Report* to Congress was particularly critical of the orientation and job placement services offered to urban newcomers. Because the BIA naively underestimated the economic and social barriers that unskilled Indian laborers would encounter in color-conscious cities, it recruited Indians ill-prepared in language, work experience, and technical skills; then, perhaps most uncalled for, it scattered them throughout strange and distant urban centers despite their desires to maintain close tribal contacts and to obtain work near their reservations. Amid concrete ghettos, they felt forsaken and confused about where to find services. At least a third of them returned home. For those who persevered, government vocational training funneled even the brightest native students into "service" occupations. Moreover, the jobs found for them by the BIA rarely lasted more than a year or offered much opportunity for advancement or cultivated skills that could be used back home.[20]

Before 1972 the United States and Canada both overemphasized programs that took tribesmen to jobs in distant cities and perpetuated poverty on underdeveloped, stagnating reservations like those in Michigan and southwestern Ontario. Out-migration thus became a grim necessity.

III

During the twentieth century Great Lakes band members traveled by the thousands to Detroit. The city projected a remarkably positive image to the world: preeminent in automobile production, a working man's haven, a dynamic industrial center that could get any job done—like becoming America's "Arsenal of Democracy" after Pearl Harbor. Millions of laborers from other regions and from other nations followed their dreams to this El Dorado, turning the Motor City into one of the most ethnically diverse metropolitan areas in the United States.

The automobile industry's insatiable demand for laborers and its handsome wages triggered immigration before 1920. News of these job opportunities was transmitted to Europe by employers and by relatives already living in the Motor City. Advertisements placed in hundreds of American newspapers also heralded the message. Detroit's Board of Commerce even requested that Ellis Island immigration officials channel newcomers toward Michigan. They came by the thousands. In 1920 nearly one-third of the city's population had been born outside the United States. Of the Ford Motor Company's employees, two-thirds were categorized as foreign born and in 1916 included fifty-eight nationalities.[21]

The 1920s saw a shift in the type of immigrants drawn to Detroit and, consequently, how the city responded to newcomers. After World War I, Washington placed strict quotas on the number of Europeans permitted to enter the country, and by 1940 the Motor City's foreign-born declined to 19.75 percent of the population. What satisfied Detroit's expanding labor needs was a massive migration from United States rural areas, particularly blacks from the South.[22]

Movement to the Motor City intensified during World War II and the boom times after that. If new arrivals had meager resources, they clustered in historic fashion throughout the inner city and became the neighbors of established residents. Prominent immigrant groups included Mexican Americans, Appalachian whites, and native Americans. Southern blacks continued to migrate north and by 1970 numbered 660,428, or 44.5 percent of Detroit's population.[23]

Detroit was more than just a Motor City or even an "Arsenal of Democracy." Like the Statue of Liberty and the American Frontier, it symbolized hope and freedom. Detroit was a place of new beginnings where schools and housing developments and job opportunities beckoned to ambitious people everywhere.

Thus, the growth of Detroit's native American community was rooted in limited reservation opportunities as well as the powerful allure of the city, (table I).[24]

TABLE 1
Detroit's Growing Native American Population

Year	Number of Native Americans	
	City of Detroit	Detroit Metropolitan Area
1880	34	—
1890	11	—
1900	14	—
1910	41	—
1920	155	—
1930	350	—
1940	434	—
1950	730	—
1960	691	912
1970	2,914	5,683

Source: United States Bureau of the Census. *Historical Statistics of the United States, Colonial Times to 1970, 3.*

The well-being of these native newcomers was by no means assured. Historically, Detroit's riches were not for the fainthearted.

23

IV

In 1805 Congress created the Michigan Territory with Detroit as its capital. Two weeks before the arrival of territorial governor William Hull, a fire destroyed the town. Former residents and the governor had such faith in Detroit and its splendid location that rebuilding began immediately. Their confidence was captured in the city's official seal adopted in 1827: *Speramus Meliora. Resurget Cineribus.* ("We hope for better days. It will arise from the ashes.")[25]

The motto was equally appropriate for twentieth-century Indians who migrated to southeast Michigan in hope of better days. Like the legendary phoenix, they had grown weak over the years. Destitute reservations sapped their physical and cultural strength. Paternalistic bureaucrats undermined their self-respect and confidence. Despairing tribal members too often found solace in mind-numbing alcohol. In search of new opportunities—of regeneration—more and more reservation residents journeyed to Detroit. Adjustments were horrendous and monumental— a fiery furnace like the pyre on which the phoenix burned itself. Yet thousands emerged phoenixlike and youthfully alive, ready to direct their fate and to fight for economic self-sufficiency with renewed vigor. They, too, had arisen from the ashes, and in Detroit they found better days.

To grasp the nature of this remarkable regeneration and to appreciate the outpouring of native pride during Michigan Indian Day parades, the historic challenges that native American migrants to Detroit faced must be examined. These included adjusting to urban life, finding a good job and a decent place to live, securing good medical care, educating their children, and maintaining a unique cultural heritage. Indians usually turned for help to other urban Indians. Thus, this study will also scrutinize the importance of personal networks as well as formal native organizations. Together they made possible the survival and regeneration of Detroit's American Indian community.

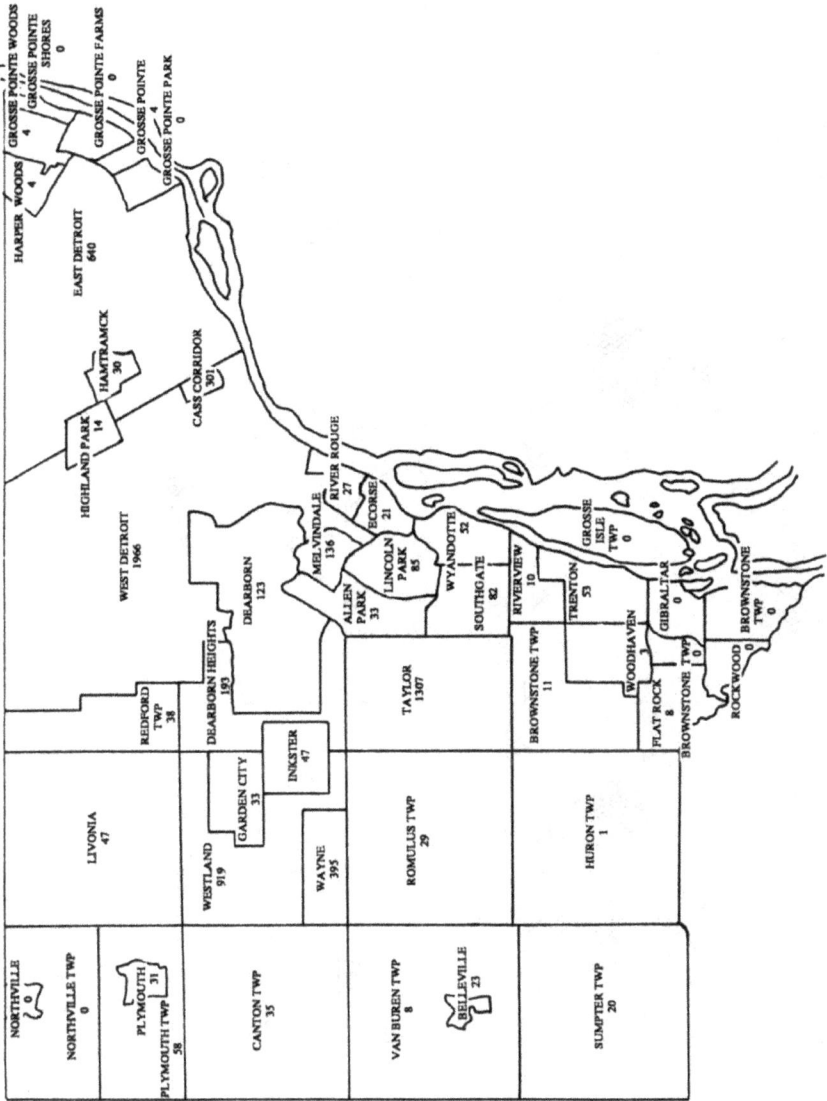

Map 1

NORTHVILLE 0
NORTHVILLE TWP 0
PLYMOUTH 31
PLYMOUTH TWP 58
LIVONIA 47
REDFORD TWP 38
DEARBORN HEIGHTS 193
WEST DETROIT 1966
HIGHLAND PARK 14
HAMTRAMCK 30
CASS CORRIDOR 301
HARPER WOODS 4
GROSSE POINTE WOODS 4
GROSSE POINTE SHORES 0
GROSSE POINTE FARMS 0
GROSSE POINTE 4
GROSSE POINTE PARK 0
EAST DETROIT 640
DEARBORN 123
RIVER ROUGE 27
MELVINDALE 136
ECORSE 21
ALLEN PARK 33
LINCOLN PARK 85
WYANDOTTE 52
SOUTHGATE 82
RIVERVIEW 10
TRENTON 53
GROSSE ISLE TWP 0
GIBRALTAR 0
WOODHAVEN 0
CANTON TWP 35
WESTLAND 919
GARDEN CITY 33
INKSTER 47
WAYNE 395
TAYLOR 1307
BROWNSTONE TWP 11
FLAT ROCK 8
BROWNSTONE TWP 0
ROCKWOOD 0
BROWNSTONE TWP 0
VAN BUREN TWP 8
BELLEVILLE 23
ROMULUS TWP 29
HURON TWP 1
SUMPTER TWP 20

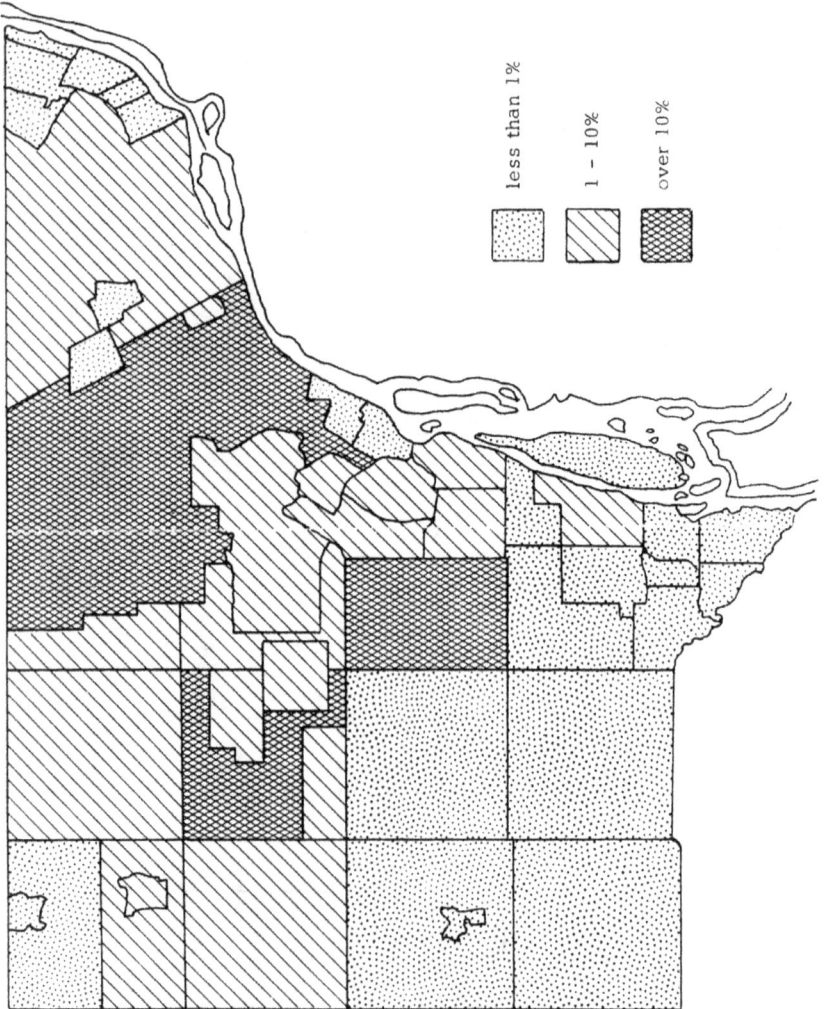

less than 1%

1 - 10%

over 10%

Map 2

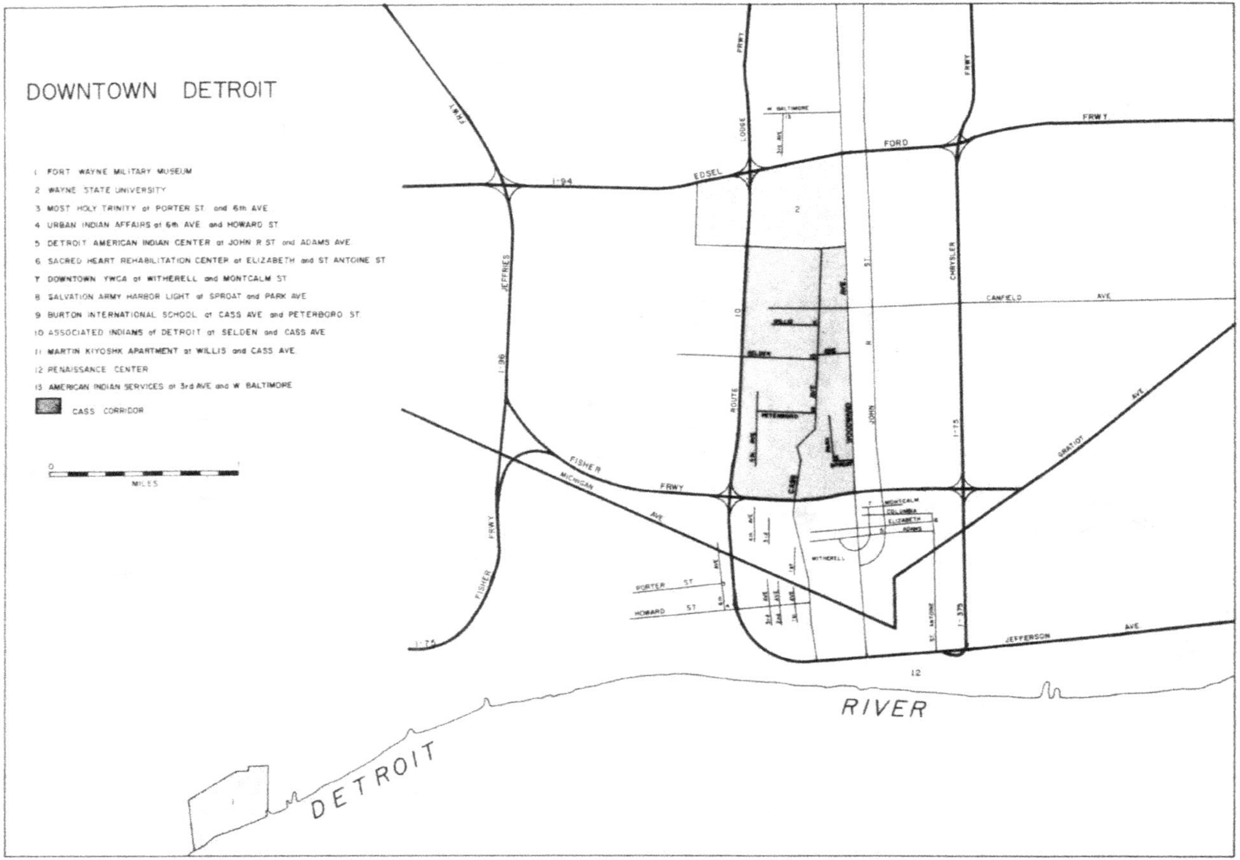

DOWNTOWN DETROIT

1 FORT WAYNE MILITARY MUSEUM
2 WAYNE STATE UNIVERSITY
3 MOST HOLY TRINITY at PORTER ST and 6th AVE
4 URBAN INDIAN AFFAIRS at 6th AVE and HOWARD ST
5 DETROIT AMERICAN INDIAN CENTER at JOHN R ST and ADAMS AVE
6 SACRED HEART REHABILITATION CENTER at ELIZABETH and ST ANTOINE ST
7 DOWNTOWN YMCA at WITHERELL and MONTCALM ST
8 SALVATION ARMY HARBOR LIGHT at SPROAT and PARK AVE
9 BURTON INTERNATIONAL SCHOOL at CASS AVE and PETERBORO ST
10 ASSOCIATED INDIANS of DETROIT at SELDEN and CASS AVE
11 MARTIN KIYOSHK APARTMENT at WILLIS and CASS AVE
12 RENAISSANCE CENTER
13 AMERICAN INDIAN SERVICES at 3rd AVE and W BALTIMORE

CASS CORRIDOR

0   MILES   1

DETROIT RIVER

Map 3

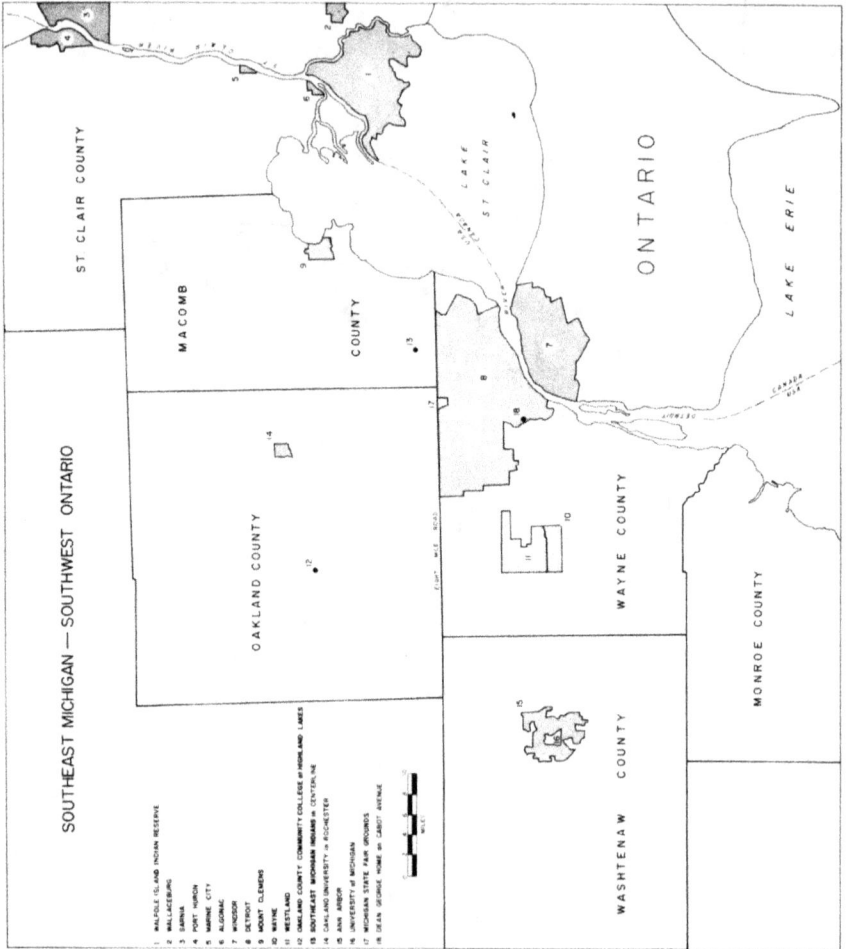

SOUTHEAST MICHIGAN — SOUTHWEST ONTARIO

1 WALPOLE ISLAND INDIAN RESERVE
2 WALLACEBURG
3 SARNIA
4 PORT HURON
5 MARINE CITY
6 ALGONAC
7 WINDSOR
8 DETROIT
9 MOUNT CLEMENS
10 WAYNE
11 WESTLAND
12 OAKLAND COUNTY COMMUNITY COLLEGE at HIGHLAND LAKES
13 SOUTHEAST MICHIGAN INDIANS at CENTERLINE
14 OAKLAND UNIVERSITY at ROCHESTER
15 ANN ARBOR
16 UNIVERSITY of MICHIGAN
17 MICHIGAN STATE FAIR GROUNDS
18 DEAR GEORGE HOME at CADIET AVENUE

ST CLAIR COUNTY

MACOMB

COUNTY

OAKLAND COUNTY

WAYNE COUNTY

WASHTENAW   COUNTY

MONROE COUNTY

ONTARIO

LAKE
ST CLAIR

LAKE ERIE

Map 4

>>> CHAPTER 1 <<<

Adjusting to City Life

Locating housing, meeting new friends, adapting to the urban environment—including changes in cultural values—finding work: these and other acute problems of adjustment faced rural Indians who came to Detroit. Not all the challenges could be met successfully.

I

During the early 1940s, John David and his friend Clarence Rogers, young Chippewa Indians from rural Sarnia Reserve in Ontario, went south to find factory work in the bustling "Arsenal of Democracy." The big city with its skyscrapers, noises, and activities at first alarmed these country lads, but after a day of knocking on doors they found an apartment. The hungry newcomers bought a few pork chops and potatoes and tried cooking supper on the apartment's newfangled gas stove. While Clarence fried the meat on a top burner, John cautiously inserted the potatoes and turned on the oven. Several times he tried to light it. Then came a loud explosion. It singed the hair on Clarence's face. Pork chops and potatoes flew through the air like grapeshot.[1] Thus began the challenge of urban adjustment.

John David's youth hardly equipped him for urban life. The death of his mother in 1934 necessitated his attending the Mohawk Institute, a mission boarding school in Brantford, Ontario, which housed more than two hundred Indian children. Besides formal classroom studies, the boys operated a farm on the grounds, and the girls learned cooking, sewing, and other domestic skills. Students were stimulated intellectually, physically, and spiritually. Yet the daily campus routine was regimented and confining. John recalled bitterly that evangelical Christian teachers also robbed him of his Chippewa culture and language. So in 1941 he ran away "to get out in the world." For Indians, the world of work in Canada meant being treated like second-class citizens; thus John and his friend Clarence moved to the United States in 1943.

The next three years brought radical changes in John's life. With help from his Detroit cousin, Chris, John got a good position in an auto plant. Then Chris talked him into joining the United States Navy. The money was alluring. So was the adventurous life. And John had no strong local ties to break, no steady girlfriends. After gunnery school in Shell Beach, Louisiana, he served with a navy guard assigned to merchant marine vessels. They carried him to colorful ports of call in South America, North Africa, and the Arabian Peninsula. The educational effect of these wartime experiences was lessened because John developed a lifelong drinking problem; when his ship arrived in a harbor he usually went right to the dockside bars and stayed. The navy discharged him in 1946. John returned to Detroit as a Chippewa veteran who had seen a large slice of the world beyond Sarnia Reserve and who was partly adjusted to the white man's life-style. No longer was he awed by big cities or bewildered by gas stoves.

Wishing to mingle with kindred spirits, John headed for the Indian beer gardens at Michigan and Third—the Torpedo Bar, Harry's, Sam Fox's—unaware that there would soon be another major change in the direction of his life. During one of John's visits, he met a beautiful Ottawa lady from northern Michigan, Leona Bailey. Love blossomed. He tried crewing on Great Lakes ore boats but missed Leona greatly. So they were married Christmas Eve, 1947. From now on, whatever new difficulties arose in adjusting to a hectic life in the Motor City, they would face them together.

Harry Command was a friend of the David's. An ex-convict, Harry likened urban adjustment to the dislocation felt by released prisoners.

Outside the walls they were "lost guys." First there was confusion over all the changes, everything from prices to new expressways. Then came intimidation; one did not know what would happen next or even what was expected of him or her personally. Naturally a native newcomer, whether just out of the 'joint" or just off the reservation, turned for help—for role models—to other Indians. Thus drinking became confused with adjustment, for many city Indians used alcoholic beverages to excess.[2]

Much of this loneliness and frustration, which amounted to cultural shock, resulted from the clash between tribal traditional values and urban industrial ones. The essence of native American uniqueness was not skin color; it was a tribally transmitted way of life, their culture. They brought this unique heritage to the Motor City from sanctuaries such as Walpole Island, and to the extent that reservation life-styles were incompatible with city ones, their identity and stability as Indians were threatened.

Conflict occurred over a wide range of principles. Many woodland Indian cultures, for example, prized the sharing of possessions with others, rather than saving for oneself. Winona Arriaga recalled that in her youth on Cape Croker Reserve in Ontario, the chiefs were always the poorest persons in the village. When an Oneida lady and her family moved into an apartment building in Detroit's Cass Corridor during the 1950s, Indian neighbors expected them to share whatever money and property they had.[3] An individual's good reputation also stemmed from avoiding competitive and aggressive actions. Whenever possible an Indian should respect and support the efforts of others, not seek to outperform them. Traditionally, the immediate welfare of the group, especially the extended family, was primary; hoarding resources for one's own benefit was improper when others were needy. One ought to live and enjoy life day by day. For reservation Indians this included relating "to nature in a unique and vital way—as hunters, fishers, mystics, cooks, priests, business-persons, and biologists—for their culture is deeply rooted in the land." Law professor Charles F. Wilkinson further noted that the "Indian seeks a harmony with all of life"; and his "measured pace permits a careful tending of many different concerns—nature, family, friends, self."[4]

Consequently, reservation residents who migrated to highly competitive, modern Detroit were immediately trapped in a no-man's-land of opposing values: poised by necessity, wrote *Detroit Free Press* correspondent Tom Nugent in 1972, "between the world they were—Navajo and Mohawk and Oneida, medicine, love of ceremony, love of being next to the earth—and the world they have been forced to become—IBM and Burger Chef and Social Security and the latest mugging at Cass and Temple."[5] Not all native newcomers resolved these discords in such a way as to preserve their identity and stability as Indians.

During urban adjustment, many reservation Indians also suffered because they lacked positive, practical experience. Walpole Island was a case in point. Before 1965 the white Indian agent and his white staff, who stifled local development, also did not prepare the islanders to compete in the economic and educational mainstreams once they left the reserve.[6] Nor was it much better in the United States. The BIA was paternalistic with its programs and just as ineffective in its administration. Reservation communities, Uncle Sam's wards, grew accustomed to bureaucrats doing the thinking and planning, accustomed to obtaining medical, dental, and other services free of change, accustomed to disdainful treatment by many non-Indian neighbors. According to Ralph West, who was reared on the Cheyenne Reservation in Oklahoma and studied postwar Detroit Indians during his graduate training at Wayne State University, what blocked their adaptation by 1950 was not so much white discrimination as the reservation Indian's underdeveloped initiative, derived from his sense of inferior education, "a defeatist frame of mind regarding relations with the whites," and a tendency to blame Washington for his problems.[7]

Finally, transition to the city was stressful because of the pronounced physical and social changes—from rural reservation sanctuary to teeming metropolis. Many Indians wrestled with the technical aspects of city life: crossing busy streets and riding buses and juggling checking accounts. In the late forties, having just come from Keweenaw Bay Reservation in remote upstate Michigan, Louise Morales was especially flustered by Detroit's traffic and city sounds. Black people, with whom she had had little previous contact, frightened her. At first she rarely left her apartment except to shop at Hudson's; even then she was easily lost if she exited through the wrong door. Martin Kiyoshk, a Walpole Island Band member, arrived in southeast Michigan about the same time. What troubled him most was the city's suspicious atmosphere—so many people who neither knew nor trusted one another. Although reconciled over the years to commonplace street crimes, Martin never got over this deep apprehensiveness.[8]

"Detroit is a jungle," asserted Fred Boyd, a city-born and streetwise Cree Indian, "and you have to be sharp to survive." Shy reservation people were pretty much on their own, unlike back home where so much was decided for them.[9]

II

How did Indian newcomers to the Motor City, cut off from reservation sanctuaries and shocked by opposing values, meet the challenges of urban adjustment? Each migrant reacted uniquely to the menacing metropolis; some personal adaptation periods took longer than others, for example, and not all went smoothly, as suggested by the poverty of many native families as well as their comparatively low educational achievement and persistent problems with alcoholism. Generally, the process involved two steps: learning about the dominant society's different values and life-styles, and cultivating new friendships to replace those back on the reservation.

For some Indians, previous significant experiences with the white man's world eased the first step of accommodation to Detroit. One such exposure was off-reservation schooling. Bill Colwell attended the Algonac public schools during the 1950s because his diligent mother supported the family with domestic work in town. Each day the two of them commuted by ferry from Walpole Island. When winter winds froze the St. Clair River, they boarded in Algonac. The first Indian to graduate from the city high school, Bill received what he called an American education. He was half reservation Indian and half white Indian. He understood the value systems of both societies, especially the white man's work ethic and such features of the workplace as unions, the seniority system, regimentation, and quotas. Consequently, when he moved for a time to Detroit, he had little trouble finding work or adjusting to the city.[10]

Not all Indian youngsters enjoyed such a healthy cultural mix. Before the sixties, if the reservation agent deemed a native home inadequate (because of extreme poverty, the death of a parent, or debilitating alcoholism), children like John David were sent to distant boarding schools. Academic training and instruction in the white man's way of life unquestionably helped their future adjustment to urban centers like Detroit, if they chose to migrate. Residential schools also caused grave and enduring cultural conflict, for their mission included the destruction of traditional Indian beliefs and practices.

Military service broadened the social and cultural lives of several future Detroiters. During World War II John David's hitch in the United States Navy introduced him to much of the world outside Sarnia Reserve. John La Pointe, a Chippewa from Keweenaw Bay Reservation, credited the Army Air Corps with teaching him to get along with a wide variety of people. His outlook broadened. He developed the flexibility necessary to adjust to the Motor City, where he moved in 1949, and for twenty-five fruitful years was employed by Borg-Warner Corporation.[11]

For tribesmen who came directly to Detroit without off-reservation educational experiences, urban adjustment was sometimes facilitated by live-in jobs at white homes. Elsie Staats and Myrtle Kiser, for example, who migrated from Ontario reserves in the twenties, felt less alienated thanks to familiar housekeeping work together with the homelike atmospheres provided. Kiser earned four dollars a week, sending half back to her large family (twelve brothers and sisters) on Muncey Reserve. Fresh from northern Michigan, Louise Morales was happily employed as a domestic servant for one and a half years in the late 1940s. Jewish neighbors at the corner of Linwood and Cortland avenues treated her well, although several youngsters, upon learning she was a Chippewa, were disappointed that she wore no feathers in her hair.[12]

Leona Bailey David, who also hired out as a domestic in the midforties, was especially fortunate to have a married sister in the city who eased the shock of urban life. Elsie Staats and Louise Morales were also helped at first by relatives and close friends from the reservation already established in the Motor City. Frank Montour explained that whenever Mohawks from his home settlement arrived in Detroit, he considered them brothers and cared for them until they found work.[13] Such hospitality was common and important in learning about city ways and developing new support groups.

Neighborly as individuals, the expanding Motor City Indian community, however, was slow to develop an institutional framework to serve the needs of new arrivals. Nor was there a close-knit native neighborhood in downtown Detroit. They simply shared skid row with several other transient, low-income groups.

III

When tribal newcomers arrived in the city before 1960 and asked about other Indians, taxi drivers and bus station attendants invariably directed them to the corner of Michigan and Third avenues; this was the port of

entry, the orientation center, for most Indians. Even if they had city relatives and friends, they congregated there in the bars, on street corners,
in second-floor apartments above the shops—just to socialize or to get
useful leads on jobs and housing. They also hoped for some news from
home. By the fifties a Michigan Avenue construction project pushed the
saloons and flophouses north a dozen blocks to the so-called Cass Corridor. This subcommunity helped recent arrivals from the reservations
to adapt to urban life during the next thirty years.

Some native Americans never left Cass Corridor. They enjoyed the
carousing and pooling of resources and the camaraderie in the middle
of a forbidding metropolis. Perhaps they could not hold good jobs or
were trapped by personal weaknesses. Most Indians (as documented by
their dispersion throughout the metropolitan area) used their urban
orientation, obtained in the corridor, as a springboard to more stable
residential neighborhoods outside its confines.

In these two Detroit ports of entry the facility that touched the most
Indians was the saloon. For most of this century no special programs or
organizations supplied an alternative social setting. Lost in the anonymity of the city, newcomers turned for recreation to a place where they
felt accepted. Ralph West had observed shortly after World War II: "The
beer taverns of Michigan Avenue provide him [the Indian] with the
means to escape and provide the companionship of others who feel as
he does, without fear of his being embarrassed by 'superiors' in the matter of language, dress and general deportment."[14] Here they found assistance and role models; they enjoyed the fellowship of old friends from
the reservation; a developing network of new acquaintances gave a sense
of belonging and stability. Historically, bars thus were important in the
migrants' entry into city life.[15]

The fame of Sam Fox's Tavern had spread to remote reserves in Michigan and Ontario. Patrons later recalled how cheerful and comfortable
the small room was, with a bar on one side and tables on the other. A
potbellied stove warmed the atmosphere during the winter months. Sam,
the ever friendly and knowledgeable host and counselor, truly cared
about the welfare of native Americans; they had been mistreated like his
own Jewish people, he claimed. Indians worked at the tavern. And at his
suburban Grosse Pointe home, Sam's wife distributed used clothing to
needy natives.[16] When Winona Arriaga arrived from Cape Croker
Reserve in 1947, she was pleased to see so many Indians at Sam Fox's
helping others, as they did back home. Here she met her husband,
Frank. Other couples such as the Davids became acquainted. Sam sold

the business in the late fifties; soon after the building was demolished. Yet his influence persisted. Two decades later several young people, whose parents had first been introduced by Michigan Avenue tavern keepers like Sam Fox, were employed by the fledgling Detroit American Indian Center.[17]

Not all consequences of the bar culture were so positive. During the stressful transition to city life, too many Indians confused drinking with adjustment. Gene Iron Shell, a Rosebud Sioux and for more than twenty years an alcoholic, experienced how the Detroit saloon clique, which became like an extended family, could also pressure a person not to sober up, not to change, not to succeed in the dominant society.[18] Back in the 1930s Teofilo Lucero, from Taos Pueblo, was among the first to realize that Indians needed a better place than the bars to congregate on paydays. An organization was required that not only eased the stress of urban adjustment but perpetuated Indian cultures, fostered unity, and provided mutual aid.

In response to these needs, the North American Indian Association of Detroit (NAIA) was founded in 1940. Most influential in uniting the original native members was Scott N. Peters, a Chippewa and a BIA educational guidance and placement officer stationed in Milwaukee. Because of the escalating Indian population, he had visited the Motor City periodically since the mid-thirties. He found automotive jobs for several men and women and counseled those with urban adjustment problems. Peters also had a dream: an Indian social group not centered in the Michigan Avenue bars.

In response to his request, the downtown YWCA finally provided rent-free space on its seventh floor for an Indian organization; then a few meetings during the fall of 1940 hammered out guidelines and a constitution for the new North American Indian Club. Its membership soon grew to 175, including young and old from many reservations in the United States and Canada. Attendance at bimonthly gatherings ranged from thirty to seventy-five.[19]

At first the club stressed recreational activities; later its aims broadened. To divert native peoples from bars and to curb their loss of Indian identity in the city, intertribal social events were sponsored: picnics, card parties, talent shows, bingo games, dances, and an annual banquet. Indian food favorites—fry-bread, corn soup, venison—were served. After World War II the men organized teams to compete in the city basketball, bowling, and baseball leagues. Simultaneously, the membership increased its area of concern. An annual Christmas program, beginning in 1947, was staged to benefit needy children; a few years later the club revised the constitution and created two new committees to foster Indian higher education and to assist the poor. In recognition of this wider focus, the club changed its name in March 1966 to the North American Indian Association of Detroit. By then it was the most important native organization in southeast Michigan.[20]

Through its relationship with the influential YWCA, the NAIA had obtained citywide attention and status, instruction in public-relations techniques, together with political support in battling for Indian causes. Yet the Y never became paternalistic, in part because the association insisted on control of its own programs. "We help Indian people," President Dean George emphasized in 1973, "and we want to keep it that way. We will accept aid, but only with no strings attached."[21]

The influx of thousands of Indian migrants to Detroit in the sixties strained the association's finances and the manpower of its welfare committee. Other Indian-controlled organizations therefore sprang up to meet the newcomers' pressing needs.

A branch of the parent group in St. Ignace, Michigan, the Indians of North America Foundation opened its office at Most Holy Trinity Catholic Church on Porter Street in 1973. It was staffed by two devoted, industrious volunteers: Carol Coulon Kawegoma and Phylis Alindayu. Additional parttime workers and donations of money enabled the foundation to offer clothing, food, and general referral services to recent arrivals from the reservations. Moreover, it staffed a cheerful drop-in center and taught in the church educational unit a General Educational Development (GED) class of twenty students as well as native culture workshops, with craft supplies paid for by the board of education. Kawegoma and Alindayu reciprocated. They made presentations to city schools; they held memberships on several commissions that assessed the employment and educational needs of Detroit minority groups. Finally, the Indians of North America Foundation served as a forerunner and catalyst for the DAIC, established in the mid-seventies. Exhausted after years of foundation work, Kawegoma and Alindayu were happy to see the center take over their services, and permanently closed the Porter Street facility.[22]

Although he had lived in the Cass Corridor since 1948, Frank Alberts never frequented Indian bars. Most of his socializing took place at the Central Methodist Church. His favorite pastor left in 1970, so Frank transferred his membership to the nearby Methodist congregation at Cass and Selden avenues; its preacher was from near Oscoda, Michigan, and knew Frank's Chippewa parents. Here he met Louise Morales, Winona Arriaga, and Isabel Dockstader, who were starting an Indian organization on the premises, much like the arrangement at Most Holy Trinity. Frank approved their goal of helping neighborhood Indians and became its vice president.[23]

The Associated Indians of Detroit (AID), led by President Dockstader, an Iroquois mother of eight, served its native neighbors much like the Indians of North America Foundation: with GED and culture classes taught by volunteers, food and clothing distributions to Indians stranded in the city, job referrals, a drop-in facility serving coffee and donuts. A Wayne State University professor gave helpful advice to AID leaders about financial sources. Enough money and goods thus trickled in to Treasurer Arriaga from the Presbyterian Church, Model Neighborhoods Program, the NAIA, donations, and auctions. One Christmas a motorcycle gang contributed presents for the children. Carleen Pedrotti, Winona's daughter, provided dynamic leadership between 1972 and 1975. The atmosphere was exciting; we were "can-do people," she recalled, "an Indian-for-Indians organization … [trying to] bring back some tradition to the people in this area." The decline of the AID dated from the involvement of some staffers in national Indian affairs, especially the controversial American Indian Movement, which took them out of town for extended periods. The FBI made such frequent inquiries that the pastor became convinced the Indian group his church sponsored was militant, perhaps subversive. In 1975 the AID was forced to move to new quarters. Winona and Carleen left the organization at this juncture. Its name was also changed and its prominence faded.[24]

A third facility to aid native newcomers was the Office of Urban Indian Affairs, established in May 1970. Russ Wright, a Cherokee social worker, persuaded the state director of social services to create this office and served as its director throughout the seventies and early eighties. His authoritative knowledge about city Indians derived in part from three consecutive terms as president of the NAIA (1964–68). From their busy suite in Michigan Plaza at the corner of Sixth and Howard, Wright and a small staff served about 250 clients a month. The office's principal functions included:

1. Obtaining emergency food, clothing, shelter, and transportation for migrants not yet eligible for public assistance
2. Establishing identification for American Indians entitled to special program benefits

3. Finding employment
4. Securing scholarships and other financial aid for Indian students
5. Interceding when the rights of native Americans appeared to have been curtailed or violated
6. Arranging, when all else failed, for travel back to reservations

The Office of Urban Indian Affairs, Wright asserted, gave native people "hope where heretofore there was only despair. They now have a tremendously improved opinion of state government that was practically nonexistent for many years.... Our people now believe that somebody cares."[25]

IV

Notwithstanding this limited help (from the Office of Urban Indian Affairs, the AID, the Indians of North America Foundation, and the NAIA), metropolitan area native Americans, at least fifty-seven hundred strong in 1970, were still plagued with underemployment, persistent health-care needs, and cramped and unhealthy living conditions. They could not even control the education of their children.

Russ Wright saw the desirability of a large Indian-staffed center where his people could get personal counseling, advice on job prospects, and could socialize with fellow Indians; other Detroit leaders visualized a place where clothing and canned goods might be stored and health information dispensed. Deborah Schuyler of Dearborn Heights, a nineteen-year-old Oneida and reigning Princess of the NAIA in 1970, spoke on behalf of the younger generation:

> There is a new awareness in young people that we must be proud of our heritage and work together for actions that will make life better for all Indians.
>
> If we had a center, there are many older Indians who would be delighted to teach us cultural aspects of our ancestry. We want to learn and preserve the Indian language, tribal dances and customs and Indian crafts so that we can pass these things on to our children and not become a lost culture.

"But we can't get together," lamented association President Dean George, "because we don't have a meeting place large enough. In fact, we don't even have a meeting place of our own. That's what we need more than anything else and then we could be of more help to each other." For many the crisis came in 1972: attendance at the NAIA meetings dropped off as muggings in the Y's high-crime neighborhood multiplied; emergency food and used clothing gathered by the association were pilfered.[26] The Indians needed their own building elsewhere in Detroit, and soon.

V

Dean George, an Oneida Indian and high school dropout, moved to Michigan in the 1950s. He and his wife, Shirley, were reasonably happy and prosperous; they had four children and Dean's work as a teamster enabled them to rent a house. Then, like so many native Americans in the 1960s, Dean became increasingly interested in his cultural heritage and in the welfare of fellow Indians. By switching to the evening work shift he freed his days for studying and aiding other Detroit Indians. He rose to the presidency of the local North American Indian Association in 1970. Later, in recognition of his prominence, the governor appointed Dean to the Michigan Indian Commission.[27]

In 1973 the living room of George's house was an important nerve center of Indian activity. Energetic community leaders conversed about establishing an Indian center amid bookcases stacked with volumes of native American history, periodicals like *Akwesasne Notes*, letters, reports, and grant proposals. One of the most respected spokesmen was Dean George, in his early forties, big as a bear yet soft-spoken. Invariably nearby and just as committed was Shirley George. Together they made a powerful team, determined to share sacrificially of their time, talents, and money. They were also willing to change and grow.

These Detroiters—the Georges, Russ Wright, Fred Boyd, Harry Command, and a few others—eventually developed a master plan for an Indian Village, influenced in part by the native American facility in Chicago and a local service center for the Chicano community. Admittedly a "monumental undertaking" with an anticipated construction cost of eleven and half million dollars, Indian Village expressed their hopes for improved living conditions and service facilities: a "physical environment within which Indian heritage may root and flourish." At its hub were an amphitheater, recreation area, cultural museum, and an administration building housing all office space through which services could be coordinated. The complex also included a mall for small businesses

40

and a larger area for industrial development, rehabilitated and new housing, and several small parks.[28]

The vigorous search for financing was protracted, frustrating, and only moderately successful. Obtaining tax-exempt status for the NAIA took more than a year and demanded rewriting the bylaws and hiring an attorney, John E. English, to prepare other necessary documents for the Internal Revenue Service. Meanwhile, the association dispatched dozens of fund-raising letters to politicians in Washington, the state capital in Lansing, and the Motor City. They canvassed civic and private groups in southeast Michigan, all to no avail. Then Willard Lambert of the Michigan Indian Commission astonished Dean with a phone call; the HEW had authorized $200,000 for Michigan urban Indians. In 1973 it sent Judy Lyons to Detroit to consult with native leaders about their needs. Aided by a grant-writing kit and the expertise of James Doyle and Associates, a local consulting firm, the association drafted in early 1974 the first federal grant proposal for a Detroit American Indian Center.[29] It requested $100,000 for the period July 1, 1974, to June 30, 1975, in order to:

1. Establish a sound organizational structure, including policies, fiscal responsibilities, rules and regulations
2. Identify the existing Detroit Indian population and document its needs with statistical data
3. Identify existing agencies that are available to service the economic, medical, social well-being, employment, and counseling needs of the Detroit Indian population
4. Evaluate the effectiveness of the project; assess strengths and weaknesses of the first-year program and revise, amend, or expand upon original goals

Late that spring the HEW approved the proposal. After interviewing several candidates who applied for the project directorship, the association chose Dean George.[30]

VI

Operations began in his living room. In October 1974, with office space obtained at the Detroit Institute of Technology on Second Avenue, the DAIC opened for business.[31] It was not a multimillion-dollar Indian Village, but it was a start.

During Dean George's administration, Indians, working within Washington's guidelines, had full responsibility for the center's success. George Holland and Courtney Scherer of the HEW's Chicago Regional Office provided technical assistance and evaluation. Their telephone calls, correspondence, and on-site visits clarified federal regulations for neophyte project leaders. As long as the center pursued its objectives as stated in the grant, Holland and Scherer responded positively to Indian ideas. Rarely did they give a flat "no," George recalled; they talked about what might happen if certain things were done.[32]

Success the first year sprang from a sound organizational structure. Personnel policies were crucial. The center began with an untrained and inexperienced staff of three in August 1974; employees totaled thirty the following June and the fledgling center financed thirty-nine more Indian positions around the city. Hiring procedures were formulated and job descriptions drafted during this time. Monday morning staff meetings, when department reports were received, common concerns voiced, and the week's priorities set, facilitated internal communication. Office efficiency and morale further improved in January 1975 with a move to roomier quarters at the Salvation Army's Harbor Light Center on Brainard Avenue. What paid for the increased rent and salaries and programs was $352,000 in federal grants; besides the $100,000 in Office of Native American Programs moneys, the center received by August 1975 $197,000 from the Comprehensive Employment and Training Act (CETA) funds and $55,000 from Title IV, Part B (of the 1972 Indian Education Act) for early childhood education. The accounting firm of Applegate and Mueller set up a simple but appropriate accounting system to prevent comingling.[33] Nevertheless, Irene Lowry, the bookkeeper, found the financial records in bad order when she started work in February 1975. Lacking money to hire an accounting consultant, she spent evenings and weekends preparing for a federal audit that summer. Her valiant efforts and intimate experience with center business transactions ultimately satisfied Chicago.[34]

Before 1974, the NAIA conducted meetings casually; then, with responsibility for more than $300,000 in grants, its board of directors, which was also the center's policy-making body, adopted more formal protocol. The ten board members learned about parliamentary procedure and federal-grant policies at Saturday morning in-service workshops. Until February 1975 attorney John English provided legal advice about grant-related matters. This knowledgeable board exercised firm control over the center from the beginning.[35]

Among the center's notable accomplishments its first year was a random sample survey of the Detroit Indian population in the Cass Corridor. Program planners from then on had some current data about Indian health conditions, education achievement, employment, public assistance received, yearly household incomes, housing characteristics, length of residency in Detroit, and marital status.[36] The center staff notified community service agencies in southeast Michigan about the needs of Detroit's Indian population. Likewise, public relations contacts were made with the local media, and a January open house attracted between three hundred and four hundred visitors to the DAIC.[37] With its CETA moneys, the Manpower Department upgraded the job skills of many underemployed or unemployed urban Indians. Its coordinators registered Indian job applicants, counseled them, and developed employment opportunities with special emphasis on work experience programs for in-school youths and dropouts.[38] Education was the key to Indian progress in the Motor City, George believed; thus he fostered maximum use of a $29,400 Title IV, Part C grant for adult education received in July 1974. Murial Youngblood coordinated these efforts efficiently. By June 1975 thirty-six Indians, including Dean and Shirley George, earned their GEDs.[39] As a final highlight, the director and a few department supervisors and board members formulated the center's ambitious goals for 1975–76 as well as the specific activities required to achieve them.[40]

The attainment of these and other successes, which included overcoming serious start-up problems with an inexperienced and untrained staff, demonstrated the power of Indian self-determination in Detroit and the effectiveness of the new center's organization. Throughout the 1974–75 administrative year, Dean George's leadership was indispensable. Lacking administrative experience he nevertheless matured in office—grasping problems and how to solve them, forcefully carrying out policies—and showed several qualities that the Iroquois most admire in political leaders: honesty, humility, courage, foresightedness, and a skin "seven thumbs thick." Dean George resigned in mid-August 1975, at the expiration of the year's leave of absence from his trucking firm.[41]

VII

Since then, the DAIC has moved to more spacious downtown quarters on John R Street, expanded its staff, programming, and financing, and preserved its independence from federal bureaucrats. The uphill path to these achievements was neither smooth nor straight. At times the center reeled from dizzying administrative reorganizations or was practically paralyzed by internal factionalism.

Detroit Indian control over its extensive service programs has been honored by Washington, which continued, since Dean George's resignation, to provide primarily technical assistance and evaluation through the HEW's Chicago Regional Office. Nevertheless, native American opinion toward Uncle Sam varied. Some cynics believed bureaucrats with their "white tape" really wanted Indian-run programs to flounder; others countered that the complex guidelines, evaluations, and audits simply stemmed from a legitimate need for accountability when expending public money.

Washington highlighted its commitment to self-determination late in 1975, when the firing of four center staff members triggered a local crisis. The DAIC was charged publicly with unfair labor practices and discrimination by Native American Strategic Services, an Indian civil rights group headed by Fred Boyd, who asked Chicago to resolve the problem.[42] Though an advocate of Indian rights, the HEW emphasized to Boyd and others its restrictive technical assistance and advisory functions as well as the great danger of intervention at the federal level in what was a local matter. Its goal was to encourage Indians to control the programs that affected their lives. Sometimes it was necessary to act as a facilitator; the HEW's Robert Chris Johns and Robert Moman therefore gathered information about Boyd's several allegations and in late December attended a Motor City meeting to investigate further the charges and seek resolution of problems concerning the center.[43] Also present were representatives of the Michigan Civil Rights Commission, the Detroit Human Relations Department, and about twenty Indians.[44] Chicago's report of January 20, 1976, concluded that many of Boyd's charges could not be substantiated. Criticisms about how the center's board of directors conducted business were considered a matter for local resolution. However, the HEW, recognizing its deficiency in not providing the beleaguered board with adequate guidelines to assure full community participation and control of the center, strongly recommended an expansion of the board to include more than just association members.[45] Detroit accepted the idea and later in 1976 increased the group by five members to be elected at large.[46]

VIII

Most administrative changes since 1975 were necessary because of the DAIC's expanded programming rather than external pressure from Chicago. Nevertheless, the changes evoked sharp criticism from the staff, whose periodic low morale seriously slowed the delivery of services. Because of its ambitious mission, the center has required vigorous leadership. Yet, within five years of George's departure, six persons held the director's position. One resigned under pressure when his alleged expense account frauds threatened to bring a Justice Department investigation and the freezing of federal grant money.[47] During the fall of 1977, while the center was in the hands of a less than dynamic acting director, several staff members characterized it as a ship adrift without a captain. The situation worsened when at least two supervisors at the center applied for the directorship and jockeyed for position during working hours. It was literally the case, as one staffer noted, that "everybody wants to be a chief."[48] The board was so unimpressed by the lot that it chose as director the relatively inexperienced office manager, Rose Silvey, an Ottawa Indian raised in the Detroit suburbs. The center's competent accounting consultant, Michael Applegate, became Silvey's resident advisor; his job was to train her and other department heads in sorely needed administrative skills.[49] What the board of directors hoped would be a forceful leadership team turned out otherwise, precipitating another period of paralysis. Led by one of the unsuccessful candidates for the directorship, several staff members denounced the Silvey-Applegate team; Silvey was just a puppet and Applegate, a non-Indian, was pulling the strings, not unlike the reservation Indian agents of past years. The whole arrangement, dissidents claimed, made a mockery of self-determination.[50] At its November 1977 meeting, three supervisors, having overcome their own differences and banded together, publicly criticized the board's decisions, and soon their resignations were demanded. This led to further low morale.[51] Their position untenable, Silvey and Applegate asked to be relieved. In January 1978 the board replaced them with James Hillman, an Oneida-Menominee and former director of the Michigan Commission on Indian Affairs, who brought considerable administrative expertise. One of his first public observations was that the center was trying to do too much with unskilled staff and not doing enough of it well.[52] The administrative drift soon stopped and more realistic goals were charted.

Serious conflicts between the DAIC's board of directors and the staff arose because of at least three factors: (1) differences in perspective, for the board tended to be middle-aged, middle-class suburbanites with limited formal education and knowledge of the inner city, whereas the staff was younger, more educated, more knowledgeable about urban needs; (2) the administrative inexperience of both groups before the hiring of Hillman; and (3) the difficulty of striking a proper balance between offering efficient, professional services to Detroit Indians, on the one hand, while maintaining the informal, drop-in atmosphere and sensitivity toward clients that made an Indian center attractive and unique.

IX

The center's survival and the expansion of its manpower, health, housing, transportation, communication, and education services by the late 1970s showed that the first challenge of urban self-determination had been met. (Between July 1980 and March 1981, the DAIC provided 11,326 services to 1,475 different clients.) Like their reservation relatives, Detroit Indians proved to themselves and others that Indians could effectively organize to promote their self-interests. At the same time much was being written about the dramatic changes taking place in downtown Detroit, highlighted by the construction of the $340 million Renaissance Center. The Indian community was part of this rebirth. Irene Lowry called it a "great awakening" among native Americans.[53] The future held many challenges for the center: development of non-federal financing sources, expansion of its physical facilities, increased staff professionalism. Yet each year it came closer to achieving the goals envisioned by Dean George and the other founders.

X

Adjustment failures over the decades were not hard to understand considering the barriers, numerous and difficult to breach, faced by rustic native people. They included the gulf between reservation and urban cultures; the Indians' lack of positive, practical experience, coming as they did from communities dominated by paternalistic government bureaucrats; and the many physical adaptations to city life—ordering one's life by the clock, the noise, traffic, understanding the layout of Detroit, using public transportation, shopping in crowded department stores, avoiding muggers day and night, apartment living. John David's near-disastrous experience with a gas oven illustrated how traumatic the transition could be.

Thousands of newcomers nevertheless accommodated successfully to city life, thanks to help from hospitable white employers as well as Indian friends, relatives, and a few key organizations. Before 1950 the Michigan Avenue bars unquestionably were the most important institutions in this process; they provided a relaxing place to socialize with other Indians, news from home, an opportunity to cultivate new friendships, especially with the opposite sex, and a clearinghouse for information about jobs and apartments for rent. Indian-run societies first appeared in 1940. A new era in adjustment history was foreshadowed. The NAIA, at first just a social alternative to the saloons and an advocate of ethnic pride, by the fifties pioneered a community effort to aid native newcomers with their resettlement needs. Self-help groups subsequently proliferated—the Indians of North America Foundation, the AID, the Office of Urban Indian Affairs—culminating in Washington's grant to the DAIC in 1974. Native-run centers from then on delivered the most vital services to Indian urbanites.

Over the years, why were some native newcomers successful in Detroit, while maladjusted ones became trapped in city slums or returned disheartened to Walpole Island and other reservations? First, "making it" must be defined as attainment of the goal that first brought an Indian person to Detroit. Successful migrants were the flexible and determined persons who developed enough new behavioral traits to (1) overcome the first urban barriers they faced with help from the evolving network of friends, relatives, bars, and Indian-run organizations and (2) then go on to grasp what they came for: the opportunities, mainly economic, not found on their home reservations. Successful participation in the dominant society basically meant obtaining and keeping suitable employment in the Motor City, becoming economically self-sufficient, and caring for one's family better than could be done at home. Second, if accommodation to city life hinged on employment, it followed that those who brought a high level of formal education and marketable skills to the city, or had a strong desire to learn, would have the best chance to succeed.

47

>>> CHAPTER 2 <<<

Social and Cultural Life in the City: The Early Years

Beginning with European migration to North America, Indians struggled to strike a balance between traditional ways of living and the newfangled yet tempting life-styles pressed upon them by expansive white neighbors. Circumstances forced most twentieth-century natives— the survivors of frontier skirmishes, deadly imported diseases, the slipshod treatment of federal bureaucrats—to stake out compromise positions between these poles. Daily lives and community histories ultimately expressed their ability or inability to be a part of two different worlds.

I

Winona Arriaga's automobile was unmistakably Indian and represented the coexistence of two cultures.[1] On the dashboard lay a yellow rope of braided sweet grass from her Cape Croker Reserve. Whenever she and her husband, Frank, left their Pigeon, Michigan, retirement house in 1981 for a trip south to Detroit or east to Canada, Winona lit one end of the sweet grass cord; as its delicate and pleasant fragrance filled the car, she offered a native prayer for their safe journey.

Winona Arriaga was proud of her ancestry, knowledgeable about native history, and allied to all creation. She also moved comfortably between rural reservation settings and frenetic city life. Refusing to be bound by bitterness over the past injustices suffered by her people, she generously shared her wisdom with those seeking assistance. Winona radiated friendliness. Her face, framed by gray-black braids and set with sparkling dark eyes, was expressive and often convulsed in raucous laughter. She dressed informally in slacks and patterned blouses by the early 1980s and was never far from her cigarettes and coffee pot. She loved many things, but especially a good story and a good time, helping others, and being surrounded by family and friends in Detroit, Pigeon, or at home on Cape Croker.

Ontario's Cape Croker Indian Reserve, located on the Bruce Peninsula overlooking the pristine, emerald waters of Georgian Bay, exerted an enduring influence on Winona. As a girl she blossomed in its cooperative community environment, which was personalized by her grandmother, "her rock," from whom she learned much about life and traditional Chippewa ways. Her modest home nurtured its children and gave them identity. Sadness also tinged Winona's recollections. Her parents' heated disagreements about certain matters, including religion, ultimately fractured the family (which she blamed on local missionaries who set Protestant against Catholic). Likewise traumatic was the memory of her sister being taken by the Indian agent and exiled to a boarding school at Spanish River because her parents did not keep "a proper home." After Winona's marriage, World War II further disrupted her bucolic world at Cape Croker. Indian men went off to battle the Axis powers. Relatives on the reserve became addicted to their monthly paychecks and the liquor they bought. Gardening was largely abandoned as well as other activities that traditionally contributed to economic self-sufficiency. After 1945 several band members substituted welfare payments for wartime wages, and continued drinking. Winona and her husband were among them. By the late forties, family life became so destructive that she left her youngsters with relatives and moved to Detroit.

Winona achieved enough stability to make a new life for her children in Detroit. At first she lived comfortably with an aunt on Seven Mile Road. Urban adjustment was also eased by visits to Sam Fox's, where natives congregated for weekend fun and to help one another find jobs and suitable housing. Winona and her second husband, Frank Arriaga, met at the tavern. While working at Abe Young's bookbindery, she became best friends with Louise Morales, another Chippewa newcomer from the north woods who had been raised much like Winona. They talked daily on the telephone before work; then they chatted after work. Each married Mexican Americans, who also became friends. Eventually Winona developed a network of new Indian as well as non-Indian friends—made at Sam Fox's, at the NAIA, the AID, her apartment house on Lincoln and Forest, and later at the AIS.

Winona resolutely clung to her Indian identity while adapting to the demands of contemporary America. As a Detroiter, she seemed to be socially integrated. For two decades she, Frank, and the children lived in a small apartment at Lincoln and Forest. Neighbors became one big family and included Nick and Louise Morales as well as other Mexican American, black, and white couples. Winona still struggled with her drinking problem, but the postwar years were pleasant, filled with the challenges of child-rearing, family milestones, and frequent parties whenever a cause for celebration occurred or was invented.

Together these friends endured the 1967 riot. Smoke from a burning city engulfed their living quarters; crazed looters dashed through the streets below. Heroic Nick Morales linked up garden hoses in time to save several structures from rapidly spreading flames. Louise vividly recalled Nick, silhouetted against the crimson sky, dodging popping power lines and spraying water onto garage roofs.

For Winona, accommodation to Detroit society had its limits. She always thought of herself as Indian and openly advocated those values she learned as a child at Cape Croker. For example, although a strong advocate of native Americans obtaining a public school education, she contended it should be supplemented with Title IV programs designed to give back to native children their histories and cultures, which once were stolen by Spanish River, Shingwauk, and other boarding schools. After youngsters' God-given special gifts were developed by families and teachers, they should be used properly. Indians must avoid greediness above all. Their good fortunes, their personal gifts as well as bounties harvested from nature, were meant to be shared. Winona remembered that before Cape Croker was altered by pervasive white influences and a money economy, those persons most respected had generously given of themselves to others. Modern America was too materialistic, too worshipful toward those who had amassed things. Hence the poor at her reserve and in Detroit received so little respect and were so mistreated.

Winona put these values into practice. She gave critical leadership to the AID, AIS, and to Title IV programs; she was generous toward old friends and newcomers to Detroit. Each summer and for special occasions she returned "home." Here Winona's beloved grandmother was buried. Here she could lead a simpler life: close to the earth and its seasons and other natural things. Here in her modest rental cottage she tried to show her native neighbors the love she had for them. She kept open house, sharing goods and herself with friends and relatives. At Cape Croker Winona and Frank were accepted. They drew strength from her cultural wellspring.

II

The white and Indian worlds that Arriaga straddled with some success had been in conflict since Iron Age Europeans first colonized North America. Indian cultures, as diverse as the continent's landforms, bewildered westward-driving Europeans who sought furs and farmlands and other resources. Conveniently, they concluded that native proprietors were culturally inferior. They must either accept the white man's "civilized" ways or perish. The upstart American nation inherited this myopia, and after 1776 persistently refused to admit notable Indian contributions to its culture.

The United States did more than ignore Indian cultural values; it uprooted tribes, herded them like cattle to isolated frontier reservations, then tried to obliterate their social and governmental structures. By treaty provisions and special appropriations, the government encouraged native wards to become farmers: educated, Christian, monogamous, economically self-supporting. Federal severalty legislation, for example, fractionalized reservation land. Various religious ceremonies and other cultural activities were also outlawed, while government agents, backed by Indian police and Indian courts, co-opted or deposed tribal leaders and intruded into every aspect of family life. Canadian government policies and programs for native people paralleled those of the United States.

Government assaults on Indian cultures succeeded only in part. Ironically, broader American and Canadian societies frustrated federal programs before the 1960s by erecting obstacles to assimilation: racial prejudice, social discrimination, and scant rewards or encouragement even

51

for natives seeking integration. Isolated reservations and limited Indian participation in the work force perpetuated the cultural gulf separating them and whites. Nevertheless, enough erosion took place so that reservation Indians like Winona Arriaga who migrated to Detroit carried with them, in varying degrees, only a part of what once had been complex and satisfying native cultures.

III

In the twentieth century the history of United States and Canadian reservations included more than stern government pressure to assimilate native peoples. It was equally the remarkable record of Indians fighting doggedly to preserve their social structures, their religions, their spiritual unity. To a degree they triumphed and greatly affected the cultural make-up of urban-bound kinsmen. Traditionalists survived through the toughest times, occasionally by going underground. These conservatives became by mid-century the teachers, medicine men, and political leaders for thousands of Indians who, amid their struggle for self-determination and their doubts about the values of the dominant white American culture, wished to revive the old ways. Among the New York Iroquois, wrote historian Alvin M. Josephy, Jr., "the traditional chiefs and religious instructors of the Longhouse acquired new followers and influence, and the institutions and heritage of the Confederacy of the Six Nations, which united traditional Iroquois of the United States and Canada, gained new vitality and strength."[2]

If wholesale Indian assimilation failed, what specific features of their old ways survived and were later incorporated into this post-World War II cultural flowering? First a few words of caution. Indians behaved so differently—because of idiosyncrasies, local variations, and contradictory cultural values among the tribes—that modern scholars have had difficulty generalizing about them. Decades of meticulous fieldwork among North American Indian tribes were required before anthropologists and historians could identify "a persisting cluster of core values and related, predictable behavior," wrote Nancy O. Lurie, that gave "Indian people a commonality of outlook they did not share with people of European cultural tradition." These customs and institutions were further synthesized, a process known as Pan-Indianism, in the twentieth century by improved transportation and communication, by the tendency of white neighbors to downplay cultural differences, and, ironically, by boarding schools, which brought together native children from widely separated tribes and bands.[3]

At the heart of the Indian core values was a sense of kinship from which all relationships branched out like arteries to the surrounding world. Immediate family, relatives, friends, fellow clansmen, townspeople, other living things upon the earth: all formed a person's family. It was a way of life neatly interwoven with the land. Plants and animals and human beings were linked and totally dependent on one another. ("That which the trees exhale, I inhale.") Each bonding formed a circle, part of a complex circulatory system like the human body's. ("So we live in a world of many circles and these circles constitute our identity.") This central Indian belief controlled subsequent thoughts and actions. One should seek harmony with all life through appreciation and respectful treatment of children, the elderly, the earth. Furthermore, if the Indian must eat his relatives (the plants and animals) to survive, he should not take more sustenance than necessary. Later, upon his death, he would in turn nourish other living things. Kinship to the extended human family also bred humility. A person should not exploit resources at the expense of others or act toward them in a dictatorial manner.[4]

Rooted in the historic need for Indian community survival and a belief that the world's goods were limited, the high value placed on sharing discouraged persons from hoarding food and material wealth at the expense of kinsmen. Generosity was fostered by towns and villages, while envious and greedy persons ranked low on the social scale. Because the world's goods should be shared, tribal members were expected to be cooperative in spirit, eschewing open aggressiveness and competition for personal, material objects. These social controls continued into the twentieth century. Indians were still distinguished by their readiness to give gifts, even prized possessions such as jewelry, to friends and by their general lack of emotional attachment to personal property. Extended families often still shared the wages of working members.[5]

Kinship promoted personal respect besides sharing. Indian esteem took several forms. Men and women tolerated peculiarities if persons acted sensibly, and at intertribal activities major cultural differences could even be accepted. Respect also included non-interference. One native expressed it cogently: "Don't butt in unless asked." Parents cautioned children not to interrupt others' conversations or, during periods of silence, to bother those withdrawn into private thoughts. The same deferential ideal guided adults. Whenever possible, confrontations should be avoided. If it became necessary to curb the actions of another

53

person, indirect yet potent weapons were preferred: gossip, humor (which ranged from teasing to devastating ridicule), cold indifference toward the troublemaker, and physical withdrawal. Direct scoldings were used only when less overt social controls had failed. Like Indian generosity, these passive techniques for channeling anger probably sprang from the historic need to safeguard community solidarity.[6] Respect for others was manifested in fundamental political and economic characteristics of Indian societies. Preferring not to coerce others, tribal council members engaged in lengthy debates that sparkled with persuasive oratory and were geared to reach consensual agreement. Political force thus became unnecessary, permitting native men and women much personal liberty. The freedom and relaxed patience nurtured by consensus politics likewise became key elements of the Indians' skillful adaptation to white technology during the past four hundred years.[7] Resourceful, free, self-reliant, respected: no wonder native Americans historically displayed such self-esteem.

IV

Soft summer rains
　　Falling all around
Soft summer breeze
　　Playing through the trees
Soft Indian ladies
　　Singing as they work
This is how our land began

Harsh concrete buildings
　　Standing all around
Harsh neon lights
　　Shining on the town
Harsh modern women
　　Screaming at their young
This is what our land has become[8]

For reservation Indians, urbanization demanded cultural change. Some alteration was enticed. Attractive new opportunities for intertribal mixing beckoned; so did a wider range of religious, recreational, and other social options. Some change was imposed. Non-Indian gate-keepers set the rules and pressured native newcomers to forsake tribal ways. Hence, their "persisting cluster of core values and related, predictable behavior," which had survived generations of governmental coercive acculturation in Canada and the United States, was again attacked when Indians migrated to Detroit. Quietness, humility, generosity, non-aggressiveness, reliance on extended families and tribal organizations—native characteristics esteemed back in the home communities—clashed head-on with behavior that white society considered normal for city dwellers.

V

Down through the decades Winona Arriaga and thousands of other new Detroiters were first welcomed into the Indian subculture by relatives. Extended urban families mitigated much of the transplantation trauma by mobilizing support—economic, social, emotional—for recent immigrants. Hence many adjusted to city life and survived as Indians by exchanging, in effect, one set of helpful reservation kin for another in Detroit. Individual friendships and acquaintance networks eventually branched beyond family members to inner-city and suburban neighborhoods, to fellow socializers in Michigan Avenue and Cass Corridor taverns, and, perhaps, to members of the NAIA or other service groups. Furthermore, reservation taproots remained sources of social and cultural nourishment.[9]

A broad range of assistance to relatives was provided by Martin Kiyoshk.[10] He was fifty years old in the late seventies, with graying, medium-length hair and a slight build. He dressed casually but neatly in slacks and sport shirts. Soft-spoken, relaxed, unassuming: Martin exuded personal control. He had first established residence in the 1940s after graduating from Shingwauk. During the next thirty years he savored Detroit as well as other cities across the continent: from Toronto and New York to New Orleans and Houston. Life on the road included lumberjacking on the Pacific Northwest's Olympic Peninsula. Eventually Kiyoshk settled again in Detroit and rented a Cass Corridor apartment. With his drinking problem under control, he was hired by Harry Command as an AIS substance-abuse counselor.

Kiyoshk's ties to the urban Indian community remained strong, particularly with fellow Walpole Islanders. Besides Harry Command, he chummed with Lance White, Carl Dodge, and Jerry Belleau, who was married to Martin's niece, Diane. Her mother, Martin's sister Helen, still lived on Walpole. Martin telephoned and visited her regularly, and while on the island he stayed at her home. The reserve itself charmed him: the soothing pace of life, the informality, and the nonthreatening atmosphere. Back in the city he also maintained a mutually beneficial relationship with a second sister, Thelma, who lived with her family near the Ambassador Bridge.

During the fall of 1980 one of Martin's nieces arrived at his doorstep in need of assistance. She had grown up on Walpole Island and attended high school in Wallaceburg before dropping out in grade eleven. Marriage to a Chippewa from Michigan's Isabella reservation took her to Ann Arbor, where she attended school and gave birth to two children. Next the couple moved to Bay City, where they worked for the Title IV Indian education program and she earned a GED. Then their marriage disintegrated. The father won custody of the children. Her car was repossessed, and she became so distraught that she lost fifty pounds. Where could she turn? Her band membership had been forfeited when she married a non-Walpole Islander. She felt she lacked enough political influence with the band council to get a job on the island, which would be too close to her parents anyhow. Because the "young people are all in Detroit," she decided to move there and searched out Uncle Martin at his Willis Avenue apartment.

The relationship that evolved over the next few months, though occasionally strained, was on the whole helpful for her. Martin generously provided her with room and board plus some spending money. He and his friends worked diligently to find her employment. One prospect required that she have an automobile; Martin loaned her $150 to buy a used car and another $100 for insurance and registration expenses. Occasionally, like a Dutch uncle, he counseled her.

Temporary salvation came when the DAIC hired the niece to work for its Title XX (of the Social Security Act Amendments, 1974) Service Program. Her spirits soared. She promptly vacated Martin's apartment. She began to dream of winning custody of her children, of finding an apartment in the suburbs (she felt the inner city was no place to raise her youngsters), and of becoming director of the center's Head Start class to make it a more culturally relevant program for native families. Thanks to help from a network of relatives and new friends, Detroit became a place for her, and historically for thousands of other Indian newcomers, to forget some of her painful past, enjoy a social fling in a vibrant new environment, take on the challenge of a new job, and formulate plans for a brighter future.

Another factor that historically enabled Detroit Indians to maintain their identities and traditional values was trips back to home reservations: to visit with relatives; to attend weddings, powwows, ceremonials, and funerals; to join in hunting and fishing expeditions; and to enjoy extended vacations. During the first decade that Charles and Mavis Jacobs lived in Detroit, they returned to Walpole Island each weekend to see relatives. And invariably the young couple was laden with homegrown produce for the return drive on Sunday. Summers, too, were spent on the island. Charles commuted while Mavis kept house and prepared meals and the children frolicked with friends along the inviting blue waters of the St. Clair River. On Labor Day weekends, despite the protests of disappointed youngsters, the family packed up and headed back to Michigan and school. After their move to a spacious Grosse Pointe home, Charles and Mavis still dreamed of returning to Walpole upon Charles's retirement.[11] Similarly, Teofilo Lucero moved permanently back to Taos Pueblo in 1983 after forty-five years of regular vacation visits.

Not all reservation returnees were longtime urban residents like Lucero and the Jacobes; some mobile Detroiters commuted, working and boarding in the city, often without their families, until they returned home on Friday nights. Prominent among them were Canadians who migrated to the Motor City during the off-season when outdoor work was slack or general employment conditions around their reserves were worse than in Detroit. Whether these commuters stayed for three months or a couple of years, the Michigan-and-Third Indian neighborhood and later the Cass Corridor had great appeal. Reservations thus remained a continuing source of social and cultural sustenance for migratory as well as the more permanent Detroiters.

Detroit Indian friendship networks branched beyond helpful reservation and city relatives. Michigan Avenue and Cass Corridor neighborhoods, particularly the taverns, became important social centers where chance meetings blossomed into pleasurable relationships. By the mid-twentieth century they were ports of entry into which were channeled streams of hopeful immigrants primarily from the Great Lakes region. The unique milieu included familiar native faces and attractive activities.

Also helpful were low rents and proximity to downtown shopping and employment opportunities. The Michigan Avenue neighborhood, moreover, was blessed by the presence of Fr. Clement Kern.

His ministry at Most Holy Trinity, which took in Michigan Avenue's skid row, began in 1943. The social and spiritual needs of Kern's new neighbors were enormous. A church-sponsored census along Michigan Avenue between First and Sixth revealed about three thousand residents. Many were Indians, but their mobility made it impossible to determine numbers. The most prominent businesses were thirty bars and an equal number of dingy flophouses. Drunkenness and poverty so pervaded these cheap hotels that even ambulance drivers refused to pick up stricken occupants. Most Holy Trinity assumed responsibility for transporting them to hospitals.[12]

Under Kern's leadership the church did a great deal more for needy parishioners of all races. It provided temporary shelter for indigents, family counseling, and a parochial school. High school and college scholarships were endowed. He also loaned Indians money during emergencies. The application process was simple: the needy person went to Kern, who usually remarked, "Well let's see what came in today's mail." Uncannily, there would often be just the amount needed by the day's visitor. Money was never a problem, Kern recalled. Those who received help repaid the gifts after their crises had passed. Amid destitution and personal difficulties, Kern offered hope and a chance to maintain self-respect.[13]

Collette Schott grew up just east of Most Holy Trinity on a street full of Mohawks (where the John C. Lodge Expressway is presently located). Her father was a Tarascan Indian from Mexico; her mother, a Caughnawaga Mohawk, became a good friend of Father Kern's (they called each other Alice and Clemmie). The children attended the church's parochial school. Schott had vivid memories of Kern's dedication to the neighborhood, particularly the Indians, and of her mother's willingness to help the less fortunate. For instance, Kern regularly stopped by in the middle of the night with babies and young children—Mohawks, other Indians, Mexicans, Caucasians—for Alice to look after until he could patch their families back together. All needy youngsters were accepted by Collette's mother.[14]

For twenty-five years Kern was a part of the social fabric around Most Holy Trinity. He adjusted to its blue-collar industrial workers, skid row perennials, and newcomers to Detroit. He came to understand the cultures of Indians, Mexican Americans, Maltese, and other urban neighbors. The services provided by his church or which it helped coordinate, such as community care for shattered families, foreshadowed the DAIC and other Indian-run programs of the 1970s. In the process Kern became an admirer of Detroit Indians. Looking beyond their overcrowded homes, large families, alcohol abuse, and poverty—"the insecurity of having nothing"—he discovered a wonderful people, if not judged solely by get-ahead standards. He saw happy families enjoying simple lives. Unlike those in the dominant society, native feelings of self-worth were not tied as much to marketplace productivity. Even after Clement Kern's retirement in 1977, former parishioners, including Indians like Collette Schott and Louise Morales, insisted that he return annually for a gala birthday party in his honor.[15]

Detroit natives historically reaffirmed their traditional identities in kinship networks, on return trips to home reservations, and in Indian neighborhood functions: the social work of Father Kern or simple tavern camaraderie. Indians also created a citywide formal organization to minister to their pressing social and cultural needs.

The North American Indian Association of Detroit, founded on the eve of America's entrance into World War II, first established a hospitable meeting center at the downtown YWCA, away from the Michigan Avenue taverns. Here members enjoyed card parties, box socials, and talent shows. Annual festivities such as the Thanksgiving dinner and children's Christmas party attracted several hundred persons. The association fought steadfastly against alcoholism and factionalism in the native community. It tried to offset the loss of Indian identity in the metropolis. New arrivals were also assisted.

Indian cultures, their preservation and their public expression, were fostered by the NAIA. From the start, it realized that many facets of native traditions had eroded, first during the reservation years and later as a consequence of urban adjustment. Cultural ignorance likewise abounded when members of several tribes converged on Detroit. Cherokee ways at times baffled the Chippewas, and vice versa. The same held true for their Six Nations, Sioux, Ottawa, and Potawatomi neighbors. The association devoted much attention, therefore, particularly during the 1940s, to cultural revitalization and sharing, to broadening the horizons of members. Indian history, arts, crafts, customs, legends, songs, dances: all were promoted by the NAIA. Fellow Detroiters, in turn, wanted native experiences interpreted for them by the association: on television and the radio, in schools and churches, before civic organizations, and at large social gatherings such as parades and powwows.[16]

in The Golden Jubilee parade. Five years later they celebrated Detroit's 250th birthday in a similar fashion. By 1968 the NAIA was featured in the St. Patrick's Day, Fourth of July, Labor Day, and Columbus Day parades. "We took pride in representing our people," recalled Russ Wright. "We were always in great demand and extremely well received whenever we appeared. This was evident because we always received the greatest amount of applause." Appreciative crowds, which lined downtown streets, were treated to an eye-catching holiday display. At the head of the column marched two men, one carrying the stars and stripes and the second the Indian flag (an eagle-feathered lance). They were followed by a medicine man and, walking four abreast, a colorful array of drummers, singers, and dancers, all in traditional dress. In their midst was a float on which actors depicted a historic scene. The performers cavalcade demonstrated to non-Indians that native people were not savage, vanished Americans; they were fellow Detroiters proud of their heritage, organized, and respectable.[17]

Powwows eventually eclipsed parades as the most popular and meaningful social gatherings. The NAIA sponsored its first such get-together in 1959. Held at the Y, it was financially successful (raising more than three hundred dollars for the association's scholarship fund) and attracted more than five hundred persons including visiting dancers from Chicago's American Indian Center and Isabella Reservation in central Michigan. A growing popularity prompted Detroiters in 1969 to stage the first outdoor powwow. It drew three thousand persons and yielded two thousand dollars in income.[18]

By then, southeast Michigan powwows had taken on distinctive characteristics. A successful two-day affair demanded greater cooperation and involvement among active NAIA members than any other annual social event. For example, the association maintained strict control over the authenticity of arts and crafts for sale. Officials permitted only natives to set up traders' booths, assuring that Indians benefited economically and that their artistic talents were stimulated. Opportunities abounded for intertribal mixing among colorful dancers, drummers, singers, and visitors of all ages. Many traveled considerable distances: from Quebec, Ontario, and the prairie provinces of Canada as well as from several Great Lakes states. The NAIA hosts, who sought to foster Indian unity, personally welcomed guests and encouraged them to mingle by providing free food and scheduling opportunities for informal conversations outside the dance arena. Intertribal exchange, greeting old friends and making new ones, so excited some Detroiters that they joined the summer powwow circuit, traveling each weekend to a different gathering in the Midwest or as far away as the northern Rockies and the American Southwest.[19]

What lay behind the powwow's popularity in the sixties? In his study of the NAIA, Gordon Northrup concluded that they were not merely theatrical performances designed to raise money; powwows provided a unique setting where participants, like farmers at a county fair, could come together and feel their identity and their common interests with other tribesmen. Proud natives also sensed they were perpetuating the traditions of their people when they enjoyed dances and singing, food and crafts. Moreover, within the dance circle Indians dressed in traditional clothing were in charge, set off from and superior in numbers to non-Indians compelled to watch from the sidelines, a reversal of the dominant and subordinate roles usually played by the two groups. Finally, like the parade, Detroit powwows conveyed a message to the public about Indian beauty and strength and unity.[20]

The NAIA's concern for preserving traditional cultures and expressing them publicly in captivating parades and powwows naturally broadened Indian perspectives. Once-provincial families showed greater concern about national native issues. Prominent, too, was an upsurge in Pan-Indianism. Beginning in 1945 national and regional Indian topics increasingly captured the attention of sophisticated association members whose interests had been expanded by World War II experiences. The need to improve the lot of Indians nationwide was a recurrent theme voiced by the NAIA leaders. If Detroiters cooperated more with tribesmen in southeast Michigan and across the continent, they could solve many of the problems plaguing their people and more effectively champion native rights. Such appeals led to significant actions. The plight of rural Navajos, devastated by blizzards during the winter of 1947, prompted not only sympathy but relief money from the Detroit native community. Washington's termination policy the following decade precipitated a special association meeting because of concern for the future of Michigan's Isabella reservation. Because the NAIA saw itself as a champion of Indians even beyond the Detroit area, it convened the membership in 1964. This time the focus of the special gathering was the Kinzua Dam controversy, which involved the flooding of Seneca reservation lands. The association dispatched two members to the upper Allegheny River on the New York-Pennsylvania border with instructions to learn about the beleaguered tribe's condition and to offer assistance on behalf of their anxious Detroit brethren.[21]

Pan-Indianism, usually associated with intertribal cooperation or simply the blending of a few aboriginal cultural characteristics, triggered a fullblown revitalization movement in Detroit with guidance from the NAIA. Since its founding, the organization faithfully promoted solidarity among metropolitan natives. Its president addressed the membership during World War II as follows: "You should all think of yourselves as Indians first, and not as belonging to a particular tribe, or as coming from Canada or from the U.S. The Club is for all Indians and not for a clique or a particular tribe. Banish from your minds any petty thoughts or jealousies, and think only of the good that will come from the unity of the American Indian." Several factors assisted the association in breaking down barriers to unity. One was the erosion of native cultural differences as a consequence of urban adjustment. Detroit's dominant society, moreover, took scant notice of band affiliations. Whether being interviewed on the radio or television, dealing with the YWCA, or appearing before local civic organizations, the NAIA leaders represented and were expected to speak for all city Indians.[22]

The preamble to the NAIA's constitution set forth the goals of its innovative revitalization crusade:

1. To establish a meeting center for North American Indians
2. To promote the study of Indian history, arts, customs, legends, traditions, songs and dances and to keep alive aboriginal cultures
3. To prove this culture was never devoid of beauty, but always full of respect for life and enriching faith in the Supreme and divine power
4. To place before the public reliable information for fuller understanding of North American Indians
5. To promote and assist Indians to attain higher education and to make every effort to elevate the environment of our Indian race
6. To lay a cornerstone of everlasting friendship
7. To assist each other in time of need

By no means was this a backward looking document, encouraging withdrawal from modern civilization and restoration of the woodland natives' pre-Colombian heyday. Nor did the association advocate a wholesale surrendering of cultural distinctiveness. It envisioned instead a compromise solution to perplexing urban difficulties. Accordingly, Detroit's Indian citizens would someday be engaged in city life as valued members: well-adapted and benefiting from contemporary American society yet proud of their heritage and practitioners of still-viable facets of the old ways.[23]

To achieve such a meaningful life, the NAIA prescribed that several steps be taken. The association's most important task, emphasized President Dean George in 1972, was "to keep the traditions, the life styles and the spiritual outlook of the American Indian alive in Detroit." In particular the NAIA sought to perpetuate native history (including a knowledge of treaty rights), arts and crafts, selected customs and values, songs and dances, and traditional dress (for use during ceremonials and special social occasions). This was the cultural foundation upon which rested the very pride of urban Indians and thus the NAIA's entire revitalization movement. Second, to upgrade the status of Detroit natives, the association advocated acceptance of some features of the non-Indian society. The key was mainstream schooling. Proud Indians (eager to be educated and to make a more satisfactory life for themselves in the city) must also be respected and accepted by the public. For this to take place, attitudes must change. Here was the final challenge for NAIA members: to provide Detroiters with reliable information about historic as well as contemporary native peoples, their neighbors who were worthy of esteem.[24]

During the postwar decades Russ Wright supplied inspirational leadership for Detroit's native revitalization movement and best personified the association's urban Indian ideal. Wright, who claimed Cherokee blood, retired from a show business career in the mid-fifties and became a crusader for Indian rights. For twenty-seven years he was a Michigan social worker. Wright wielded great influence: as president of the Michigan State Employees Association (the first United States labor organization to be headed by an Indian), a director of WTVS-TV, and for nine years a board member of the Greater Detroit Chapter of the National Council on Alcoholism. Most critical for the Motor City Indian community during the sixties was his presidency of the NAIA. Combining skills as a magnetic and charming entertainer with his earnest desire to improve the lot of urban natives, Wright urged fellow Indians to unite behind his leadership for the common good. He called upon all to follow the association's principles by returning to the true Indian way of honor, truthfulness, and integrity; proclaiming with pride their Indian identity to fellow Detroiters; and, with help from the NAIA, doing "missionary work among your people," too many of whom had developed feelings of inferiority because of slipshod treatment by the dominant society.[25] Wright's evangelism attracted a large following. He was a living testimony that the association's revitalization goals could be achieved. Charismatic Russ Wright had a good education, success, and much influence with the non-Indian community, yet still associated with Indians and was exultant about his identity. Obviously city life could have new meaning for native people.

VI

Predictably the association's call for cultural compromise was not heeded by all Detroit Indians. By 1970 they were more than five thousand with kin groups occupying different positions on the continuum between two cultural poles: reservation life and city life.

One small cluster on the social-cultural continuum truly became urban Indians. Disinterested in reservation roots, submerged in competitive and fast-paced city life, divorced from fellow Indians, accepting of industrial values and life-styles, they became merely Detroiters of a particular ancestry. Indian identity was abandoned or at least was no longer a driving force in their lives.

A second group, numerically the most important for this study and which included Russ Wright and Winona Arriaga, selected strategic compromise points between polar extremes. Consciously pluralistic, they mixed cultures and maintained a dual orientation, resisting total surrender to either the urban white or the Indian reservation milieu. Working-class and professional suburbanites with steady jobs, they exploited Detroit for economic purposes and seemed committed to city life. Some married outside their tribes and race. Generally they adapted to prosper. But they did not become brown white people. Even after many years in the city, they remained traditionalists and in varying degrees continued to look toward their home reservations. Here they owned land. Here kinship ties were strongest, and they spent many weekends and summer vacations. Here was the touchstone of their unconquerable Indian identity.

A third set of families rejected outright the dominant society's lifestyle and compromised minimally to survive. Like flotsam they drifted about the inner city: the poorest and least educated of the metropolitan natives, coming and going seasonally, sinking few roots. Traditional reservation alignments still governed their lives and often eventually caused abandonment of urban outposts and a return to rural home communities.

Russ Wright acknowledged that historically some suburban Indians were so engrossed in competitive, mainstream Detroit economic and social life that they became separated from inner-city cohorts, the NAIA, and, sometimes, from reservation roots. Cecil Rodd, born on the Sarnia Reserve in Ontario, was a prosperous and skilled Michigan industrial worker until his retirement in the mid-sixties. He and his wife and children lived in suburban Romulus during most of his working years. All signs pointed to complete social assimilation. Rodd lamented that he had abandoned the Indian way of his youth, but he really had no other alternative than to walk the white man's road. In 1944 Rodd became an evangelical Christian and joined a local Baptist congregation. A self-described loner at work, he avoided taverns on Michigan and Cass. Contacts with downtown Indians were limited to inviting some to attend his suburban church. Only a few accepted the offer. Although he was fairly knowledgeable about Indian history, Rodd's ties to Sarnia withered with the passing years. He surrendered band status; eventually he knew few persons living there. Home was Romulus, where he raised his children, where his wife was buried, where he was accepted and respected.[26]

A variation on this pattern of assimilated suburban Indians was the Jacobs family. When Charles and Mavis first migrated to the city from Walpole Island, they not only visited the reserve each weekend but participated in NAIA social functions. But after their move to Grosse Pointe in 1952 and enrollment of the growing family in neighboring schools, the parents became so absorbed locally that they lost touch with the metropolitan Indian community. The Jacobs were involved in church work besides school parent-teacher associations and athletics. There was no question about their social integration. Teachers and school officials treated the youngsters respectfully. Because the boys were excellent athletes they were courted by coaches and admired by classmates. Neighborhood boys and girls always congregated at the Jacobs's, whose children were in great demand as overnight guests. The Jacobs family, mirroring Charles's success as an engineer, was committed to developing skills that would help them succeed in Detroit's mainstream while simultaneously preserving their sense of Indian identity. Even though contacts with inner-city natives lapsed, Charles and Mavis and the children nevertheless maintained their affiliations on Walpole, particularly during the summer months.[27]

Of the Indians who lived away from downtown Detroit, Russ Wright most admired those who never lost touch with the NAIA, who regularly mixed with inner-city natives, and generously assisted the less fortunate. Teofilo Lucero was determined to succeed in the white man's world while preserving his culture and helping needy urban relocatees.

Lucero was a man of contrasts. Stepping out of his blue pickup truck onto a Detroit Street, sporting a western shirt, tooled leather belt, blue jeans, and boots, he appeared to be a new arrival from New Mexico. But he was not a cowboy. He was a full-blooded Pueblo Indian and a respected elder who had lived in the city for more than forty years. His muscular torso, long black hair, and smooth skin belied his seventy-five years. Around non-Indians his face was often expressionless, but at a native gathering his eyes sparkled and he became outspoken. Though he lived and worked in the Motor City, he remained at heart an Indian: in his strong tie to his Taos home, his vast knowledge of native southwestern and woodland cultures, his spiritual beliefs, and in his willingness, as head of the DAIC's Arts and Crafts Department, to share generously his reservoir of wisdom with others.[28]

As one of the NAIA's early members, Teofilo Lucero stimulated cultural revitalization and sharing. He taught classes on Pueblo-style dancing, drumming, singing, and costume making, infusing a distinctive southwestern influence into metropolitan Indian activities. Lucero beseeched native parents to pass on their heritage to the children. He strived to strike a balance between Indian and white ways. For example, Teofilo recognized that to succeed in the Motor City, one must have a solid, mainstream education. He encouraged his own children as well as other native youngsters to stay in school and develop employment skills for their urban-industrial world. Yet Lucero made sure that his religious beliefs remained at the center of his life. Like those of many other urban Indians, Teofilo's adjustments were mandated by the dominant society. Otherwise he would simply have been swallowed up, assimilated; or, if all change was resisted, he could have become (1) totally alienated and dependent on the dole or (2) forced to return to his Taos reservation. Teofilo's compromise did not signal deep respect for the white man. In Lucero's heart and in the hearts of many Detroit Indians there burned a fierce anger over the loss of native lands more than a century earlier. Obsessed with time and money, whites had since shown scant regard for mother earth and her bounty, he claimed. They squandered resources. They grew fat upon the land. They hoarded it and fenced it and even became contemptuous of its aboriginal inhabitants. Ironically, both the Indian sense of brotherhood and cultural closeness to the earth were worthy of emulation, if only the white world would slow down, would look, and listen. Yet Teofilo Lucero made his peace with the dominant society. He wore its clothes, drove one of its pickup trucks, worked in its factories, owned a home on one of its residential streets, paid its taxes.

But like so many NAIA members, he never lost his Indian identity. It remained the internal, spiritual compass directing his social-cultural life.[29]

Teofilo Lucero, like Russ Wright, Dean George, and others who did not live downtown, still retained a deep concern for the welfare of inner-city Indians and did not consider even down-and-outers to be riffraff. The reluctance of so many to acquire a formal education and to work long and hard when jobs became available mystified Dean. He was not sure what they really wanted out of life in Detroit. Rampant alcoholism, even among the downtown youth, also distressed him. But when the opportunity arose to help those in need, such as the establishment of an Indian center or a new educational program, no one in Detroit worked with more dedication than Dean George.[30]

Inner-city natives historically divided into two groups. First were the families whose downtown residence turned out to be temporary. Household heads had enough formal education to obtain steady employment and thus support the family. Children were encouraged to complete high school and, if necessary, to go on to college. Diligence and frugality by all members were expected so that the family's resources would multiply, even if this meant partial withdrawal from traditional kinship networks and their attendant responsibilities. Optimism about life in the dominant society usually culminated in the purchase of a house on the city's fringes or within the suburban ring. Here native families followed lifestyles of their choosing: either maintaining contact with the Indian community through the NAIA (like Russ Wright, Teofilo Lucero, and Dean George) or becoming more separated and assimilated (like Cecil Rodd and the Jacobses).

For a second Indian group, the inner city was never a springboard to suburbia. Instead, these families remained trapped in poverty pockets on Michigan avenue or along the Cass Corridor, plagued with the same difficulties that originally drove them from rural reservations: unemployment or underemployment, overcrowded and substandard housing, health problems (particularly substance abuse), and low educational achievement. Hardship abounded. They eked out a living by working part-time jobs and by pooling resources with close kin and friends. Some accepted public assistance. Over the years a few families sank urban roots, perpetuating a cycle of poverty and self-destructive behavior down through the generations. More often, these large households were like migrants in search of seasonal employment, drifting back and forth from reservation to city and back again. Even within Detroit they were constantly on the move, escaping from crowded apartments and rent increases or looking for quarters closer to friends and relatives.[31]

Downtown natives not destined for suburbia exhibited distinctive social and cultural characteristics. One was a strong sense of Indian identity, although by 1970 most no longer spoke their native languages and public expressions of pride were confined to special occasions such as parades and powwows. These Indians repressed a wide range of feelings. School officials thus characterized native children as shy and withdrawn. They rarely laughed or cried with their classmates. Another example was the tendency, once an adult started drinking in a friendly neighborhood tavern, for pent-up emotions to gush out.

Linked to un-demonstrativeness was the preference for avoiding confrontation with landlords, employers, school officials, medical personnel, and other non- Indians occupying authority positions in a city geared to competition and aggressive advocacy. If offended by a set of circumstances, Indians simply walked away from Detroit apartments, jobs, and schools, often at great cost to themselves. Native passiveness, their tendency to ignore problems and troublesome people, even placed them at a disadvantage in dealing with welfare agencies. Admittedly a few unscrupulous families manipulated the system to their advantage, obtaining assistance checks, for instance, from both Detroit and Walpole Island. But they were extraordinary. Far more common were the frustration and discouragement felt by needy inner-city families required to fill out endless forms, jump through bureaucratic hoops, and grapple with computer errors as well as with caseworkers who assumed their clients were fraudulent and must be investigated. To avoid such confrontation and rejection, downtown Indians frequently turned to one another for assistance, another distinguishing trait. Michigan Avenue and later the Cass Corridor appealed to them not just because rents were low; Indian friends lived and socialized in these neighborhoods. Here one could get help: money, a place to sleep, personal support during a crisis time. Here native youngsters buddied together, roaming the streets and going to movies, just like their parents did in apartment buildings or on the job.[32]

Individual beliefs of inner-city native families about Detroit society and the future fueled a stubborn adherence to their own life-styles. They avoided integration with whites and declined to reveal deep thoughts to them. Aggressive whites, whose institutions suppressed Indians, also seemed to take life too seriously; they were overly concerned about the future, unable to enjoy life one day at a time because they were so obsessed with hoarding money. For these Indians, keeping up with the

Joneses had little allure. Inevitably, this refusal to compete in the metropolitan mainstream led to social isolation. Although many downtown natives never lost their sense of humor and even joked about themselves and non-Indians, they nevertheless evidenced much despair and frustration over their poverty and the unlikelihood, given America's history of broken promises to Indian people, of conditions improving for them or their children in the future.[33]

Indian family life drew discerning comments from fellow downtown residents. Father Kern, for example, who looked beyond overcrowded native homes and apartments, past the alcoholism and itinerant fathers, recognized the happiness they shared. He saw the spiritual quality of their close-to-nature way of life. Particularly admirable, he felt, was the fortitude of Indian mothers and the close ties they forged among their children, who often numbered five or six.[34] Other observers noted the lack of support for formal education among these Indians as well as the variety of family composition. Besides the nuclear household consisting of a married couple and their children, many men and women were separated from their spouses and lived with "boyfriends" and "girlfriends." Others, not married, also lived together. Native neighbors made no differentiation among them.[35] Nevertheless, the abundance of broken homes exacted a social price, particularly from the children as evidenced by household poverty, debilitating health problems, and abusive behavior.

VII

The three Detroit groupings, which jelled by 1970, were the results of individual Indian decisions. Because people and the times in which they live change, the alignments were not always permanent. The pull of both polar extremes on Indians living along this continuum generated a long-term tension and instability. With the passing years, some urban Indians predictably shifted, perhaps radically, the degree to which they maintained their ethnicity and tribal heritage. Socially integrated Indians, for example, became militant traditionalists; cultural conservatives might marry non-Indians, obtain well-paying jobs, start families, and disappear into suburbia. Such shifts were especially prevalent in the 1960s and early 1970s.

For both Canada and the United States, the sixties and early seventies was an era of social turmoil when the pressing needs of poverty-stricken and neglected native citizens were called to the attention of society at large. The grass-roots civil rights movement together with great-society initiatives emanating from Washington prompted thousands of North American Indians to rethink the meaning of their identity. Many Motor City natives fought valiantly to preserve what remained of their heritage and to bolster a sense of community. Other Detroiters came out of the closet. No longer hiding and hoping to be overlooked, they acknowledged with pride their Indian-ness. All seemed bent on taking their rightful place in American society.

CHAPTER 3

Working

Because of the chronic lack of jobs on Walpole Island Indian Reserve during this century, many residents chose off-reserve work. The glass and sugar factories in nearby Wallaceburg, Ontario, have hired Indians at least since the 1920s. Burton Jacobs, a former chief, grew up there. During World War II, he and sixty to seventy other band men commuted daily across the St. Clair River to Algonac, Michigan, where Chris Craft and the Warner Foundry enjoyed boom times because of defense contracts. Also on the ferry were about forty women. Well-to-do Detroiters employed them as domestics in their vacation homes. One was Roseline Fisher, the mother of Bill Colwell; for forty years this trusted and faithful housekeeper supported herself in the resort town where her son graduated from high school.[1] Algonac and Wallaceburg maintained their economic importance to Walpole through the 1970s, as verified by the still busy *Lowell D.* car ferry and heavy traffic on the swing bridge linking the island to the Ontario mainland. As far back as islanders can remember, Detroit also offered economic attractions. Indians were drawn to the city first to sell their furs and crafts; after the automotive boom, they worked for wages in the factories. Also, Detroiters had regularly journeyed upriver to Walpole—buying Indian-made products, enjoying outdoor fairs and powwows, renting riverside cottages, and hunting ducks. In the early 1920s Henry Ford docked his yacht at the island. He spoke to 71 band members gathered at a nearby meeting hall about the economic development of their reserve and the need for natives to have a sound technical education. The wealthy industrialist added that he would like to hire some Indian factory workers.[2] From then on, the image of Detroit as a cornucopia of opportunity for underemployed Indians was indelibly fixed in their minds.

Notable among those attracted to the Detroit job market were Charles and Mavis Solomon Jacobs. Both were born and raised on Walpole Island. Mavis's parents, prominent merchants and farmers on the reserve, sent her to a convent boarding school at Chatham, Ontario, for her high school education. The academic training was excellent. She mixed freely with an exclusive student body drawn from several countries. Unlike some repressive government and mission boarding schools composed entirely of Indian children, this institution treated Mavis with respect, and she internalized no negative feelings about her race or culture. After graduation in 1939 she accepted a job with a Detroit friend of her father's and roomed with a cousin. In 1941 Mavis married Charles Jacobs, who had also received a fine off-reserve education and then had to move to the Motor City to make a living. He did so well in art and mathematics at the Sarnia Collegiate Institute that Charles reckoned he should get more training as a draftsman. So he worked nights at a sugar factory in Mt. Clemens to pay for daytime classes at Detroit College of Applied Science. He graduated in 1940. He, too, found work, as an apprentice draftsman with help from an employment service. The war forced a two-year hiatus in his career, while he served in the Canadian armed forces; otherwise he rose steadily to the top of his field. Between 1946 and 1980 he was a hard-working employee of Erie Engineering Company. "The Indian" (as he was affectionately called) was referred to by the company's automotive clients, including the Big Three, as the best layout man in the city. Lots of work came his way, including Saturday and Sunday overtime; the company claimed it just could not get along without him. Rarely could the family gather for dinner before 7:30 in the evening. Such determination and sacrifice eventually enabled the Jacobses to buy a comfortable home in Grosse Pointe. Here they raised seven children. All have fond memories of summers spent on Walpole Island. When the youngest was fourteen, Mavis went back to work, and for eleven years was a comparison shopper for J. L. Hudson.[3]

I

The economic success achieved by the Jacobs family was not unique. By mid-century Indian migrants to Detroit found employment in nearly every occupation. During the twenties, thirties, and forties most women began their careers as domestic servants; schools had trained them for such work and they preferred a homelike atmosphere when first moving to the city. At one time Elsie Staats, Myrtle Kiser, Leona David, and Louise Morales were housekeepers. Edith Beaulieu, a Mohawk-Delaware from Muncey Reserve in Ontario, arrived in the mid-twenties with her father, a railroad engineer for the Pere Marquette who was transferred to Detroit. The following decade she did housework around the city and also met her future husband Roman, a Minnesota Chippewa, at Sam Fox's. Increased industrial production plus the local labor shortage caused by America's entry into World War II drew many Indian women into factories for the first time. Edith worked at Packard Motor Company on fighter airplanes to be shipped to Great Britain.[4] Among those Indians already in the plants was young Teofilo Lucero; he had been employed by Midland Steel since 1937. Before Pearl Harbor his assembly line made Chrysler car frames; then the plant converted to Sherman tank production. He recalled that about one hundred other Indians worked at Midland by 1941. Teofilo remained on their payroll more than twenty-one years.[5]

For thousands of other Indian men and women, automotive production, allied industries, and construction remained economic mainstays. Six Nations ironworkers, for example, have included Ron DeLeary, Dave Miracle, and Guy Doxtator. Elmer Sebastian, former president of the NAIA and a board chairman of the DAIC, worked in the building trades during the postwar years. John David was an industrial painter. Maynard Kennedy, president of the association during the late 1970s, belonged to the riggers and machinery erectors local union. Dean George drove a moving van throughout the eastern United States for eight years; then he went to work for Hare Cartage, delivering car parts to assembly lines in the metropolitan area. Frank Alberts also was a teamster.

Flexibility characterized the careers of some Indians. Martin Kiyoshk, dead set against long-term commitments after a restrictive boarding school experience, apprenticed himself in a Detroit upholstery shop to learn a good trade. Afterward he moved from city to city, always able to find employment. When Carol Coulon Kawegoma, Elsie Staats, Winona Arriaga, Louise Morales, and Leona David needed jobs, they drew on a variety of skills; periodically they were housekeepers, barmaids and hotel maids, department store clerks, waitresses, assembly line workers, postal clerks, and bookbinders.

The Detroit Indian community likewise included small-business owners and well-paid professionals such as Charles Jacobs. Among the small-business owners were Harry Command, operator of a window-washing company, and John David, whose pet supply business grossed more than a million dollars a year by the late 1960s. Architect Sylvester Stone, a childhood friend of David's from Sarnia Reserve, based his firm in Utica, Michigan; he specialized in commercial commissions with Indian motifs during the seventies. Health-care professionals included Edith Beaulieu, who obtained her GED and LPN certificates later in life to help children, and Bill Memberto, head of the Indian center's health department since 1978. Two licensed social workers, Russ Wright and Harry Command, regularly counseled clients at Urban Indian Affairs and the AIS. Equally prominent were college-educated native administrators like Jim Hillman of the DAIC and Judith Mays, director of the Detroit Indian Educational and Cultural Center. Attorney Beverly Clark was another noteworthy professional. She, too, had Sarnia Reserve roots, and in the late 1970s volunteered her expertise to the NAIA as well as Michigan Indian Legal Services.

II

Despite these professional successes and the variety of employment found by urban migrants, most Indians were clustered in low paying positions. In his 1950 Detroit study, Ralph West observed that limited education confined about half the male and 15 percent of the female workers to unskilled or semiskilled auto factory jobs. The construction industry, especially iron-working and rigging, employed another quarter; many were Six Nations tribesmen who obtained their skills back East before moving to the Motor City.[6] The 1970 census classified precisely, for the first time, Indian occupations in metropolitan Detroit. Drawn from this data, table 2 reveals native concentration in poorer-paying jobs.

TABLE 2
Distribution of Detroit Indians,
by Occupation and Sex (Age 16 and over) (1970)

	Males (%)	Females (%)
Professional, Technical, and Kindred Workers	9	9
Managers, Officials, and Proprietors	7	1
Clerical and Kindred Workers	6	25
Sales	2	5
Craftsmen, Foremen, and Kindred Workers	24	1
Operatives and Skilled Workers	30	16
Laborers	13	2
Service Workers	9	31
Miscellaneous Groups	0	10
Total	100(1,238)	100(750)

Source: United States Bureau of the Census, *Census of Population: 1970 ... American Indians*, 168–77.
Note: Figures in parentheses are the numbers of respondents.

Only 14 percent of the work force were professionals and managers. Work in Detroit was still advantageous in 1970 if one noted that only 11 percent of the male work force on all reservations could be considered professionals and managers. However, when urban Indian males were compared with white counterparts across the nation (27 percent of whom occupied the top two employment categories) the native Detroit worker clearly was disadvantaged and underemployed.[7] At the close of the 1970s, the DAIC's survey of Wayne County again documented how few people (8 percent) were employed as professionals and managers (table 3). Moreover, most males still worked as craftsmen, foremen, operatives, skilled workers, and laborers.[8]

TABLE 3
Distribution of Wayne County Indians,
by Occupation and Sex (Age 16 and over) (1978)

	Males (%)	Females (%)
Professional, Technical, and Kindred Workers	4	6
Managers, Officials, and Proprietors	4	2
Clerical and Kindred Workers	3	28
Sales	2	4
Craftsmen, Foremen, and Kindred Workers	36	10
Operatives and Skilled Workers	19	6
Laborers	17	5
Service Workers	11	32
Miscellaneous Groups	4	7
Total	100(1,007)	100(574)

Source: Bashshur et al., *Native Americans in Wayne County,* 102.
Note: Figures in parentheses are the numbers of respondents.

At least these underemployed Detroiters had jobs. What about those unable to obtain work? During the 1940s wartime boom, anyone who wanted a job could find it, according to Russ Wright. Not until the fifties did the local economy sag and substantial Indian unemployment occur. The worst was yet to come: the sixties saw a phasing out of many unskilled and semiskilled jobs held by Indians, especially in small plants, and no federal programs or Indian centers existed to help out-of-work tribesmen acquire new skills. By 1970 Wright estimated that many city Indians were unemployed and poor. The census that year showed that 9 percent of Detroit Indian men and 10.5 percent of native women in the labor force were jobless.[9] These figures represented a great improvement over the general reservation scene, where the unemployment rate for males reached 41 percent. On the other hand, only 4 percent of white American males fit this employment category.[10] The Detroit American Indian Center's survey of Wayne County revealed persistent high unemployment as late as 1978 (tables 4 and 5).

76

TABLE 4

Selected Reasons for Not Working among Wayne County Indian Males, by Age (1978)

Reasons for Not Working	16–20 (%)	21–30 (%)	31–40 (%)	Age Groups 41–50 (%)	51–60 (%)	>60 (%)	Total (%)
Retired	—	—	3(1)	11(5)	21(10)	78(45)	13(61)
Student	71(138)	11(10)	—	—	—	—	31(148)
Disabled	2(4)	9(8)	26(10)	29(13)	52(25)	17(10)	15(70)
Unemployed	25(47)	63(55)	51(20)	39(17)	19(9)	—	31(148)
Laid-off	2(5)	10(9)	12(5)	5(2)	—	—	5(21)
Sick Leave	—(1)	7(6)	8(3)	16(7)	8(4)	5(3)	5(24)
Total	100(195)	100(88)	100(39)	100(44)	100(48)	100(58)	100(472)

Source: Bashshur et al., *Native Americans in Wayne County*, 97.
Note: Figures in parentheses are the numbers of respondents.

TABLE 5
Selected Reasons for Not Working among Wayne County Indian Females, by Age (1978)

Reasons for Not Working	16–20 (%)	21–30 (%)	31–40 (%)	Age Groups 41–50 (%)	51–60 (%)	>60 (%)	Total (%)
Retired	—	—	—	1(1)	6(6)	47(32)	4(39)
Student	67(158)	8(18)	2(4)	2(4)	—	—	18(184)
Housewife	13(31)	57(125)	81(204)	79(130)	67(65)	42(29)	56(584)
Disabled	1(2)	2(5)	1(3)	7(12)	13(13)	4(3)	4(38)
Unemployed	17(39)	29(63)	14(35)	10(17)	13(12)	7(5)	16(171)
Laid-off	1(1)	1(3)	1(3)	—	—	—	1(7)
Sick Leave	1(3)	3(6)	1(3)	1(1)	1(1)	—	1(14)
Total	100(234)	100(220)	100(252)	100(165)	100(97)	100(69)	100(1,037)

Source: Bashshur et al., *Native Americans in Wayne County*, 98.
Note: Figures in parentheses are the numbers of respondents.

TABLE 6

Distribution of Non-working Wayne County Indian Males Who Looked for Work during the Four Weeks before the Survey, by Age (1978)

				Age Groups			
	16–20 (%)	21–30 (%)	31–40 (%)	41–50 (%)	51–60 (%)	>60 (%)	Total (%)
Looked for Work	33(62)	61(56)	50(21)	43(81)	8(4)	2(1)	35(225)
Did not Look	67(124)	39(35)	50(21)	57(24)	92(44)	98(55)	65(303)
Total	100(186)	100(91)	100(92)	100(105)	100(48)	100(56)	100(528)

Source: Bashshur et al., *Native Americans in Wayne County*, 100.
Note: Figures in parentheses are the numbers of respondents.

TABLE 7

Distribution of Non-working Wayne County Indian Females Who Looked for Work during the Four Weeks before the Survey, by Age (1978)

| | | | | Age Groups | | | |
	16–20 (%)	21–30 (%)	31–40 (%)	41–50 (%)	51–60 (%)	>60 (%)	Total (%)
Looked for Work	20(42)	26(55)	12(29)	7(10)	6(6)	3(2)	15(144)
Did not Look	80(165)	74(156)	88(205)	93(140)	94(89)	97(66)	85(821)
Total	100(207)	100(211)	100(234)	100(150)	100(95)	100(68)	100(965)

Source: Bashshur et al., *Native Americans in Wayne County*, 100.
Note: Figures in parentheses are the numbers of respondents.

Among twenty- and thirty-year-old Indians, whose jobless rate was more than 50 percent, most were looking for work (tables 6 and 7), highlighting the shortage of suitable jobs for their modest skill levels.

University of Michigan consultants who analyzed this data for the center concluded that for twenty-one- to thirty-year-old males the unemployment rate was about three times the national average.[11]

The Detroit American Indian Center's 1978 census of 1,639 Wayne County native families revealed widely varied incomes (table 8). At one end of the scale, 433 families exceeded $20,000 a year; at the other end, 32 percent had earnings of $7,000 or less, a percentage nearly double the national figure.[12]

TABLE 8
Distribution of Family Income among
Wayne County Indians (1978)

Family Income Level	Percent
$3000 or less	14(229)
$3,001–5,000	11(185)
$5,001–7,000	7(118)
$7,001–10,000	8(134)
$10,001–12,000	5(90)
$12,001–15,000	9(153)
$15,001–18,000	12(191)
$18,001–20,000	7(106)
$20,001–25,000	13(206)
over $25,000	14(227)
Total	100(1,639)

Source: Bashshur et al., *Native Americans in Wayne County*, 105.
Notes: Median family income category =$13,001–$14,000.
Figures in parentheses are numbers of respondents.

The Wayne County survey also focused on poverty levels, which took into account income and family size. Based on State of Michigan guidelines, 26 percent of the Indian families lived below the poverty line (table 9).

TABLE 9
Distribution of Wayne County Indian Families below Poverty Level, by Selected Characteristics (1978)

Characteristic	Families below Poverty Level (%)
Overall	26(428)
Area of Residence	
Cass Corridor	65(96)
West Detroit	37(190)
East Detroit	27(47)
Suburbs	12(94)
Family Size	
One Member	46(113)
Two Members	36(81)
3–5 Members	20(182)
6+ Members	20(52)
Age of Family Head	
17–20	67(35)
21–30	32(114)
31–40	20(101)
41–50	18(62)
51–60	26(61)
60+	37(51)
Employment Status of Head	
Employed	10(114)
Unemployed	58(311)
Education of Head	
0–7	40(52)
8	36(61)
9–11	33(170)
12	18(94)
13–15	17(29)
16+	12(6)
Sex of Head	
Male	18(231)
Female	59(197)

Source: Bashshur et al., *Native Americans in Wayne County*, 113.
Note: Figures in parentheses are the numbers of respondents.

Area of residence was tied in with poverty (65 percent of Cass Corridor families were in this category as against 12 percent for the suburbs); likewise significant were family size and the age, sex, education, and employment of the family head. What kept these disadvantaged Indians functioning was public assistance. Nineteen percent of their families received help in the form of Aid to Dependent Children, food stamps, medicaid general assistance, and social security.[13]

III

The clustering of Indians in low-paying positions, the community's high level of unemployment, the distressful number of poverty-stricken families by the 1970s: all originated from a persistent cycle of native working problems. First there was the difficulty of finding a good job. Upon arriving in the city nearly seventy years ago, Elsie Staats and Myrtle Kiser accepted modest pay and unskilled positions because of their limited education.[14] This became the pattern in Detroit. During the late forties, Martin Kiyoshk, having graduated from Shingwauk, likewise discovered that his boarding-school skills did not mesh well with the Detroit marketplace. Some newcomers like Charles Jacobs, driven to excel, temporarily endured poor-paying jobs in order to finance more education; another was architect Sylvester Stone, who paid for his training with ghetto pool-hall winnings. But they were exceptional. "I became an architect," Stone recalled, "but many of my friends, who didn't have a skill like mine, are alcoholics now. They were all laborers and could only hold day-to-day jobs. I come back to the old neighborhood now and find them broke."[15] This observation was confirmed in the early 1970s by the AID's Carleen Pedrotti. Most Cass Corridor Indian residents, she estimated, lacked the education and skills to hold a good job; some were so discouraged that they had stopped looking.[16] The DAIC's Wayne County survey emphasized not only the general under-education of the native community but specifically the many workers in lower occupational categories with less than twelve years of formal schooling (Table 10).[17]

TABLE 10
Distribution of Occupational Group among Wayne County Indians, by Years of School (1978)

Occupational Group		Years of School						
	<7 (%)	8 (%)	9–11 (%)	12 (%)	13–15 (%)	16 (%)	>16 (%)	Total (%)
Professionals	—	1(1)	—(2)	4(25)	10(19)	50(18)	67(12)	5(77)
Managers	—	3(3)	2(10)	4(27)	4(8)	11(4)	11(2)	3(54)
Clerical Workers	—	5(5)	7(34)	17(110)	19(36)	6(2)	—	12(187)
Sales Workers	—	1(1)	3(15)	3(22)	3(6)	—	—	3(44)
Craftsmen/Foremen	40(21)	33(32)	27(132)	24(160)	29(55)	11(4)	11(2)	27(406)
Operatives	26(14)	29(28)	17(80)	13(84)	7(14)	6(2)	—	14(222)
Laborers	13(7)	15(15)	15(71)	12(78)	8(16)	3(11)	—	12(198)
Service Workers	21(11)	12(12)	26(125)	18(120)	11(21)	11(4)	—	19(293)
Armed Forces/ Miscellaneous	—	1(1)	3(16)	5(36)	9(17)	2(1)	11(2)	5(73)
Total	100(53)	100(98)	100(485)	100(662)	100(192)	100(46)	100(18)	100(1,554)

Source: Bashshur et al., *Native Americans in Wayne County*, 103.
Note: Figures in parentheses are the numbers of respondents.

Ignorance about employment information also hampered Detroit Indians. Russ Wright observed how inefficient their efforts were for more than three decades. The recent arrival, usually with little money, "doesn't know where, or how, to look for work in the city. He doesn't know what agencies can offer help or how to approach them. Even if they find out about welfare or unemployment benefits, Most are too proud to ask for help. They'd rather die than walk into a government office and ask a white man or a black man for help." Mavis Solomon Jacobs, like her husband-to-be, was unusual; she sought help from an employment agency in the 1930s and could afford to ride about the city for two months with a list of potential employers until she found the right job. More often the Indian's lack of education, lack of money, and lack of knowledge about the competitive employment process, as Wright lamented, "combine to trap him at the bottom of the barrel."[18]

The convenient day-labor agencies were the dregs at the bottom of the barrel in which many Cass Corridor breadwinners floundered. Wages paid were less than for permanent jobs, often just enough to meet immediate expenses. It was difficult to save enough money for emergencies or even to accept a good position, which meant surviving two weeks until the first paycheck and might also require new work clothes, tools, and transportation. Money for education certainly would be in short supply.[19]

Aware that employment information obtained in bars, through friends and relatives, or found in newspaper advertisements rarely yielded the best match of talents with jobs, the BIA stationed vocational guidance officers, like Scott Peters, in several cities. His success was limited. Unemployed Detroit natives met Peters at a downtown hotel during his periodic visits in the late thirties. He was unimaginative with the men; he merely accompanied them to factory employment offices, identified himself, and asked for job application forms. Too often he referred women to domestic jobs even if they had other skills. Washington abandoned its modest employment counseling effort in 1942, and more than three decades would pass before it started another federal job program for Detroit Indians.[20]

Discrimination against Indians was another prominent part of their Detroit employment history, although evaluating the dimensions and intensity of personal experiences is troublesome. One impediment was the lack of in-depth research. Detroit racial histories focus almost exclusively on the black experience. Corporate and union records are also disappointing. Industries either neglected to note the full range of racial diversity in the factories or have denied researchers access to employment files. Unions like the United Auto workers championed fair employment practices. Yet their archives contain few references to native Americans. Over the years the economic gate-keepers of Detroit, corporate employers as well as union officials, harbored ambiguous attitudes toward native people.

Disagreement in the Detroit Indian community about economic prejudice also blurs the picture of their twentieth-century experiences. For several years after her arrival from Walpole Island, Elsie Staats felt she was the victim of job discrimination. Early in World War II, as many Detroit plants retooled for wartime production, Teofilo Lucero waited with other laid-off workers outside one busy factory, only to see blatant discrimination against blacks and Indians. Only whites were hired. Martin Kiyoshk sensed a negative Indian stereotype in postwar Detroit. Police harassed Indians and he was denied employment in the automotive industry.[21] Other urban Indians perceived things differently. For Myrtle Kiser the city was heavenly compared to the nasty treatment she got from whites near the Muncey Reserve. Detroit streets were safe; she traveled about inexpensively; she was treated well on the job. Edith Beaulieu experienced no prejudice during more than thirty years as a domestic servant, factory worker, S. S. Kresge clerk, and nurse. Nor did Leona David, who also kept house and clerked for a department store. Fred Boyd held half a dozen factory jobs after the war without incident.[22] Perhaps, as one knowledgeable Indian lady suggested, some over-sensitive natives just looked for discrimination over the years.

Most tribesmen could speak only of their own experiences. Ombudsman Russ Wright, whose knowledge was wide-ranging, emphasized that because of corporate fair-employment policies, the only on-the-job discrimination by 1980 was personal harassment by some foremen who did not like Indians. When such an incident occurred during the construction of the Joe Louis Arena, Wright and the local ironworkers union intervened, shut down the project, and eventually got the offending supervisor reassigned.[23]

Anti-discrimination policies and legislation notwithstanding, big corporations as well as individuals continued to offend sensitive Indians. Cary Severt, public relations officer at the DAIC in the late seventies, sported a mod haircut and dapper business suits. A major firm once kept him waiting in its office for more than an hour. An official finally apologized for the discourtesy; they had been looking for an Indian. Feisty Harry Command also suffered from such ignorance. When dressed in a suit he was once told by a white person that he did not look like an Indian. Command countered: "You don't look like a Pilgrim, either!"[24]

Recently, another variety of discrimination against Indians and other unskilled workers has taken a toll that is easier to enumerate. Institutional discrimination theoretically took place when the occupational structure became less favorable to Indian employment. In the urban areas of the United States and Canada this has happened since the 1960s; technological innovations severely reduced the number of unskilled jobs and, conversely, expanded the opportunities for white-collar workers. The economy became increasingly prejudicial toward semi-skilled and unskilled workers, who did not adjust readily to these changes. The system created demands for skills they did not have. It required ever higher levels of education. It even expected persons to alter their dress, speech, and manners; to complete lengthy application forms; to buy expensive tools and pay high union membership fees. Institutional discrimination had a major impact on Detroit's work force.

One other source of Indian employment troubles over the years, which partly explained their relatively low economic status, was cultural traits brought to the Detroit economy. It is difficult to distinguish and measure just how important were these uniquely Indian factors, as opposed to characteristics native people shared with many other urban migrants: poverty, under-education, rural backgrounds, and vulnerability to institutional discrimination. Cultural features, like employer prejudice, also hinged on personal perceptions. Some evidence of their significance emerges, nevertheless. One Chippewa, raised off the reservation and for forty years a successful union laborer, noted that reservation workers often lacked a sense of responsibility toward their jobs. Perhaps it was encouraged at home, where the government provided so much. Over the years he recommended several of them for jobs in the construction industry, but finally quit helping; their tardiness and absenteeism threatened his own career.[25]

Another Chippewa, Winona Arriaga, explained that Indians would not slave just to make a lot of money. They valued giving away, not acquiring. Because money was historically foreign to Indians, the two did not mix well on reserves like Cape Croker or in the city. Money matters usually caused hard feelings in Indian organizations. For her people it has been the cause of much discontent. Daughter Carleen concurred.

The financial position of Thurman Bear, a mutual friend who was prominent in the native community during the seventies, must have been affected by similar thoughts:

87

Being an Indian is really a frame of mind.

I love to dance. Five days a week I live and work like a white man, but I spend my free time dancing. I'll drive all the way to Oklahoma on the weekend just to dance.

One boss I had gave me trouble. He wanted me to work overtime on Saturday. But I told him I would quit rather than not dance.

Being an Indian is to be free. I don't want to be saddled with the white man's values of "work hard, save your money and buy material things." I don't care about the new house or the color TV.[26]

Dean George, Teofilo Lucero, and many others espoused these values and lived by them. They would never become materially successful city citizens according to census bureau criteria.

IV

The ability of some Detroit Indians to resolve long-standing employment problems was exemplified during the late seventies by Joe Mesheky. An Ottawa from northern Michigan, Joe attended Holy Childhood Boarding School until 1942, then came to Detroit at age sixteen "to survive—that's all there was to it." Back home in Harbor Springs there was nothing; both parents were dead, he was too young for welfare, and did not want to be "adopted out." Manual labor was plentiful in the Motor City until after the war. He, too, learned to enjoy the beer gardens. Joe then served four years in the air force, which trained him in jet-engine mechanics and sent him to the Pacific. These and many subsequent years were largely "wasted."[27]

Nearly sixty years old, Joe had the scars to prove it. His long hair, brushed straight back, was graying fast. He pointed, while chain-smoking Pall Malls, to the several scars on his forearms and deeply lined face—on the nose, eyebrow, and temple—the results of bottle and knife fights while intoxicated. A drunk once stabbed him in the chest, barely missing his heart. Joe vowed he would never drink again. The promise was kept for two weeks, until he got out of the hospital.[28]

Drinking and other personal problems escalated after discharge from the service in 1950. Twice the courts sent him to prison. Later in the decade he got a Ford factory job, married, and fathered two children.

his drinking drove them away. Joe Mesheky ended up on skid row in the mid-sixties: picking up cigarette butts, rummaging through garbage cans, running numbers, working out of Cass Avenue day-labor shops.[29]

It was good to get moving early after sleeping in a cold, abandoned building. Besides, day workers had to report by 5:30 A.M. Other Indians were among the regulars who sat around just looking at the clock until the dispatcher sent them off to job sites. The work was hard. Joe especially recalled assignments at U.S. Cold Storage, where he handled frost-covered packages all day. Minimum hourly wages were paid by check each afternoon. Recipients with drinking problems, like Joe, promptly got them cashed at the nearest bar, where the evening drinking commenced. Afterward they got supplies—bologna, bread, wine—from a grocery store and looked for "the cheapest damn room" available. Day after day it was the same. Not all could survive the physical abuse; some could not get by financially and borrowed against forthcoming wages for lunch money and transportation. Joe was still drinking heavily and surreptitiously when the DAIC hired him as a janitor in the late seventies. Shortly after that he touched bottom physically and spiritually.[30] Joe turned his life around with support from other recovering alcoholics. He reestablished communication with his grown children. He became a successful Indian center counselor, helping other urban natives plagued with alcoholism and poverty. If only the Indian employment and drug abuse programs of the 1970s had been available thirty years earlier, Joe observed rather sadly, perhaps so many precious years would not have been lost.[31]

V

Particularly helpful in lessening the employment problems of Mesheky and other urban tribesmen was the Comprehensive Employment and Training Act (CETA), passed by Congress in 1973. Its purpose was "to provide job training and employment opportunities for economically disadvantaged, unemployed, and underemployed persons, and to assure that training and other services lead to maximum employment opportunities and enhance self-sufficiency." Section 302 of Title III specifically dealt with Indian Manpower Programs. Federal legislators, aware of the financial plight of native people, committed Washington to support the economic and social development of native communities in accordance with their goals and life-styles. Manpower services would include, for example, on-the-job training, public service employment, classroom training, and summer youth programs emphasizing work experience. To ensure a flexible and decentralized delivery system, Congress also instructed the Secretary of Labor to use local Indian tribes, bands, or nonreservation groups as prime sponsors.[32]

What was the economic goal of the southeast Michigan native community that CETA addressed? "The Manpower Program has been and will continue to be an integral part of the Detroit American Indian Center's services," stated an NAIA brochure, "since employment is essential for self-sufficiency."[33] Self-sufficiency: so often unattainable on the reservations; in quest of it many tribesmen migrated to the Motor City throughout the twentieth century. Many attained their goal, but 26 percent lived in poverty during the seventies. CETA was designed primarily to alleviate their employment problems.

From the start, the DAIC's Manpower Program fostered economic self-sufficiency with a variety of services; however, some client characteristics made the task arduous. Ninety percent of the 867 American Indians who were offered services by the manpower staff between October 1979 and September 1980 were in the prime employment ages of sixteen to forty-four. Yet 458 had not completed high school; 69 were offenders; 695 were classified as economically disadvantaged; three-fourths claimed to be unemployed.[34] Many even acted disinterested in the special training opportunities CETA offered; a few of them naively looked for fast and easy money. (Dorothy Goeman, department head during the mid-seventies, smiled when recalling one who wanted to be a race car driver—right away—and another a Hollywood movie star.) Others, ranging from 30 to 60 percent depending on the season, only sought temporary jobs, not an education. Canadian Indians, for example, often came to Detroit for the winter months, when seasonal work at home was slack; in spring they headed back across the border. Tribesmen from the Southwest followed a different cycle, wintering on the reservations and working in southeast Michigan during warm weather. In either case they lingered no longer than necessary. Some year-round residents simply did not want regular work, would not accept the work ethic of the urban dweller, and refused to pay the price of succeeding in the white man's world. Getting by with short-term employment was their goal. Finally, staffers were challenged by the discouraged, down-and-out clients. Plagued with low self-esteem, inexperience, little training, and urban cultural shock, they were pessimistic about ever finding a good job.[35]

Communication between the Indian center and its clients was tenuous. What attracted needy natives to the manpower office during the seventies was at best a loose recruitment network consisting of newspaper and radio advertisements, referrals (from Urban Indian Affairs, the Salvation Army, churches, parole officers, and social workers), and staff members' personal contacts in the city. Unemployed or underemployed tribesmen dutifully completed job application forms, but many were such vagabonds—no telephone, constantly on the move—that manpower counselors could not always contact them promptly when a suitable position opened.[36]

Manpower's training and employment programs usually were attractive enough to overcome weak communications and flexible enough to meet the short-term needs of some clients as well as aid others who desired career training and placement. For those requiring limited but speedy help, employment counselors, sensitive to street problems, created a flexible, friendly drop-in atmosphere in their small office. At their disposal were emergency money, food, clothing, and transportation. The small staff helped with urban adjustment as well as health problems (medical, dental, vision). They facilitated certification of Indian status. Vocational counseling, referral, and placement services were offered.[37] Within one seven-month period the center dispensed, among other benefits, 100 gallons of fuel oil, 240 bus tickets, $380 in food vouchers, 33 food packets, and $2,040 to buy 34 pairs of eyeglasses.[38]

Its rapid response to a Mohawk construction worker during the autumn of 1980 was a source of pride. A fine job had just opened but would be lost if he did not immediately get a special tool belt priced beyond his means. Within eight hours, the center obtained union and employer confirmation that the position was his, provided he came properly equipped the next morning, processed the necessary requisitions forms, and bought the belt.[39]

Manpower offered different services, with less emphasis on speed, to Detroit Indians desiring more permanent employment, "GREAT NEWS," reported the *Native Sun* in May 1980:

> Females can be welders too! Catherine Primeau has proven this is a very profitable alternative to the stereotyped [*sic*] female occupations. She has completed the Welding Training Course offered through the Center and the job search position of this training has provided her a job. She starts at $7.00 per hour as an apprentice [*sic*] in eight weeks she will be making $15.00 per hour.[40]

The center, which stressed vocational training, negotiated agreements with private and public contractors to teach Indians highly marketable skills. Manpower's 1979–80 fiscal year budget included twenty-seven thousand dollars for instructional costs. Unemployed clients without a high school diploma could thus be directed to GED classes provided by Ross Institute right in the center; and as another inducement, CETA paid a stipend to the forty-nine students enrolled in May 1980. Their success rate was 100 percent. To upgrade Indian education and employability, manpower also paid for clerical and bookkeeping instruction at the center. Those who desired technical training, like Catherine Primeau, got financial help to attend the International Truck Drivers School, MoTech (automotive training), WeldTech (welding), and similar institutions. Not counting hourly student stipends, the WeldTech course cost the center forty-five hundred dollars per pupil. By May 1980 seventeen Indians were registered for training programs. Information about money for higher education, such as NAIA scholarships, was also available in the manpower office.[41]

Other types of assistance given to long-term urban settlers included job counseling and placement. The former was a three-step process. Before clients enrolled in CETA training programs, they had to take a five-day self-evaluation course taught at the center by Ross Institute. Students, who received a stipend for the week, clarified short-range and long-range career goals. Next, each met with a manpower counselor to discuss job-market realities and what training programs would best fit their plans. Then the center alerted all *Native Sun* readers to specific openings and long-range employment trends.

Manpower's toughest task was placement. Client training during the late 1970s helped, but institutional discrimination simultaneously raised job entry qualifications. Detroit's 1979–82 economic slump further reduced employment opportunities. "It's disastrous," lamented Joe Mesheky. Moreover, many Indians, recently hired through affirmative-action programs, were laid off in 1980 because of low seniority. The Michigan Employment Security Commission (MESC) was supposed to assist these unemployed. It issued a daily list of available city jobs. But few native clients benefited; they usually lacked either the required experience or training. And positions demanding limited skills were almost always filled by the time manpower telephoned its clients and they in turn applied. If new job opportunities were to open for Detroit Indians, center counselors would have to develop their own business contacts. Before hard times in 1980 they succeeded modestly, and placed thirty to forty workers per month.[42]

During the summer of 1978 the center's Gail Chakur persuaded Chevrolet to hire 144 Indians for its local gear and axle plant. Those who survived the company's demanding orientation sessions and ninety-day probation period worked on assembly lines in different sections of the complex, which contained different ethnic and racial groups. The work was rugged but the pay was good: more than eight dollars an hour to start plus plenty of overtime and fringe benefits. Native employees got strong support from both the UAW and Chevrolet, which modified some plant procedures once Gail explained the unique cultural backgrounds and needs of native employees. One Indian lady had to remind black colleagues, resentful about natives hired through affirmative action, that blacks received special economic help in the sixties; now it was the Indians' turn. At least two Indian men were threatened with knives. Even office workers in the personnel department seemed bitter about the new employees, though they were only a few and certainly did not threaten blacks. These factory jobs gave many Indians a new sense of financial security as well as cash to buy automobiles and other material goods they had never been able to afford. (Some Great Lakes tribesmen who moved to Detroit just to get one of the Chevrolet positions were so poor that they had to sleep in cars and eat Indian center emergency food rations until receiving their first paychecks.) Nevertheless, many Indian workers did not endure. For some the work was too physically demanding, too dirty, too confining. A few went off to celebrate with their first big paychecks and never returned. Others developed health problems or refused to endure harassment from blacks, who controlled the union stewards. Chevrolet informed Gail that Indians were their best and worst workers; they had a very high dropout rate, yet those who stayed outperformed all others. The manpower office was encouraged. It continued to place Indian workers at Chevrolet, Cadillac, Chrysler, and other automotive plants until the 1980 economic downturn.[43]

Staff members like Gail Chakur, essential to the success of an Indian manpower office, had to be (1) knowledgeable about city agency services, (2) sensitive to native cultural backgrounds, (3) aware of both the problems and opportunities in urban life, and (4) able to fashion new programs for the changing needs of off-reservation tribesmen. Joe Mesheky also had these attributes. With the center's help he conquered alcoholism. Then he earned a GED and in January 1980 found rewarding work in the manpower department. His face beamed when describing how good it felt to awaken each morning and not be sick, not have to worry if he had hurt someone in a bar the night before, to realize that he had a helping

93

job. This metamorphosis also became an effective counseling tool. Joe's clients got a persuasive, double-barreled message: career advice plus living proof that center programs could solve Indian employment problems. With counselors like Joe Mesheky, urban natives responded; they knew they were with their own people and could get help. There were some discouraging moments. Particularly disheartening were the training-school dropouts. For some the course was beyond their intellectual grasp at the time; for a few others alcoholism and drug abuse probably were involved along with a disinterest in this type of education (perhaps they only wanted the $3.10 an hour stipend plus allowances for transportation and baby-sitting). Some discontented students were salvaged by Joe and his colleagues, who regularly visited the training sites, chatted with teachers, and provided helpful advice.[44]

Over the years the manpower office employed several effective counselors besides Gail and Joe. Linda Isaac-Halfday knew the streets (what it was like "to have nothing but air in your pockets") before taking advantage of the center's GED classes. Beginning as a receptionist at the front desk, she eventually earned a supervisory position in manpower. Linda and Joe worked closely and productively together. They assisted each other's clients and jointly visited training sites.[45] Trained in business at the University of Michigan, Mike Dashner maintained strong Walpole Island roots and interacted well with other Great Lakes natives. He was not put off by long hair, checkered work records, or blue jeans; he sympathized with Indians who wanted to socialize with peers at weekend powwows or back on the reservations. Dashner avoided placing clients on assembly lines where, he believed, they could not perform their best. He also tried to make employers sensitive to Indians' cultural backgrounds. Rolando Garcia had blood ties with both the Spanish-speaking and Indian communities. He worked especially hard with Indian teenagers, encouraging them to stay in school and helping them discover what careers they really wanted, rather than pushing them into jobs they would quickly abandon.[46] These workers, and a dozen others in the seventies, believed that the manpower office—small, friendly, helpful, staffed by fellow Indians—offered native job applicants a unique and indispensable service.

VI

For CETA programs adequately to meet client needs, immediate as well as long-term, external relationships had to function smoothly. Liaison was the principal responsibility of the project director. Most essential was cooperation between manpower and the DAIC's executive director. The mutual understanding achieved by 1980 had not come easily. Discord characterized the early years because (1) the head of manpower reported only to the board of directors and (2) the entire department operated with personnel policies different from the rest of the center. This ultimately undermined morale. It also weakened the administrative team concept advocated by Director James Hillman. In August 1978 he confronted the board and threatened to resign; it was impossible to function any longer, Hillman asserted, unless he supervised all programs under the center's roof. The board concurred.[47] Then it selected an efficient new manpower head, Rose Silvey, who could work harmoniously with Hillman. When teamed with counselors such as Joe and Linda, Rose's administrative skills were formidable, the department's progress marked. Center staff had a special responsibility to Detroit's Indian community, she claimed: a chance to prove it could work together for something important.[48]

Relations between the United States Department of Labor and the Indian center generally were satisfactory, despite Detroit's desire for more autonomy and Washington's insistence on complete accountability. In practice, federal administrators excused minor local snafus as long as the manpower staff corrected mistakes and continued to aid disadvantaged urban natives. The only cause célèbre was triggered by the government's 1979 requirement that Indians from Canada, to be eligible for CETA services in southeast Michigan, must register as aliens with the United States Immigration and Naturalization Service. General indignation erupted among Detroit native Americans. The NAIA had always insisted there was no such thing as a "Canadian Indian"; it was "founded on the principle that all Indian people, regardless of their tribe's location in North America should be part of our service population." Efforts to reverse Washington's policy were channeled through the center's board of directors, but it was warned that money spent on nonregistered clients would have to be repaid. At first solicitations for help from the Native American Rights Fund and the Institute for the Development of Indian Law availed nothing. Finally, Hillman reported to the *Native Sun* readership that the Michigan Indian Legal Service Corporation from Traverse City responded with a case which proves that American Indian people born in Canada are exempt from the Immigration and Naturalization Service registration as aliens. In fact the case proved that the INS has no power to deport a North American Indian since the Jay Treaty has been interpreted by the courts that the right to cross means Indians are entitled to be here without the "permission" of the Immigration and Naturalization Service.

With the case in hand which proves our point, the board of Directors of the North American Indian Association of Detroit, Inc. has adopted a resolution requesting a waiver of this requirement of the CETA rules, and has directed the staff to no longer require alien registration as a necessity for getting services under CETA.[49]

In January 1980 the matter was resolved satisfactorily. The Department of Labor issued new CETA regulations that did not require Indian registration with the Immigration and Naturalization Service.

VII

Like its ambivalence about Washington, the Indian community's appraisal of CETA programs, from emergency help to training for the trades, was mixed. One Ottawa businessman scornfully referred to the "organized begging" of downright lazy tribesmen at the DAIC. Natives needed to be more ambitious, like him. Their model should be the Poles and other industrious Eastern Europeans who arrived in Detroit dirt-poor. By the time many of them retired they owned small businesses and homes. Their children attended colleges. Another prominent Indian leader accused the center of paternalism; it offered too many handouts (dead-end jobs, food, transportation, clothing) rather than fostering economic independence. He likened it to a Chicago drop-in facility for alcoholics that fed the same Indians each day. This was counterproductive; it only bred dependence, not unlike the old reservation system, which reduced Indians to wards of the government. A successful program should give its clients fishing poles rather than free fish. The manpower office's most glaring defect, according to another knowledgeable critic once highly placed at the Indian center, was that the CETA director as well as the counselors lacked training in how to develop unsubsidized jobs for Indians. Thus too many staff members sat around not knowing how to proceed. Even hard workers like Joe Mesheky were unimaginative; they thought mainly of factory jobs and channeled clients into trades without much future. The victims of such inept administration were the unemployed and underemployed and untrained native workers of southeastern Michigan, for whom the program was intended.

Russ Wright, aware of these and other criticisms, was a Detroiter long enough to take a historical perspective. CETA at least surpassed an earlier era when there was no special help for urban natives who needed new skills or to polish old ones. Like any office, manpower had room for improvement, Wright maintained; yet if Indians used CETA's financial aid and worked hard, they would do well. Besides, what were the alternatives? His Office of Urban Indian Affairs, although it had found work for dozens of Indians over the years, could not make employment training and placement a major thrust.[50]

Even more unsatisfactory was the MESC: notoriously slow, impersonal, inefficient. One knowledgeable manpower counselor condemned the MESC outright as the worst state agency, noting that even Detroit's Department of Social Services sent clients to private job-finding firms. Hillman, like Russ Wright, realistically assessed CETA's strengths and weaknesses. Without question, poverty-stricken Indians got better help from manpower than from the MESC: shoes, clothing, lodging, transportation, even stipends and free training. Yet there was no denying that most manpower assistance was short-term. The Indian center's goal (helping clients improve their lives through skill development and placement in permanent, unsubsidized jobs) often was not achieved. This was obvious during Detroit's 1979–82 economic slump when so many factories, like Chevrolet Gear and Axle, laid off Indian workers with low seniority. Until the economic skies brightened, Hillman saw no alternative to what were, admittedly, federal welfare programs like CETA.[51]

VIII

Some Canadian and United States Indians who settled in Detroit during the twentieth century achieved economic success: they supported their families in relative comfort and without government assistance. Detroit native people entered nearly every occupation—as domestic servants, factory and construction workers, teamsters, painters, clerk typists, nurses, engineers, small-business owners, architects, lawyers, social workers, and schoolteachers. Edith Beaulieu, Charles and Mavis Jacobs, Sylvester Stone, and Russ Wright were among the successful ones, the industrious ones, the fortunate ones. Ingredients that fostered their career success included: 1) solid academic education, at least through the high school level; (2) pursuit of additional training when needed, including college credits; functional orientation to urban life and the dominant value system; self-confidence; pride in their Indian heritage; (5) no debilitating health problems; (6) high motivation to work and determination to do well; (7) good job performance; (8) dependability; cooperation; (9) strong network of professional contacts; and (10) supportive family ties.

Most Motor City tribesmen clustered in low-paying positions by mid-century. Moreover, native unemployment escalated after World War II, especially among young adults; for Wayne County twenty-one- to thirty-year-old males, the rate was three times higher than the national average by 1978. Thirty-two percent of Indian families, nearly double the national figure, earned seven thousand dollars a year or less. Twenty-six percent lived below the poverty line in 1978. They, too, had come to Detroit with high expectations. Reality was disappointment, deprivation, despair.

At least two factors helped alleviate the burden of these economic difficulties. First, people like Joe Mesheky, for years bogged down by alcoholism and low day-labor wages, turned their lives around physically and spiritually. They mended broken family ties, launched new careers, reached out to others plagued with substance abuse and poverty. A second factor was CETA. The manpower office at the DAIC offered both short-term and more enduring services. Among the more enduring services, the GED and training programs were notable. Knowledgeable and helpful counselors like Joe Mesheky and Linda Isaac-Halfday were of critical importance. CETA, though a vast improvement over Washington's prior neglect of off-reservation natives and the ineffectiveness of the MESC, still had its shortcomings. Critics castigated everything from the Department of Labor's excessive interference and manpower's paternalism to the alleged laziness of CETA clients. Unemployment or underemployment, they pointed out, was partly due to the passive and self-destructive attitudes of poor Indians. No one and no amount of money could rescue them until they were ready to help themselves by working hard and using federal assistance effectively.

Assessing the progress made by southeastern Michigan Indians in the workplace was difficult in 1980. Besides the controversies swirling about the DAIC's CETA office, the setback in the national economy devastated

Detroit, which suffered a 14.6 percent unemployment rate in July of that year. Especially hard hit were native Americans. Even in good times they were plagued with a host of employment difficulties discussed in this chapter. When the census bureau gathered data on Detroit's 1980 native population, the profile that emerged revealed striking, persistent problems. Of the total American Indian, Eskimo, and Aleut population in the six-county area (12,487), its labor force (persons sixteen years of age and more) was 9,812. Those unemployed numbered 1,146, or 18.8 percent. Wayne County Indian unemployment was 18.6 percent and in the city of Detroit the percentage was slightly higher, 19.7. The 18.8 percent rate for metropolitan Detroit was nearly twice that of whites (9.5) and roughly comparable with blacks (21.9). The seriousness of Indian economic trouble was also highlighted by their incomes, 16.6 percent of which fell below the poverty level in the metropolitan area. Downtown, in the city of Detroit, the percentage of persons in this category jumped to 26.4. Of those employed in metropolitan Detroit, only 710 held managerial and professional positions; most (3,128) were employed in the census-taker's lower-paying, lower-status occupational categories: service, precision production, craft, repair, operators, fabricators, laborers. This census data, gathered during a recession year, documented that the Indian community's recent economic progress had been tenuous—highly dependent, as Director Hillman observed, on a robust automobile industry as well as special federal programs like CETA to upgrade the native work force.[52]

IX

Dean Jacobs, a son of Charles and Mavis, grew up in Grosse Pointe, Michigan. He remembered being "the darkest person in the whole school district. Once I had a teacher come up to me after a basketball game and ask me where I was from. I told him I was an Indian and he asked me 'how do you like living in this country?' I think he believed I was from the Far East." After high school he attended Eastern Michigan University. Then he quit to become a draftsman with his father's firm. The pay was good. But the work was not fulfilling. In 1973, while still in his twenties and unmarried, he took a hundred-dollar-a-week pay cut to become an Indian land-claims researcher. "People were a bit skeptical of me, coming from Grosse Pointe to Walpole. They thought I was running from something. It was a big move for me." Dean quickly reestablished the Jacobs family presence on a year-round basis: moving into their yellow bungalow overlooking the scenic St. Clair River, marrying an island woman, winning election to the band council. Land-claims work assumed increased importance, involving travel across North America and to Europe, and by the end of the 1970s he established on Walpole an impressive archives, which supported historical research for several Indian bands. At first, "I had the same questions people are asking now—why bring up the past, why go back, why not worry about the future. Then I found what my ancestors had gone through, I felt proud they survived obstacles that faced them after the [land] surrenders. I was proud to be an Indian."[53] He was also happy to have a meaningful job on Walpole Island Indian Reserve, which his parents had been forced to leave nearly forty years earlier.

Dean Jacobs's return was not unusual; for as the local saying goes, people always find their way back to Walpole. Whenever island job openings were advertised, for example, many off-reserve band members applied—attracted not just by the work but by the chance to live at home. During the late seventies the band council, trying to get the island moving, implemented a master economic development program designed to protect the fragile marsh environment, on the one hand, while also making the island more attractive and generating new jobs. An ideal result, according to Chief William Tooshkenig, would be the establishment of a shoe factory: small, nonpolluting, labor intensive.[54] Yet he and other native leaders in Canada and the United States realized that it would be a while before local resources could fulfill the economic needs and career hopes of all tribal members. Thus a goodly number continue to migrate to urban centers. And they wait, like Dean Jacobs, for meaningful jobs to be generated among their people.

Charles and Mavis Jacobs moved back to Walpole Island in 1980. Erie Engineering opposed his retirement, but Charles insisted; so the company sponsored a farewell dinner and presented him with an engraved fishing rod.[55] After decades of off-reserve work the Jacobses and other retired seniors headed for home. In the autumn of their lives, days were more relaxed. Charles tended his large riverside acreage and used his new fishing gear. Mavis, attractive, more fashionably dressed, friendly, and gregarious, supervised the remodeling of their two-story homestead, played with Dean's children, and renewed old friendships. Together they had much to offer the struggling island community; they were knowledgeable and anxious to work on some local project. Once decided, theirs would be a major effort that doubtless succeeded. Charles and Mavis Jacobs, returning Detroiters, had entered a new stage in life. For them and their Walpole neighbors it could be springtime again rather than autumn.

ILLUSTRATIONS

Michigan Indian Day Parade

Detroit American Indian Center at John R. and Adams

Dean George

Frank Alberts

Winona Arriaga

Martin Kiyoshk

Dean Jacobs

Charles and Mavis Jacobs

Cecil Rodd

Russ Wright

Teofilo
Lucero

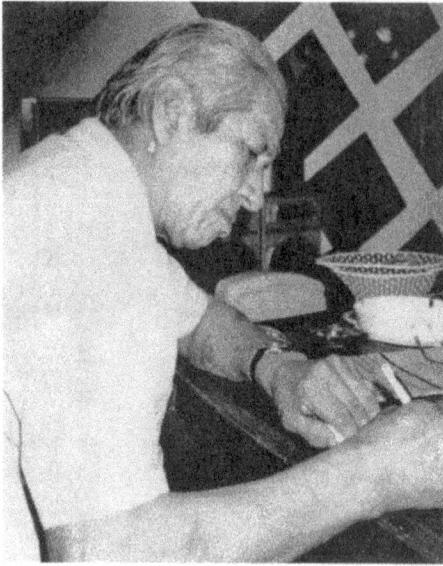

Joe Mesheky

Edith Beaulieu

American Indian Services at W. Baltimore and Third Avenue

Bill Memberto

Harry Command

Jane Johnson

Judy Mays

Louise Morales

Walpole Island Powwow

Fred Boyd

Rose Silvey

Elmer
Sebastian

>⟩⟩ CHAPTER 4 ⟨⟨⟨

Living in the Motor City:
Health and Housing

i seem walking in sleep
down streets grey with cement
and glaring glass and oily wind
armed with a pint of wine
—An Acoma Indian

But to every man there openeth
a High Way, and a Low
And every man decideth
The Way his soul shall go.
—John G. Wenham

The offices of American Indian Services (AIS), a licensed outpatient substance abuse clinic, were stationed strategically in a two-story green building on the busy midtown corner of West Baltimore and Third avenues. One neighbor was the huge General Motors complex, headquarters for a mighty corporation; another was skid row, the Cass Corridor, one of Detroit's most poverty-stricken areas and home for hundreds of Indians.

There was nothing ostentatious about the old green building in February 1978, and AIS exuded the friendliness and informality of a drop-in center. Upon entering the lobby through a bright red front door, clients were greeted by wall posters and stacks of pamphlets proclaiming the importance of higher education and the dangers of alcohol and drug addiction. Beyond were the modest offices of the secretary-receptionist and the director; to the left, up the wooden staircase to the second floor, visitors could find the small but private counselors' offices and an assortment of recreation facilities: a television set, pool table, piano, magazine rack, bookcases, three easy chairs, a comfortable couch, and a big coffee pot. Seven tables were arranged conference-style for alcoholics' self-help meetings and community lunches served each Wednesday. Lest the purpose of AIS be forgotten, two upstairs walls displayed, under the colorful banner "Remember When," photographs of staff activities throughout the city and state.

To look at Gene Iron Shell, a tall, handsome Sioux and one of the AIS counselors, it was difficult to imagine that drinking nearly ruined his life. Weight lifting kept him physically strong. Dressed in a bright western shirt, Indian-beaded leather belt, blue jeans, and cowboy boots, he sat behind a big wooden desk smoking a dark cigarette. His friendly tan face and open manner exuded informality yet seriousness of purpose. Office typewriter, file cabinets, handy gray telephone, a sizeable library of reference books, certificates of achievement decorating the pale green walls: each added to the image of an organized, middle-aged professional very much in charge of his life.

Thirty-five years earlier, as a youngster on the Rosebud Reservation in South Dakota, Gene Iron Shell had set off on a suicidal course. He modeled himself on a father and older brothers, who were already in the insidious grip of alcoholism, an addictive and progressive disease, which, if not arrested, for there is no cure, ends in permanent mental and physical damage or early death. Thanks to a traumatic boarding school experience, Gene also internalized the drunken Indian stereotype. For him it became a self-fulfilling prophecy. Booze was his friend; it enabled him to socialize, overcome shyness with girls, and dance well. Even with his wife he had to drink to "own certain feelings of adequacy." He drank to become what he wanted to be and to blot out fears.[1]

Instead of a delightful social whirl, Gene Iron Shell's youth attested to the self-destructiveness of alcoholism: frequent blackouts beginning at age nineteen, courts-martial and eventually dismissal from the U.S. Army because of his drinking (in ten years he never rose above the rank of corporal), bloody barroom brawls in downtown Denver and other western cities, work and money troubles. Moral values decayed as Gene alternately exploited and deserted his family—wife, children, brothers, parents. Drinking and drugs obsessed him. The year was 1969: defiant yet persistently remorseful, he arrived in Detroit.[2]

Four years later he touched bottom. Alcohol so jeopardized his factory job and relations with his wife that Gene Iron Shell committed himself to a detoxification center. On June 11, 1973, his first sober day, he was reborn. He endured a difficult seventeen weeks of physical withdrawal from drugs, followed by therapy and alcoholism education. Eventually he became such an advocate of a self-help program for addicts that Sacred Heart Rehabilitation Center of the Archdiocese of Detroit, where he sobered up, hired him in the hope he could influence other Indian problem drinkers. Later Gene Iron Shell took a counseling job at AIS.[3]

I

Alcoholism ate away at the fabric of life in Michigan through its involvement in 20 percent of all divorces and 60 percent of reported child abuse. Regarding the Detroit metropolitan area, the National Council on Alcoholism reported that it "accounts, directly or indirectly, for 40 percent of the problems brought to family court.... Between 30 and 40 percent of delinquent youths come from alcoholic homes."[4] Particularly astonishing was the human suffering among native Americans in the Motor City; it was estimated that 60 percent of Indian males and 40 percent of the females had drinking problems. AIS branded alcoholism "the most critical and frequent underlying factor in the high unemployment rate, lack of education, breakdown in the family unit and legal problems, etc. of Indian people today."[5] The disease was also an important facet of the broader story of Indian living conditions.

II

Over the years Detroit Indian housing and health care echoed the reservation scene. Tribesmen fleeing overcrowded homes on Walpole and in other Indian communities, for instance, often moved in with Motor City relatives and cramped their quarters. Rural problem-drinkers drifted into the city, quickly located Indian bars, and compounded personal troubles. For ambitious as well as skilled reservation migrants, willing to accept many mainstream values, the hustle-and-bustle of urban life was exhilarating and rewarding—a cozy home in the suburbs plus superior health care. Yet, as has been shown, life in Detroit simultaneously presented insurmountable difficulties for other Indians. Their maladjustment and low incomes brought a poverty that permeated every facet of life.

In 1950 historian Ralph West observed that many families rented small, inexpensive inner-city apartments in which crowded rooms served combined functions. Often in need of repair, typical quarters were sparsely furnished with miscellaneous used sofas, chairs, and appliances. Two features particularly reminded West of the reservation housing he knew as a child: Detroit families gathered around kitchen tables during their leisure hours (a holdover from the reserve where this was probably the only heated room) and they seemed oblivious of housekeeping. Walls, curtains, and shades were badly stained and in poor condition; a variety of mementos cluttered tables and stands; frayed rugs and worn linoleum covered the floors. West was struck by "the disorderly accumulation of years of neglect."[6]

Two decades later Detroit Indian housing showed marked improvement. Fifty-nine percent of the families owned or were buying their dwellings, the average value of which was $ 15,700 in 1970.[7] Homes were scattered throughout southeast Michigan and, as might be anticipated, ownership was highest among suburban families with substantial incomes (tables 11, 12).

The quality of Indian rental units likewise was enhanced. Half of these structures had been built before 1939, but nearly all had modern water and sanitary facilities. Native census-takers rated 85 percent as "satisfactory" by 1978, with another 11 percent "needing minor repairs." Only 4 percent required major remodeling or were judged "dilapidated," the most being in the Cass Corridor (table 13),[8] where tribesmen exhibited "the typical deprivation characteristics of Indians who moved to urban areas in search of a better life, but instead ended up in the city slums."

Only 49 percent of the Cass Corridor housing units seemed "satisfactory." Nineteen percent were either beyond repair or needed substantial renovation. These quarters contained the highest density of persons per room and the fewest units with telephones, complete kitchens, flush toilets, and bathing facilities. Unvented room heaters were observed in 14.5 percent of these apartments.[9]

TABLE 11

Distribution of Indian Home Ownership in Wayne County, by Area of Residence (1978)

Home Ownership	Cass Corridor (%)	Other West Detroit (%)	East Detroit (%)	Suburbs (%)	Total (%)
House Owned or Being Bought	1(1)	43(238)	49(91)	81(741)	59(1,071)
Co-op/Condo Owned or Being Bought	—	—(1)	—	—(1)	—(2)
Rented for Cash	94(143)	55(301)	47(87)	19(171)	39(702)
Rented in Return for Work	3(5)	1(6)	1(3)	—(2)	1(16)
Occupied without Payment	2(3)	1(4)	3(5)	—(2)	1(14)
Total	100(152)	100(550)	100(186)	100(917)	100(1,805)

Source: Bashshur et al., *Native Americans in Wayne County*, 130.
Note: Figures in parentheses are the numbers of respondents.

TABLE 12
Distribution of Indian Home Ownership in Wayne County, by Family Income (1978) Income

Home Ownership	<$5,000 (%)	$5,001–$10,000 (%)	$10,001–$15,000 (%)	Income Group $15,001–$20,000 (%)	$20,001–$25,000 (%)	>$25,000 (%)	Total (%)
House Owned or Being Bought	23(94)	41(104)	59(143)	78(230)	81(166)	92(208)	58(945)
Co-op/Condo Owned or Being Bought	—(1)	—	—	—	5(1)	—	—(2)
Rented for Cash	73(300)	57(143)	40(98)	21(63)	18(38)	8(19)	40(661)
Rented in Return for Work	2(9)	1(3)	.5(1)	.5(1)	—	—	1(14)
Occupied without Payment	2(8)	1(2)	.5(1)	.5(1)	.5(1)	—	1(13)
Total	100(412)	100(252)	100(243)	100(295)	100(206)	100(227)	100(1,635)

Source: Bashshur et al., *Native Americans in Wayne County*, 128.
Note: Figures in parentheses are the numbers of respondents.

TABLE 13
Distribution of Indian Housing Conditions in Wayne County, by Area of Residence (1978)

Housing Conditions	Cass Corridor (%)	Other West Detroit (%)	East Detroit (%)	Suburbs (%)	Total (%)
Satisfactory	49(74)	77(414)	77(140)	97(875)	85(1,503)
Needs Minor Repairs	32(48)	17(89)	18(33)	2(22)	11(192)
Needs Major Repairs	12(19)	4(24)	4(7)	1(8)	3(58)
Dilapidated	7(11)	2(10)	1(2)	—	1(23)
Total	100(152)	100(537)	100(182)	100(905)	100(1,776)

Source: Bashshur et al., *Native Americans in Wayne County*, 131.
Note: Figures in parentheses are the numbers of respondents.

III

The Cass Corridor was one of several Wayne County locations where Indians lived. Historically, they were a mobile and culturally diverse people, an uncrystallized collection of dispersed individuals who maintained strong social ties to home reservation communities. Detroit had no Indian colony. The Michigan Avenue neighborhood between Second and Sixth functioned as a port of entry for reservation migrants before 1950. Its skid row milieu included pawnshops, flophouses, and walk-up apartments above businesses like Sam Fox's tavern. Along the thoroughfare native newcomers lodged with relatives. They gradually oriented to a kinetic urban life. New friends notified them about rooms for rent besides job prospects. Limited to domestic work before World War II, young women met pressing housing needs with such live-in work; men who obtained factory jobs across town usually took up residence near these plants. Both groups returned to Sam Fox's and other taverns on the weekends to socialize with Indian friends. Others continued to live and work along Michigan Avenue until urban renewal projects razed the neighborhood early in the fifties, whereupon skid row bars, flophouses, Indian families, vagrants, and alcoholics moved north to the Cass Corridor. (Only the long line of Michigan Avenue pawnshops was prevented from joining this relocation en masse.) The corridor's heyday as a popular place to live, shared by hundreds of Indians and other groups, lasted two decades. Unquestionably it was the most well-known and important native American subcommunity in Detroit. Its apartments also epitomized the housing problems plaguing off-reservation band members in the mid-twentieth century. Downtown Detroit Indians subsequently joined thousands of others in scattering to southeastern Michigan suburbs: Taylor, Westland, downriver areas, and other municipalities (see map 4). By 1981 fewer than sixty native families lived in the Cass Corridor, which once had teemed with tribesmen.[10]

A rectangular section strategically located on the near west side, Cass Corridor stretched fifteen blocks (1.8 miles) north from the Fisher Freeway to Wayne State University; along its eastern perimeter extended Woodward Avenue, and six blocks (.5 mile) to the west the bustling Lodge Freeway formed another flank. A drive or stroll along the corridor's streets in the seventies presented amazingly diverse buildings; dingy bars, transient hotels, small restaurants, and grocery stores were juxtaposed with day-labor offices, a few light industries, a cheery elementary school, and senior citizens' residences. Rooming houses and apartment buildings honeycombed the entire area. Once fashionable residences, these turn-of-the-century brick and stone structures had become dilapidated, a telling testimonial to neighborhood blight. Loyal residents stayed on because the corridor was convenient to downtown stores, culture centers (Detroit Institute of Art, Fisher Theater, Masonic Temple, Wayne State University, Detroit Public Library), and city bus lines. The cost of living also stayed relatively low. Nevertheless, renters knew about their neighborhood's reputation as the tenderloin district (noted for vice, drugs, and prostitution) and Detroit's dumping ground (for alcohol and drug abusers and its poverty-stricken families.) Bleary-eyed drunks staggered down the streets day and night, reeled in and out of taverns, huddled passively in doorways, and passed nights in burned-out or abandoned buildings. The Gold Dollar Bar, just across the street from the Burton Elementary School, touted "Female Impersonators Nightly." Another epithet was "the forgotten area." Crime and unemployment rates were high; so was resentment and disillusionment. Yet money for new construction or renovation seemed unavailable. Cass Corridor had fantastic potential, emphasized Rose Mary Robinson, who represented the area on the Wayne County Board of Commissioners. Neglected by powerful political and economic leaders, however, it had become a disgrace to Detroit.[11]

By 1970 seventeen thousand Cass Corridor residents formed a striking mosaic set into the predominantly black central city. University students, teachers, executives, retirees, and factory and construction workers lived beside destitute families, derelicts, hustlers, hippies, prostitutes, alcoholics, and dope dealers. Most were white. But they also included Orientals, East Indians, Arabs, some blacks and native Americans. Besides the vice vendors, who preyed on local inhabitants and visitors, were those who prayed for the corridor with word and deed: social workers, schoolteachers, the Salvation Army's Harbor Light Center, the Glorious Freedom Mission. "It is one area of Detroit where brothels and churches compete for patronage," a reporter remarked, "and often the same patrons visit both places." What particularly caught the eye was (1) the overriding poverty of the people, whose median family income was $3,600 to $4,500 and (2) the high concentration of senior citizens.[12] Elderly as well as poor tenants in two Henry Street apartments, for instance, struggled unsuccessfully to subsist on welfare or social security payments. Building managers observed that after deducting monthly rent, not enough money was left to eat properly. Afraid of muggers and ripped off at a neighbor-

110

hood store, many simply withdrew to their rooms and went hungry, and drank.[13]

Martin Kiyoshk rented a third-floor apartment in 1980 next to the Third Street vice strip. His rooms resembled those of other neighboring tribesmen back through the decades. The four-story dark brick building, a former hotel, was in moderately good repair thanks to its energetic owner-manager, who tried to refurbish each dwelling unit in between tenants. In return for a substantial deposit and $150 to $200 a month rent, he promised quiet and safe quarters. Each occupant got two keys: to the formidable front door and to his or her apartment. Upon climbing the winding, wooden staircase to the third floor, especially at meal times, pungent smells from a dozen kitchens triggered visions of the corridor's international residents. Martin's apartment was off to the right, along a hallway and beyond the fire door. Sunlit, the combined living room and kitchen (with a small General Electric refrigerator, Robert Shaw gas stove, counter, and sink) overlooked noisy Willis Avenue and the building's tiny front yard. Off to the north and beyond the university loomed two mid-town land marks: the General Motors and the Fisher buildings. The atmosphere in Martin's front room was warmed by hardwood floors. He furnished the three rooms (living room-kitchen, bedroom, bath) quickly because, as a busy bachelor, he did not require or desire much. Nor were the selections obviously distinctive. Voluminous literature stacked about on dressers, tables, and counters derived from his work as an alcohol and drug abuse counselor; a plaid couch and matching easy chair, bentwood rocker, a black-and-white television, a throw rug, and a couple of seascapes in the front room sufficed for entertaining; and the kitchen cupboards were minimally stocked, for most of his meals were eaten out. Gazing about, was the occupant obviously native American? If one looked carefully—at the *Akwesasne Notes* wall calendar, framed photographs of dark-skinned nieces and nephews, at miscellaneous pieces of Indian craftwork—and analyzed the content of each room, it could be argued that Kiyoshk's values, reflected here, were not those of a typical Detroiter. He was a Walpole Island band member living in the city.

Whenever Martin ventured from his comparatively secure apartment building, he reentered the brutal battle for survival in the Cass Corridor. In January 1981 his boss, Harry Command, visited the old neighborhood. While sipping coffee at a corner cafe he recognized in the passing parade of Indian acquaintances alcoholics, dope peddlers, and con men. Danger and drugs had aged them. Once again Harry marveled at the miracle that spun him off this fast and deadly track nearly twenty years earlier so that he could start life anew. He survived the corridor, like Joe Mesheky and Martin; yet none could forget those unfortunates still on the track or those who perished of malnutrition and in fires, who froze to death in deserted buildings, who were beaten up in bars and stabbed on the streets. Comfortable inside the warm restaurant, Harry Command glimpsed in the gaunt faces of street Indians what his own fate would have been.[14]

For decades Indians tolerated substandard Cass Corridor housing because it was cheap, an important consideration for impoverished tribesmen just off the reservations, and because it was convenient to downtown stores, jobs, and (for a few predators) to potential victims. For problem drinkers, the undereducated and unemployed, the neighborhood offered plenty of relatives and friends to bunk with and borrow money from, day labor offices, Indian bars, and news about home communities. Unfortunately, lamented one young man who somehow shared a small apartment with twenty to twenty-five other Indians, "the worst part of the city [the Cass Corridor] is the best part to live in." His buddies lived just as they desired: having fun, pooling limited money, assisting native American derelicts who came their way.[15]

Yet life on the cheap had its price. The local crime rate was sky-high. Police regularly rousted Indians. Welfare payments, cramped living quarters in decaying and unsanitary facilities, and other pernicious features of daily life bred many social and psychological pathologies, notably addiction to alcohol, a slow form of suicide.

IV

One spring evening in 1980, a Detroit native American alcohol-awareness group held an open house and prompted several Indians to share with the audience what alcohol had done to their lives. A middle-aged Iroquois woman related how, during three decades, she had been robbed of her adolescence as well as three husbands, each of whom died prematurely from alcohol-related illnesses. The memories of raising seven children were largely lost. Unforgettable, however, were the times she ended up in jail, beaten and robbed. For more than two decades, Morris, a Chippewa, drank himself out of jobs across Canada and the United States. Alcoholics always demoted themselves "from penthouse to poorhouse," he observed; it was never the reverse. Burton first tasted liquor at age four. From then he loved the feeling it imparted and prided himself on how many other Indians he could outdrink. Booze became his "medicine of life." Don, another speaker, admitted that not too long ago people refused to let him in their homes. As a diffident teenager he found in a bottle what he first thought were confidence and freedom—to raise his hand in high school, to attend dances. Ironically, he lost the very qualities he pursued. As he became increasingly violent and ill tempered, he stole from his friends to pay for hard liquor. Robbery, assault, and breaking and entering climaxed in his "touring stone buildings" (prisons) between ages seventeen and twenty-six. Down in solitary confinement, bereft of family and friends, his spirit broken by alcohol: Don "walked through the doors of Hell." A final Detroit speaker, one of several with Walpole Island roots, also described how drinking had so robbed him of clear thinking that he could not even get "honest with his dishonesty." All personal difficulties, which were considerable, he blamed on judges and attorneys and parole boards. For years the delusion persisted that he was too smart, too young, too tough to have to quit drinking.[16]

Harry Command and other recovering alcoholics realized how long-standing and widespread were these personal problems in the southeast Michigan Indian community. AIS estimated that alcoholism, a total disease, touched about 60 percent of area Indians. "It follows that the social and family disorganization are attending to these rates feeding each other in circular patterns; economic and social status problems followed by family disorganization and mental illness followed by unemployment, alcoholism, around and around."[17] Gene Iron Shell witnessed the fate of several clients unable to stop self-destructive drinking. Some froze to death along the highways; others became "vegetables" in state institutions, dressed each day in rubber bags and fed by nurses' aids. Problem drinking also was linked to crime. Gene calculated that many natives in the state prison in Jackson, whom he advised regularly, had abused drugs and alcohol. Equally tragic were those who only worked enough to buy an evening bottle and some groceries. Finally, there were the suicides: teenage Indian alcoholics who isolated themselves, then fought depression, until finally they "give up and give in." "We have to get rid of the 'drunken Indian' image," Gene insisted. "Alcoholism robs us of ourselves-of being who we are. It is the most devastating disease Indians suffer from today."[18]

Victims extended beyond group-drinking males in Cass Corridor bars. While he was an AIS counselor and a frequent participant in citywide self-help groups for alcoholics, Rod Wulff assisted many suburban natives. As teenagers during the sixties, when it was socially trendy to be Indian, they donned K Mart beads, followed the powwow circuit, and had developed harmful addictions to alcohol and other drugs. Also an AIS employee, Martin Kiyoshk counseled "closet alcoholics" from throughout the metropolitan area. They included women who pulled the blinds after husbands left for work, took out hidden bottles, and drank alone.[19]

A therapist underscored the seriousness of urban Indian drug abuse, especially in the Cass Corridor. They drink to ventilate, she explained: to release pent-up, normal emotions, which, as children, they learned to suppress. They also took drugs to self-medicate themselves out of the real world. Hence, at local Indian bars a wide range of saved feelings bubbled up to the surface. Some quiet customers, for example, soon were effusive; later they became argumentative; and eventually they picked fights. Others acted maudlin and then started crying. A few passed out onto the cluttered floor in their own vomitus.[20]

Recovering Detroit alcoholics agreed that, before the 1970s, the Indian community lacked programs to mitigate excessive drinking problems. Particularly needed was a group of educated, dedicated, sober role models to provide social services leadership. Nor were there any Indian-run agencies that offered specialized counseling and referrals. Also lacking were native health workers to (1) change community, family, and individual attitudes toward alcoholism, (2) develop leisure-time activities for alcoholics, (3) find employment for alcoholics, and (4) encourage youth, who often lived amid alcohol-abuse situations, to stay in school. There simply was no organization, as AIS later lamented, "to intervene on this vicious cycle for the Indian population."[21]

Nor was there a native-controlled clinic to meet other unmet health needs of Detroit Indians as of 1970. Those living outside the urban core (on comfortable incomes, in homes with all the modern conveniences, situated along safe streets) predictably enjoyed good health, like their neighbors. Easy access to family physicians and neighborhood hospitals was taken for granted. But inner-city Indian families, struggling for existence on lower incomes and living in less wholesome environments, became excessively troubled by illness. Traditional Indian medicine as well as the city's mainstream health delivery system oftentimes proved inadequate.

Traditional medicine, brought to Detroit from home reservations like Walpole Island and Six Nations, was clouded in mystery. Indian people disliked discussing it, in part because of the negative attitudes of white missionaries, physicians, and federal officials back through the years. Natives who could cure an illness understandably were reluctant to reveal their medicine; some also feared that talk about secret ceremonies might cause a spell to be put on them.

Down through the years, most Detroit natives apparently accepted Western, scientific medicine, although evidence about patterns of use remained sketchy. Traditional health practices played a supportive role. No medicine man lived in the city by the 1970s; for their services Detroiters traveled to Six Nations, the Dakotas, and as far as Oklahoma. At times practitioners visited the Motor City to conduct ceremonies. But, as knowledgeable informants explained, the "concrete buildings and population concentration of urban areas are considered inappropriate for a ceremony setting whose primary purpose is to become attuned to nature." Six or seven herbalists lived in the metropolitan area in 1977. During ceremonies in patients' homes they administered herbal teas as preventative agents (to internally purify a baby, for example) and as cures for diarrhea, upset stomach, and skin rash.[22]

Perhaps 25 percent of the native population used these remedies during the 1970s. Mainly they were older tribesmen who, together with some young people, saw this as a way to preserve aboriginal woodland cultures. Medical requirements partly explained their visits to home reservations. Those married to non-Indians were least likely to follow customary techniques. Men preferred traditional medical help, perhaps because they disliked hospitals and were not as familiar with physicians as their wives, who required prenatal and postnatal care. Ruth, a forty-two year-old Iroquois grandmother who lived in Detroit most of her life and who took Indian medicine every Sunday, recalled how sick she became during a pregnancy. Her father's response was to drive to Six Nations and buy medicine, which relieved her symptoms. The baby was born healthy. Ruth's mother also traveled to the reserve for medical assistance. Besides birth complications, Indian medicine was practiced on other special occasions, including deaths, important days in the lunar calendar, and even Christian holidays. In short, the importance of these activities, as a supplement to the white man's modern medicine, cannot be denied. The rub was that Detroit's mainstream health-delivery system, an impressive network of hospitals, clinics, and social agencies, was not entirely satisfactory for inner-city Indians.[23]

By the 1970s Mayor Coleman Young's administration, recognizing the need for better mobilized human services, prodded the City Council to create the Neighborhood Services Department (NSD). Improving family and neighborhood life in four target areas was its major goal. One area was southwest Detroit, including the Cass Corridor—home for at least forty-two thousand needy persons. Based on the community action concept first advocated by Washington's Office of Economic Opportunity, the NSD delivered a wide range of social services (medical-dental, employment, housing, counseling, transportation, food cooperatives, hot meals for senior citizens) at four major area centers and five subcenters. Furthermore, in area II, where many native Americans lived, the NSD staff in 1976 organized seventy-two community meetings to disseminate information, sponsored 238 GED classes, and provided casework services for 5,944 new clients and to 6,233 returning clients. That year nearly fifty thousand residents visited the department's four neighborhood clinics and three thousand received emergency dental care. Clinics also provided family planning services and, in cooperation with the city's Health Department and local hospitals, comprehensive alcohol and drug abuse help for more than five thousand low-income persons and families in 1976.[24]

The facilities of the NSD were not the only options available for impoverished Detroiters. The city's Bureau of Substance Abuse, to take but one example, listed twenty-two treatment centers and six inpatient institutions for alcoholics. Notable among private facilities were the Salvation Army Harbor Light Substance Abuse Treatment Center and Sacred Heart Rehabilitation Center and Half-Way House.[25]

The "Place of New Beginnings," Harbor Light provided a therapeutic community for persons in advanced stages of addiction who required a residential program out of the mainstream. Here, after alcohol and heroin detoxification, they engaged in group and individual therapy sessions, supervised by staff professionals. Harbor Light offered "soup, soap, and salvation." More specifically, free meals, lodging for a few nights each month, occasional new sets of clothing or a bus ticket, vocational services, a community drop-in center, an outpatient clinic for substance abusers, daily chapel services, spiritual guidance: all were available free of charge at the Salvation Army's Brainard-and-Cass facilities, in the heart of Cass Corridor.[26]

Sacred Heart sponsored similar programs, in an atmosphere of Christian living. Begun in June 1967 by six chronic, down-and-out alcoholics, it served 1,500 men over the next decade, expanding out of its rehabilitated parochial school building into three other downtown branches until it developed a capacity for 180 men. Many types of therapy were employed for the rehabilitation of patients—physically, psychologically, spiritually—during a typical ninety-day stay. Thanks to Sacred Heart, the staff claimed, more than a thousand of "the forgotten men of the city" received "care, concern, consideration and human dignity that has been lost sometimes as long as 30 years."[27]

The Neighborhood Services Department and other mainstream health organizations obviously aided thousands of needy Detroiters. But too few were native Americans. Teachers at the Cass Corridor's Burton Elementary School witnessed daily the tragedy of untreated Indian medical problems. In 1970 a *Detroit News* reporter commented

> Where drink isn't the enemy, sickness often is.
> A teacher at Burton Schools says:
> He had an Indian family here awhile ago with five children....
> ' "The father died of tuberculosis, and shortly after the mother died of cancer. The grandmother took the kids in, but never said anything to us or asked for any help. She was too proud.
> "Then she got TB, and the state finally took the children away to foster homes. They were beautiful children, too."
> Mrs. Yvonne Walker, a kindergarten teacher at Burton agrees.
> "They're beautiful kids, ... but they have a lot of problems. One little girl, five years old, has been in a youth home twice. Her parents abandoned her.
> "One boy's mother is on ADC. He has trouble with his eyes, but she won't see her caseworker about finding a doctor. Another little girl came in here with an infected ear. It was draining and smelled and she must have been in terrible pain.
> "But she didn't say anything to us....
> "Some have problems with their teeth, and rarely smile because they're ashamed of it. A boy in my class just sits and cried all morning. He has problems at home, but won't talk about it."[28]

After living in the Cass Corridor for a year, a University of Michigan doctoral student in anthropology concluded

> Indian people in the Cass Corridor rarely discuss their aches and pains or any of their health problems. Many go to doctors only in cases of emergency. Regular health checkups are unheard of... except with babies ....
> The most noticeable sign of poor health care is the area of dental health. The majority of adult Indians ... have bad teeth. They do not have regular checkups. They wait until a tooth aches so much that it must be pulled.[29]

Painful tooth decay, an infected ear, reluctance to talk with a caseworker or schoolteacher: why were the poverty-stricken Indians of downtown Detroit so hesitant to seek help from social agencies designed to serve the community? Part of the explanation lay with the transplanted natives. "Too proud," like the school child's grandmother, was a factor; more likely they were too uninformed. Newcomers to the city simply were ignorant about the multiple social services available. Undemonstrative Indians with special health needs, struggling to cope with an urban environment, balked at candid conversations with non-Indian counselors whom they distrusted. Moreover, Detroit social institutions, whether by intention or ineptitude, alienated clients. They lumped all poor minority people into one category. No wonder agency personnel, unaware of unique Indian problems and their cultural and historical backgrounds, failed to establish rapport with native people. Indians complained bitterly about the bureaucracy: the brusk and impersonal atmosphere, required medical referrals and appointments, lengthy forms to complete, intimate talks with hurried strangers (in health clinics where they rarely saw the same physician twice). When Detroit Indians needed prompt help in a medical emergency, too often they experienced extended suffering in crowded hospital emergency rooms.

V

During the 1960s, mounting public concern for the disadvantaged, whose condition a wealthy nation had neglected for decades, climaxed in a series of social reforms known as the War on Poverty. The poor health of many Appalachian whites, urban blacks, Mexican Americans in barrios, and Indians on and off reservations was an inextricable part of their neediness; therefore, Washington stressed the expansion and improvement of health-delivery systems. The Medicare and Medicaid programs subsequently gave America's poor better access to these facilities. After conclusive investigations rated native American economic and health conditions the lowest in the nation, presidents Kennedy, Johnson, and Nixon pressed Congress to set up Indian-run programs that would lift native living standards while simultaneously respecting their cultures and sense of community.[30]

Responding to White House special messages, Congress enacted legislation that ultimately improved Indian health in Detroit. The Comprehensive Alcohol Abuse and Alcoholism Prevention, Treatment, and Rehabilitation Act of 1970 created the National Institute of Alcohol Abuse and Alcoholism (NIAAA) to meet the needs of millions of American problem drinkers, including native people. By the mid-seventies the NIAAA paid for 153 Indian alcoholism programs to provide direct services to native drug abusers.[31] One center was Harry Command's American Indian Services. To establish more general health-care programs for urban Indians, including outreach, referral, and direct services, Congress passed Title V of the Indian Health Care Improvement Act (1976). Thirty million dollars was authorized for these local programs over the next three years.[32] One was Bill Memberto's Detroit American Indian Health Center.

VI

In 1959, at the age of twenty-nine, Harry Command was a five-time loser with a lengthy police record of armed robbery and violation of parole, which had led to more than ten painful years in Michigan prisons. His maladjustment to urban society had begun a few years after birth to Chippewa parents in a Detroit ethnic neighborhood. His mother was from Walpole Island; his father, a window washer by trade, had migrated to the Motor City from Leech Lake Reservation in Minnesota. Harry harbored a few fond memories of summers spent on rustic Walpole with his blind grandfather, but chiefly he recalled an early dislike for education—it "was for dummies"—and persons in authority who told him what to do. Thus he spent a rebellious youth in the ghetto, cutting classes as early as elementary school. "I grew up with a lot of hatred in my life, and I took it out in fighting." At age fifteen he was permanently expelled from school. Imprisoned at eighteen, Harry took up boxing. He also became an alcoholic.[33]

One day while sitting in solitary, for the ninth time, he touched bottom; recently he had learned of his mother's death and had killed a fellow prisoner in the boxing ring. "Harry," he asked himself, "how long are you going to continue hurting people?" Convinced he was gradually going insane, he contemplated suicide. But, drawing upon some deep, inner strength, he began to build a new life from the ashes of the old. Night classes, reading, and intensive therapy engaged his thoughts; he came to believe that there must be a way out for people like him and to understand how alcoholism stymied his personal development. Only part of his hellish bondage had been the stone walls and iron bars.[34] Particularly helpful during this rehabilitation were visits from ex-convict George ("Chi") Walker of Kalamazoo. A boxer who had also lost the battle to the bottle, Walker introduced him to the philosophy and the fellowship of a self-help group for alcoholics.[35]

Alcoholism and prisons remained a part of Harry Command's life after his release in June 1959. The personal struggle with excessive drinking persisted until March 1966, when he took the last drink. That year he also launched his own window washing business. It quickly expanded and yielded a substantial profit. This second life, as he labeled the post-prison years, included enjoying a stable marriage, raising two daughters, and buying a pleasant home on the city's northwest side. Moreover, inmates and ex-inmates who knew Harry Command in prison started corresponding with him, requesting his help and advice. Many were native Americans. He conscientiously answered hundreds of letters. He visited prisons and vouched for ex-convicts in the courts. Command recalled that by 1972 he got so busy "giving talks, attending alcoholism seminars, visiting inter-tribal groups and reservations, that my home life began to suffer, and the need became apparent for additional help."[36]

Because of Harry Command's background, he and eight friends focused their abundant energies and limited finances on native American alcohol and drug problems in the city. With editorial help from Eugene Begay of the Chicago Indian Center, they submitted a fifty thousand-dollar grant proposal to Health, Education and Welfare's NIAAA in February 1972. Then they established AIS at a Victor Avenue storefront in Highland Park while awaiting Washington's decision. "For five months it was a constant struggle just to keep our heads above water," Harry recollected. As director he constantly scurried back and forth from window-washing jobs to AIS, where Indians received alcoholism and employment counseling. Indian volunteers contributed their evenings and their own money to continue these services and to pay the rent. Harry, for example, cashed in his life insurance, exhausted his savings account, and borrowed fifteen hundred dollars from a credit union; helping needy Indians, many of whom were newcomers to the city, also cost him several window-washing customers. In late September, the NIAAA rescued AIS by approving its grant request.[37]

As stated in its lengthy grant applications over the years, AIS battled alcoholism and drug abuse in Detroit by seeking to (1) "change community, family, and individual attitudes regarding alcoholism through a

structured program of preventative education and community outreach,"
(2) "provide specialized counseling and referral for treatment services
to Native American alcohol abusers," (3) "reduce the unemployment
rate of the service recipients," and (4) "motivate youth who are subject
to alcohol abuse situations and who themselves are or may be potential
alcohol abusers."[38] Harry Command was allowed considerable administrative freedom in pursuit of these goals because the NIAAA's small staff
had so many Indian alcohol centers to supervise.

Harry Command felt blessed. Besides a good home and family, he had
an urgent job to do, helping his people. "We're becoming involved in
politics, unions, every phase of community life," he noted confidently to
one reporter. "You're going to hear a lot about us." With such a goal,
much was demanded from the director, his staff, and from alcoholics
seeking salvation. Harry insisted on and got sound fiscal management,
hard work, and dedication from the staff. Particular emphasis was placed
on education as the key to working within the system.[39] Harry led the
way by obtaining enough workshop hours and college credits to get state
certification as a social worker. Staff members were encouraged to do
likewise. The AIS even offered educational programs for its clients. Harry
provided local backup support for staff counselors, developed new programs and financing sources in Lansing, Washington, as well as corporate offices, and carried the message about the dangerous consequences
of Indian alcoholism to legislators, penal institutions, local civic and
church groups, national conferences, and colleges across the Great
Lakes country.

The immediate recipients of the plentiful energy and vision pumped
into AIS operations by Harry Command were the staff counselors, whose
salaries, together with the director's and secretary's, consumed most of
the federal grant money received since 1972. Counselors came from
several tribes with different cultures, yet they worked effectively together
because they accepted Harry's approach for improving urban Indian life.
Most were recovering alcoholics. Professional counseling also demanded
continuing education, and those engaged in it were promoted up
through the AIS ranks.

By the late seventies the staff advised about thirty-five active clients
and their troubled families and answered dozens of telephone calls each
day. Their growing number attested to increased community awareness
that AIS was a critical link between Detroit Indians and service agencies.
Indian alcoholics felt comfortable with the informal atmosphere of
AIS, although they often hung around for several days before seeking assis-

tance. Here they needed no doctor's referral, no appointment, filled out no forms, did not have to bare their souls or talk much at all, and were not rushed. (This was quite a contrast from busy and bureaucratized city and state agencies.)[40] Nor did Indian alcoholics get sympathy. This was the worst thing you could give any person, asserted Wulff.[41] The AIS staff understood, because of their professional training and personal experiences, that the decisive first step in arresting alcoholism must be the client's desire to help himself or herself. Only then could counselors design a workable ninety-day nondrinking program that ministered to their three needs (spiritual, mental, physical) and included continuous personal support and weekly meetings.

At self-help (SH) meetings Gene Iron Shell, Rod Wulff, Harry Command, and hundreds of others discovered "The Twelve Steps," the core of the whole program. Humility, or ego reduction, was stressed by the first seven steps; these included admitting that "we were powerless over alcohol—that our lives had become unmanageable," believing that "a Power greater than ourselves could restore us to sanity," making "a decision to turn our will and our lives over to the care of God as we understood Him," and humbly asking "Him to remove our shortcomings." Salvation for the alcoholic lay in prolonging this humble spiritual state, which alone could neutralize the obsession with alcohol. Steps eight through twelve did so by integrating it with a more responsible life-style: making amends to "all persons we have harmed," continuing to take personal inventory, seeking "through prayer and meditation to improve our conscious contact with God," and finally "having had a spiritual awakening as the result of these steps, we tried to carry this message to alcoholics." Even the anonymity of SH derived from "The Twelve Steps" and was intended, according to one of the cofounders, "to keep those fool egos of ours from running hog wild after money and public fame at SH's expense. It really means personal and group sacrifice for the benefit of all SH."

AIS was committed to twelve-step work: carrying the lifesaving message to other alcoholics. Often this began when the Central Detroit SH Office notified Harry Command that an Indian requested help. The person was escorted to five or six different group meetings a week to keep him or her dry for a succession of twenty-four-hour periods and also to find other members with whom the newcomer could form common bonds. If the newcomer was especially comfortable with one group from among the roughly sixty SH organizations in metropolitan Detroit, it became his or her home group. For native Americans this was often the Thunderbirds.[42]

The continuing fellowship at these weekly gatherings helped self-confessed alcoholics in several ways. Convincing testimonials from the membership proved that personal transformation was possible. The seriousness of alcoholism was discussed and how each of "The Twelve Steps" was important in rehabilitation. Group guidance (therapy) was given to those experiencing severe personal problems while trying to lead sober lives. For Indian members who, like Gene Iron Shell, had internalized the drunken reservation Indian stereotype, SH leaders from AIS personally demonstrated that native Americans could make it in the system, that SH offered a better road for the future, that their uniqueness, their Indianness, could be a source of pride and achievement rather than an excuse for defeatism and escapism. As Harry Command often emphasized, drunkenness came from booze alone, not from being Indian. The SH group concern for individual needs, especially its commitment to come to a member's aid anytime the compulsion to drink became too strong, was a powerful social force that replaced the old drinking buddies and, like the spiritual dimension of SH, helped the chronic alcoholic stay sober, one day at a time, until his or her self-destructive illness was arrested.[43]

Alcoholism could be held in check only when one understood it was a total disease, claimed Gene Iron Shell. Not just because it eventually affected every aspect of one's life—health, family, friendships, job, and the like—but because the alcoholic "must be involved with it for the rest of his life if he wants to stay sober." Complacent ones who felt they could go it alone and leave SH usually started drinking again. Alcoholism could not be fought alone. And the alcoholic must never forget that he or she would always be "one drink away from being a drunk.v"[44]

Once a Detroit native American alcoholic was regenerated through SH, his or her new strengths were nurtured by an assortment of AIS activities. A cheerful drop-in center on the premises, a community lunch served every Wednesday, and sponsorship of an Indian bowling league encouraged healthy socializing away from Cass Corridor bars. Because AIS also understood that meaningful work was crucial to the recovery of its clients, it emphasized employment counseling and by the summer of 1978 had found jobs for more than four hundred Indians.[45] Still another thrust of Harry Command and his staff was educational programming designed to qualify underemployed native Americans for higher-paying jobs with greater responsibilities. During the 1976–77 academic year thirty ambitious Indians attended night classes at AIS to earn GEDs or to refresh their skills; moreover, the Michigan State Board of Education paid for AIS's postsecondary career development program, which, with help from Wayne State University's Community Services Division, increased Indian use of educational and career development resources at several Detroit agencies and community institutions.[46]

The Native American Alcoholism Therapist Training Program, the first of its kind in the nation, was the AIS education project of which Harry Command was most proud. It assisted needy Midwest Indian communities by training local native American mental health workers in alcoholism treatment and prevention. Their $300,000 two-year college program was designed by AIS, offered by Detroit's Wayne County Community College, and paid for by an NIAAA grant. The forty-two trainees, who were employed by or gave volunteer help to Indian communities in Canada, Michigan, Wisconsin, and Illinois, took course work in Detroit every third weekend of the month beginning in September 1975. Thus their valuable home services were not interrupted. Student travel, living expenses while in the Motor City, tuition and fees were paid for by the grant, as were staff salaries.[47] Gene Iron Shell, one of the instructors, warned, "I don't believe in pulling punches in this program. Our people have to see what this disease [alcoholism] is doing to our culture. I believe in laying it right on the line."[48] Specifically, the sixty-nine-credit curriculum integrated classroom work (in communication skills, sensitivity training, Indian cultural heritage, and technical expertise for the mental health field) and supervised field experiences at their home agencies. It culminated in an associate of arts degree at the end of the second year. Thirty-five native Americans completed these requirements. That they enriched their home communities was undeniable; ten former volunteers obtained jobs and sixteen who were already employed won promotions.[49]

Ernest Tootoosis, a Cree Indian elder from Saskatoon, Saskatchewan, and a recovering alcoholic, was an AIS consultant for the Native American Alcoholism Therapist Training Program. While in Detroit he remarked that although alcohol once had divided Indians, it was now drawing them back together.[50] The history of AIS illustrated this trend in the Motor City. Established in the early 1970s by a few native Americans who sacrificially donated time and talents, AIS had since provided valuable and varied programs for the city's Indian alcoholics and other community members: social activities, specialized counseling, referral services, job placement for hundreds of natives, continuing education curriculums tailored to Indians' needs, and twelve-step work in connection with SH.

VII

Bill Memberto was born and raised in Muskegon, Michigan; his mother was Dutch and his father a full-blooded Ottawa from the Grand River Band. Poverty gripped the family. Neighborhood white youth discriminated against Bill. Most degrading were the schools, which made him feel like a nonentity. Teachers seemingly had no knowledge of woodland cultures or the historical contributions of native peoples; they stifled his artistic expression and slotted him for vocational training. Bill dropped out instead. The army then diverted him from a life of petty crime and drug abuse primarily because it respected his potential and gave him responsibility. Within eighteen months he made sergeant, at age eighteen. Bill became an army medical specialist and, knowing that an Indian could succeed in such a structured system, went on to complete his high school training and earn some college credits. After being discharged, he took his bachelor's degree at Western Michigan University. For a decade he worked in the mental health field. This experience and training Bill brought to Detroit when he assumed the directorship of the Indian Health Center in 1978.[51]

The center's programs were already well established. Seven staff members, with offices at the DAIC on John R, included the project director, a nurse-coordinator, a health planner, three community outreach workers, and an executive secretary. Outreach workers aided ten to fifteen persons daily by the fall of 1977. They sought the best medical help for native people. They set up individual appointments, frequently provided transportation, and tried to gain patients' confidence (many were still treated by medicine men and disliked visiting medical doctors). The staff also dispensed emergency food and clothing. They referred clients to other Indian offices such as AIS and Russ Wright's Urban Indian Affairs. In accord with federal requirements staff members made a preliminary health-needs assessment; then they visited city agencies to share their findings and assist them in helping the Indian community. For example, through the Indian center newsletter the department notified natives about the twenty-four-hour emergency dental care available to anyone in pain because of tooth problems and who was unable to pay to see a dentist.[52] To improve native health more directly the department sponsored an Indian Free Clinic at 120 Parsons Street, just off Cass Avenue, and staffed by volunteer physicians and a registered nurse. "Indian people feel better if they can come to an Indian clinic and be served by Indian people," explained Elizabeth Smith, R.N. and a Makah

Indian. "They feel they have a better relationship with me and can express themselves better."[53] Besides volunteer doctors, a dozen agencies donated their time, assistance, and supplies to the clinic, which served 140 native patients during one year. Indian senior citizens benefited nutritionally and in other ways from the Health Department's food and friendship program. It provided one free hot meal per day, five days a week. Finally, the staff instituted a health advisory board to assure community participation in the program and to aid in establishing specific objectives.[54]

Before leaving Detroit, Bobby Crooks, a college-educated Choctaw and Memberto's predecessor, reflected on the health status of urban Indians. Their major problems, closely associated with poverty, included: high infant mortality; lack of immunization among children; improper nutrition; untreated dental, vision, and hearing maladies; alcohol and drug abuse; street-fighting injuries; inadequate emergency care. His Indian Health Department provided 5,470 services during the 1976–77 administrative year, and closely cooperated with other center offices. (Manpower once obtained a factory-job interview for a client, only to have the company refuse to hire him because of impacted wisdom teeth. Crooks sent him to a dentist to determine the extent of the problem; then the department convinced Wayne County to pay for the extractions. Ultimately the fellow got the position.) Echoing the thoughts of Joe Mesheky, Crooks emphasized that Washington should have started urban health programs forty years earlier, for by 1977 deep-rooted native needs were frightfully complex and nearly overwhelming in their extent. Several years would elapse, he predicted, before anything but a dent could be made, even by Indian-run agencies.[55]

Bill Memberto comprehended the magnitude of this challenge and charted an ambitious course for Detroit's Indian Health Center. This involved expanding free clinic services, increasing the outreach staff to maximize home visits, and breaching the access barriers, that is, convince more clients to use center services and tailor its care to be even more acceptable to native people. After six months on the job his detailed report to Washington, noting 3,931 services between June 16, 1977, and May 31, 1978, affirmed that the staff "have not lost sight of the great unmet needs in the Indian community in Detroit, and are moving as rapidly as possible toward a solution of the major health problems facing them."[56]

Memberto was confident that Detroit Indians, backed by the government's self-determination policy, could best supply their health care needs. To be sure, native project directors in Michigan must abide by the dominant society's rules. There simply were not enough Indians to alter this political reality. Nevertheless, he believed native people could become skillful lobbyists in Washington, Lansing, and locally; they could tap more effectively public goodwill toward them and educate Detroiters about Indian needs; they could learn about government offices that had money for Indian programs and about how to pressure recalcitrant bureaucrats to modify restrictive regulations. Another challenge of Indian self-determination was accountability: Washington's insatiable demand for numbers to document fully how a program spent the previous year's moneys and why it needed more in the future. To complete these required forms and also to make intelligent long-range program decisions, Memberto needed to know, not just how many people were assisted by his staff, but the health status of native persons whom the center could not aid because of inadequate resources.[57] To develop this data the Detroit Indian Health Center undertook its most ambitious enterprise.

Like the 1978 special census of all known Indians living in Wayne County, the health status survey was professionally planned and executed (in consultation with Memberto's office) by Dr. Rashid Bashshur of the University of Michigan's School of Public Health. He selected a study sample of 205 native families from the Wayne County population for a comprehensive examination of their health status and use of mainstream services.[58]

The information about the health status of Detroit's Indian population was critical to Bill Memberto's planning. How did the survey population appraise their own health, for instance? If they judged it as very good, they probably would not seek care. The data was striking: only 27 percent of Indian respondents considered their health "excellent," whereas 49 percent of a sample of the national population (as determined in 1980 by the United States Department of Health and Human Services) believed they were in excellent health. Indian physical well-being was linked to family income and residence. Perceived poor health was most common among the lower-income group and greater in the city than in the suburbs and downriver areas.[59]

The accuracy of Wayne County Indians' perceptions was validated when they pinpointed the presence of specific diseases. Two illustrations from the survey convey the seriousness of their situation. Diabetes, a debilitating disorder prevalent among Indians, was found at a high rate in the Detroit native community: 52.2 cases per thousand, compared with a national average of 20.4. These represented only the diagnosed Indian cases. If their entire population were screened, evidence from a Pima tribal study suggested that the rate might be closer to 100. The implications were obvious: so life-threatening a disease should be addressed in Indian health programs with early diagnosis and treatment as well as education about diet and nutrition. Indian dental hygiene was also alarming. Only 43 percent of the study sample used dental services during the previous year; less than 20 percent received prophylactic care. And without checkups and professional cleaning, their health had to suffer, although it was impossible to gauge this without complete screening. Low-income families living downtown reported the least amount of prophylactic care and dental repair work.[60]

Besides urban Indian illnesses, the survey revealed the extent of unmet health needs. Most of the Indian sample claimed they had a usual medical provider and a regular dentist, yet these practitioners were not always called on in time of illness. Nine percent of the families experienced medical problems for which they received no care. And during the year before the survey, 15 percent endured untreated dental difficulties. Data on both types of care documented a greater unmet need in the inner city than outlying areas. Low family incomes doubtless contributed to this suffering. Roughly 25 percent of the households received public assistance and experienced difficulty paying for health care. A quarter of the Indian families in the sample had no form of health insurance (compared with about 12 percent of the United States population).[61]

Finally, the 205 Detroit Indian families outlined their principal priorities for health care and related community matters. Respondents realized the information requested was for a health study, yet they rated six problems more pressing than medical and dental care. In order of importance they were: cost of living, jobs, education, crime and vandalism, housing, and environment. These "community-wide views reflect a rather distressed condition wherein people are generally alarmed at the seriousness of many problems they have to face," the Michigan researchers concluded. "Nonetheless, the major problems are economic in nature." When asked to rank their most vexing health troubles, again money loomed large. Survey families were most concerned about financially needy fellow Indians, followed by drug addiction treatment, nursing care for the elderly, aid for alcoholics, the environment (clean air and clean water), traditional medicine, and the like. For example, 63 percent of the sample rated alcoholism and drug abuse as "very serious" or "serious" concerns. Anxiety about the less fortunate and the elderly,

which reflected both current Detroit conditions as well as Indian humanistic traditions, meant that a "health care program designed to meet the
needs of this Indian community should consider these problems as its
highest priorities." What barriers did needy Indians face in obtaining
medical and dental services? For 80 percent of the respondents the cost
was either a "very serious" or "serious" difficulty, distressing alike to suburban and inner-city residents. Service hours and transportation were
also notable access problems. What was the best way for planners like
Bill Memberto to help? Three-fourths believed it was "very important"
or "important" to establish an Indian health center.[62]

The 1980 needs assessment, documenting the low health status of
Detroit Indians and suggesting ways to promote Indian well-being, fostered further expansion of the health department's services. Using part-
time, contract physicians who were coordinated by Agatha Jenkins, an
Ottawa public health nurse, Memberto transformed operations into the
Detroit American Indian Health Center with its own board of directors.
At 360 John R, its free clinic services were impressive: immunization,
nutritional counseling, obstetric-gynecological examinations, transportation to other nearby medical facilities, and senior citizens health screening.[63] Outreach worker Ben Bearskin, Jr., was particularly enthusiastic
about adaptation of the center services to native needs, like those at AIS.
No one foisted mainstream values on sick Indians.[64]

VIII

No 1970s federal legislation comparable to CETA or the Indian Health
Care Improvement Act tried to alleviate the housing problems of destitute urban Indians who were victimized because of their inexperience
as renters and the shortage of suitable low-income housing. Their living
conditions became the worst in the city: overcrowded, substandard apartment buildings in deteriorating neighborhoods characterized by crime,
transiency, and poverty. Yet natives were notoriously reluctant to con-
front landlords about code violations; they preferred, it seemed, to walk
away rather than fight, even if it meant abandoning personal possessions.[65] Their need for effective advocacy was truly pressing.

Since January 1976, the DAIC's housing officer, Frank Alberts, has
upgraded housing conditions for some native Americans. He obtained

city-financed emergency shelter for newcomers who arrived without re-sources. Once they obtained steady work, he helped them find suitable apartments close to job sites or public transportation, and if they main-tained good work records, he could draw upon extensive lists of owners willing to lease houses to stable Indian families. Encouraging a landlord to extend a few weeks of rent credit, helping with the relocation, busing some used furniture stored at the center—all were part of his job. Urban neophytes also got information on tenant responsibilities and their right to clean and healthful living conditions. If negligent landlords refused to make repairs, Alberts at times upgraded the place himself and billed them; he also reported code violations to the city Housing Commission and Legal Aid's Landlord-Tenant Clinic. Albert's intimate knowledge of the Cass Corridor, where he lived for more than thirty years, and his bighearted concern for fellow tribesmen have helped hundreds of urban Indians. But with so many county natives poverty-stricken and low-in-come public housing monopolized by blacks, families continued, on into the eighties, to settle for substandard rentals.[66]

Poverty further blighted the living conditions of Indian center clients scattered outside the Cass Corridor. Staff members like Alberts and Mem-berto and Mesheky ministered to their needs, but the task was overwhelm-ing. The center's brown passenger van transported native people from east side and west side neighborhoods, which conjured up images of Watts: row upon row of one-family frame or brick houses on tiny lots, dilapidated or vandalized or boarded up or burned out; streets and al-leyways and vacant lots choked with garbage and litter and the rusty re-mains of abandoned automobiles. Occasionally an oasis loomed, an ele-mentary school perhaps: well-maintained and fenced in, with the newer model cars of teachers and the bright-eyed enthusiasm and potential and playful innocence of children. Outside the chain-link barriers life looked downright Hobbesian: "solitary, poor, nasty, brutish, and short."[67]

Cary Severt, the Indian center's energy crisis coordinator in 1980, got a close look at several low-income native households while he aided them in paying heating bills. With a home near Woodward Avenue and Eight Mile Road, one Chippewa widow struggled to live on $300 a month from Social Security. She allotted $144 for her home mortgage; the rest went for food and other bills. Clearly she could not meet all her needs. The small, one-level home required extensive exterior repair. She owed $431 to the gas company; she was indebted to a hospital for artificial hip sur-gery; she did not eat well. Severt helped her complete the forms for utility assistance payments, described Indian center services, then drove her downtown to eat a hot lunch with the seniors and pick up commodity food donated by the Gleaners. Another native woman lived just west of the Lodge Freeway in equally wretched circumstances. A car on the vacant lot next door was home for one neighbor. Fierce-sounding dogs offered some protection and she admitted no strangers. Inside, the aged family head, a stroke victim, lay bedridden. A pension and Social Security enabled the two to survive. They received wheeled meals as well as nursing care for the husband, and each day the daughter stopped by to bathe and care for the invalid father. She, four young children, and her illiterate, out-of-work husband needed Aid to Dependent Children money to exist. At least one of her brothers was unemployed and lacked a high school education. Severt pleasantly explained the Indian center's services and how it might help with, among other things, obtaining a wheelchair for the disabled father.[68] Cary then said good-bye to the old couple and the young mother—a dutiful and loving daughter, spirited, desperately trying to aid her parents and brothers and her husband. Yet, for the time being, all were trapped in a Detroit ghetto.

Jane Johnson, a Cass Corridor resident for a dozen years and a professional counselor who claimed Indian ancestry, reflected one day about the interconnections among employment, housing, and health and on the dilemma they posed for social engineers and do-gooders. Poverty pervaded most of the Cass Corridor Indian households and was often accompanied by substandard living conditions and serious health problems. Overcrowded quarters, inadequate heat, faulty plumbing, rats and roaches: native families endured these difficulties because they had to (they occupied the city's cheapest apartments) and because they were near their friends. Jane depicted one corridor apartment where winter winds continually rattled and bypassed loose-fitting windows, the disconnected kitchen sink sat like a discarded toy on the floor, and a bucket of water was needed to flush the toilet. Moreover, the owner had just raised the rent to two hundred dollars a month.[69]

Amid what some would call this miserable scene, several adults who eked out a living on welfare and day labor and Aid to Dependent Children money engaged in self-destructive behavior: alcohol and drug abuse, child abuse, the physical mistreatment of spouses. Parents seemed not to value formal education. At times children missed classes because they lacked adequate clothing, food, or had to care for siblings in the place of temporarily incapacitated parents. One pretty grade-school girl, a prizewinning powwow dancer, had taken tranquilizers since age seven because of the abusive action she witnessed at home.[70]

To suggest that society remove the children from this seemingly harmful situation was to misconstrue the dynamics of Cass Corridor native life, Jane contended. First of all, such urban Indian behavior was deep-rooted; it existed for at least two generations in some families and was largely an extension of reservation communal ways. Nor was life in Cass Corridor bars and apartments and on the streets without redeeming features, if one looked carefully. Jane saw beauty as well as blight, the sharing of clothes, food, cars, and beds as well as booze. No matter how austere a family's finances became, some mother in the apartment building made sure that the children were fed.[71]

Since the sixties Rita Kiyoshk, one of these unsung mothers, kept open house for Walpole Islanders new to the city and for their friends. She fed them together with her four children. On a given night from ten to fifteen guests slept on the floor. While job hunting, each person contributed what he could from limited resources and also helped with housework. An Indian preschool educator, upon entering Rita's untidy apartment, threatened to call the health department. Perhaps it was justified. Yet Jane and others quickly pointed to all the good things that happened at Rita's: Indians helping other Indians (reminiscent of the days at Sam Fox's tavern), needy Indians surviving the initial shock of urban life, native people living together as in the old days and in the old ways.[72]

Apartments like Rita's also posed a dilemma for social workers. Removal of a child from this situation and placement with a black foster family would solve the problem of substandard physical conditions. But cultural insiders like Jane comprehended the equally devastating psychological and social effect on young ones if they were wrenched from homes where they always slept securely two to seven in a bed, lived communally with other native children (roaming the streets together, attending movies together, eating their meals together), where they understood they were Indians, and were surrounded continually by Indian "aunties" and "uncles."[73]

The closer this social-cultural dilemma was examined, especially in the light of its historical roots, the more complex it became; the pat answers seemed increasingly dubious; and the realization dawned that probably there were no white man's and black man's remedies at all. After a century of destructive BIA paternalism, a similar concept was discerned by Washington policymakers in the 1970s, who then instituted a self-determination policy for Indians across the United States.

132

IX

The Detroit American Indian Health Center and American Indian Services rose to this challenge. Supported by federal grants and spurred on by the native community's pressing health problems, they offered a wide range of services beginning in the 1970s: identification of unmet and severe native health needs, assisting clients in using public and private resources, counseling alcohol and drug abusers, and providing direct medical care. Planning for and managing of these services, together with housing help supplied by Frank Alberts, involved the maximum participation of Indians as called for by Congress.

AIS, in particular, showed the power of Indian self-determination unleashed, which nationwide was the most dynamic force in native American life during the seventies. "This is not anything Washington has handed us on a platter," insisted the AIS director. "Our program is thoroughly Indian, from top to bottom. We feel we have some realistic answers put together by concerned Indian people.[74]

The keys to the success of AIS in Detroit included clear and practical goals for improving the future of native Americans, adequate federal moneys, sound fiscal management, and enthusiastic community involvement. Finally, one cannot survey the AIS story and the many lives it saved and enhanced without being struck by Harry Command's decisive role. Two of his friends expressed it quite simply: this organization's accomplishments demonstrate what one determined fighter, when given another chance, could do for his people.[75]

>>> CHAPTER 5 <<<

Education for the Concrete Reservation

By 1969 Indian education policy (historically motivated by a desire to exploit Indian lands and by a "self-righteous intolerance of tribal communities and cultural differences," and implemented through persuasive and coercive techniques) reaped a bitter harvest throughout America. Effects on the education of Indian children according to United States Senate Subcommittee investigators (in the so-called Kennedy Report) were disastrous. Public schools and BIA facilities had failed "to understand or adapt to, and in fact often denigrate, cultural differences." Classrooms had become battlegrounds "where the Indian child attempts to protect his integrity and identity as an individual by defeating the purposes of the school." Whether examining national data, an individual BIA school, or native performance in public institutions, the outcome was "a dismal record of absenteeism, dropouts, negative self-image, low achievement, and, ultimately, academic failure for many Indian children."[1] By the time native students reached grade six, their verbal ability, reading, and mathematics achievement slipped one and a half grade levels behind white students of nonmetropolitan areas. The twelfth grade found them two and a half to three years behind. Regional and national dropout rates ranged from 43 to 60 percent.[2] Almost 75 percent of In-

134

dian household heads surveyed in Michigan, for instance, had not graduated from high school, and most had less than a ninth grade education.[3] Undereducated young people perpetuated the poverty cycle. Yet Indian communities felt powerless to influence or control school boards.

I

The schooling of Detroit's Indians was strikingly like national conditions disclosed in the Kennedy Report. Education also mirrored the general shortfalls in urban life: families who sought jobs in the Motor City and instead became trapped in the Cass Corridor; those wishing better living conditions who ended up in overcrowded, substandard apartments along a vicious vice strip. Thousands of Indian newcomers who funneled into the downtown during the postwar years likewise wanted a richer life for their children. The dreams of many were dashed when urban blight and racial tension and skyrocketing crime rates chased middle-class neighbors out to secure suburbs. By default, decaying inner-city schools were left to the poor and the elderly, to the Arabs, Orientals, Mexican Americans, Appalachian whites, and native Americans. The census revealed in 1970 just how serious the undereducation of Detroit's Indian population had become. Only 35.2 percent of metropolitan area adults were high school graduates, compared with 52.1 percent of the general population; the median school years completed by Indians was 10.4, nearly two years fewer than the general population.[4]

Detroit Indian home surroundings were closely connected with school performance. Besides the shock of adjusting to urban life and, sometimes, the persistent clash between tribal values and those of the urban-industrial dominant society, parental economic instability was a critical environmental factor for hundreds of Indian children over the years. A quarter of Wayne County's native population had incomes below the poverty level during the seventies. Furthermore, financially hard-pressed families of necessity lived in the cheapest sections of the city. Sixty-five percent chose the Cass Corridor. Deteriorating housing in dangerous neighborhoods and not enough money for food and clothing clearly discouraged high achievement in school. Apparently, so did the notably low achievement of household heads among the neediest families; 68.7 percent of them had less than a high school education. Statistics gathered by Indians in the 1970s showed that the fewer years of formal schooling an Indian had, the less likely he or she was to obtain gainful employment and, by implication, provide a home atmosphere supportive of education[5] (see table 14).

TABLE 14
Distribution of Wayne County Indian Family Income, by Education of Head of Household (1978)

Family Income	Years of Schools Completed						
	<7 (%)	8 (%)	9–11 (%)	12 (%)	14–15 (%)	16 (%)	>16 (%)
<$5,000	42(54)	35(59)	31(164)	18(94)	14(24)	10(3)	15(3)
$5,001–$10,000	16(20)	17(28)	16(83)	17(87)	11(19)	3(1)	5(1)
$10,001–$15,000	9(12)	14(24)	14(71)	15(81)	17(31)	20(6)	15(3)
$15,001–$20,000	16(21)	15(26)	19(98)	19(98)	19(34)	17(5)	30(6)
$20,001–$25,000	7(9)	11(18)	11(60)	16(84)	14(24)	10(3)	—
>$25,000	10(13)	8(14)	9(47)	15(81)	25(44)	40(12)	35(7)
Total	100(129)	100(169)	100(523)	100(525)	100(176)	100(30)	100(20)

Source: Bashshur et al., *Native Americans in Wayne County*, 108.
Note: Figures in parentheses are the numbers of respondents.

Of the 867 clients seeking employment assistance at the Indian center's Manpower Office between October 1979 and September 1980, more than half were school dropouts.[6]

The actions of inner-city parents also demonstrated that they harbored negative feelings toward local public schools. Only a few of their children attended regularly, achieved at their intellectual capacity, and continued through high school. At Burton Elementary School in the heart of the Cass Corridor, for example, native parents rarely visited classrooms during open houses or conferred with teachers. Also they neglected to answer teachers' letters or communicate with the principal about their youngsters' absenteeism.[7]

Were these parents disinterested, embarrassed about their poverty and lack of education, fearful of academic failure, or bitterly opposed to Burton School and its program? Longtime Cass Corridor resident Frank Alberts explained that transient parents did not have enough time to get deeply involved with neighborhood schools. Sometimes they even left their children in Canada (living with relatives on the home reserve) while temporarily working in Detroit. Writing in 1950, historian Ralph West attributed parental attitudes to their bad experiences in Indian schools, when "students were 'broken' with leather straps, or by confinement in the school jail, in an effort to remove 'everything Indian' from them." Moreover, minimally educated fathers and mothers believed that an elementary or junior high education was enough. Twenty-four years later anthropologist Beatrice Bigony still heard this viewpoint expressed. Besides, schooling was a bother because of:

> getting the children to school on time, making sure that they have decent clothing to wear, and countering the teasing and discrimination by other children. Moreover, the parents are usually bogged down with problems of their own: finding or keeping a job, feeding the family, making the living quarters inhabitable, keeping off the bottle. At times the children are left to fend for themselves while one or both parents go off drinking in the bars day or night. In such families the issue of education is of minor or no concern.[8]

Nonsupportive home surroundings thus sparked in-school problems, which lasted for decades.

Another contributing factor was the size and location of the native population. In 1970 the metropolitan area Indian school enrollment, including those in college, was only 1,515—far less than 1 percent of the total Detroit figure. So scattered were youngsters that in the fall of 1973 they attended classes in twenty-seven school systems. Within the Detroit school district's eight regions, only Burton had more than forty Indian children. Its 1973 enrollment was 1,121, with Indians making up a mere 3.7 percent.[9] Consequently, even at Burton, urban Indian youngsters did not get the attention they needed.

Before the sensitizing of teachers in the 1970s about their students' racial and ethnic backgrounds, teachers, upon discovering a native person in a Detroit classroom, at times treated them like curiosities, or worse. Priscilla Sands remembered pleading with a history teacher at least thirty years ago not to tell her classmates she was an Indian. But it was to no avail. Mary Left Hand described similar feelings:

The ignorance of many of her childhood friends shocked her. They sometimes refused to join her on weekend visits to the Sarnia Reservation, fearing, she says, that "we lived in teepees."

"I always considered myself just like any other kid. But the teacher would make me stand up and she would say 'Mary is an Indian.' I wanted to be proud but they'd be lookin' at me like I was some sort of specimen, like you look at little germs under a microscope. How's a kid in the fourth or fifth grade supposed to react to that?"

Wounded by an uninformed teacher, one of Harry Command's daughters once asked him if he were one of those "bad Indians" they learned about in school.[10]

Indian students further diluted their classroom contribution through chronic absenteeism and tardiness. Undemanding, transient parents partly explained the phenomenon. Low-income families could not always provide appropriate clothing for their youngsters as well as money for school lunches or to pay a sitter when a child became ill. Marital difficulties and the need for young people to help support the family also contributed to prolonged absences. Youngsters offered other explanations: about how they were teased and ostracized, about the boring class materials, and how school just did not seem important to them as Indians. Most city natives endured these unhappy conditions only until age sixteen. Then they dropped out.[11]

The personal characteristics of Indian children presented another vexing challenge to well-meaning teachers. To examine but one school: the record of Indian students at Burton before 1990 was undistinguished. Not that natives were a behavior problem; they adhered closely to the institution's code of conduct. Instead, it was the undemonstrativeness of both boys and girls, as kindergarten teacher Yvonne Walker commented in 1970:

> All the Indian children do neat work. They're very exact and, at least at first, eager to learn. But they are shy and withdrawn. One boy only speaks if you speak first, and then it's in a low voice, almost a whisper....
>
> You can't get them to talk about the reservation, either, or about their culture. Almost as of [sic] they were ashamed, they refuse to go into detail.[12]

Because they were reluctant to ask for assistance, the only special talents they willingly displayed were artistic. Understandably, teachers interpreted this behavior as signifying a disinterest in formal education as presented at Burton school.

Parents have explained part of the mystery behind this alienation. The highly individualistic and competitive classroom environment ran counter to cooperative values taught at home. Over the years teachers' attempts to motivate youngsters by giving personal, positive reinforcement ironically were counterproductive. Indians disliked being singled out for praise. Placing one child above others was inappropriate from the native standpoint and led to accusations of being a show-off. Indians also preferred to sit in a circle, where they could see one another, rather than in rigid rows; they enjoyed helping one another with especially difficult lessons. But Detroit educators considered this cheating. Without communication between teachers and parents about these and other cultural differences, nonassertive native students showed their displeasure by staying away from school.

Race and culture separated Indians from classmates as well as teachers. At Burton, relations were peaceful during the last four decades, with no bloody clashes between Indian and non-Indian students. Natives kept to themselves or palled around with a few Indian friends. Lack of social mixing extended beyond the school to Cass neighborhood playgrounds. One teacher remarked that any minority student coming from a culturally different background and entering a white school was "going to get a hard time." Indians were hazed and bullied at Burton and at other inner-city schools. A few stood up to it and even returned the aggression. More often they played hooky until age sixteen.[13]

Low academic achievement was the most serious consequence of (1) the lack of full participation in the schools, (2) the small and scattered Indian population, and (3) a home environment that was not supportive of the city's educational system. Seemingly disinterested as well as docile, Indians did not perform well in any Burton School activities. Some seemed promising in the early elementary grades, but each year their achievement declined. Most slipped so far behind that they gave up and quit. For years the staff was baffled about how to alter the situation. They knew it was not a matter of intelligence, but motivation. "The Indian child in Detroit is definitely culturally different, and is a square peg trying to be put into a round hole by the school system," wrote one scholar in the early seventies.

> It seems ironic that a large school system that is populated by minority group children with long historical records of non-achievement could not design a successful strategy of education for these children.

[B]y the third grade in reading and math the child was almost a full year behind and ... two years later had even lost more ground.... [F]or every ten months of school the Indian child usually only makes five months of academic progress. In Detroit schools, which are almost lock-step in grade promotion, it is especially important for a child to keep pace or the curriculum will get ahead of his abilities and skills. Without a doubt, many Indian children sit passively in Detroit classrooms undergoing frustration in a curriculum in which they cannot achieve.[14]

The deterioration of Detroit schools since the sixties further fueled the adults' sense of alienation. An Oneida lady from Canada, who moved into the corridor in 1968 with her husband and three children, commented: "I don't trust my kids around this neighborhood.... Even in the daytime, it's not safe. My kids have been beaten up on the way to school.... In London, Ont[ario], they refuse to rent to Indians, and jobs are harder to find. [The family thought] we'd make out better here, but I don't know how we got stuck in this neighborhood. We tried to find a place in Dearborn, but there was nothing we could afford."[15] Hundreds of Indian families nevertheless found a way to move to the suburbs by 1970.

Exodus from the central city yielded its rewards: safer schools, smaller classes, diminished racial tension, a more affluent atmosphere for ambitious parents to raise their children's expectations and prod them on to higher academic achievement. Escape to the suburban ring was not a panacea for Indian education troubles, however. Inner-city youngsters who were left behind amid a crumbling downtown core found it increasingly difficult to live like Indians and succeed in the schools. Families in the cozy suburbs also became disenchanted, not so much with their children's basic education, but with the schools' inability or unwillingness to teach Indian students—widely scattered, small in number—about their history and cultural heritage. Not until the three Indian Education acts of the seventies did the federal government address these urban Indian education problems. Meanwhile, Detroit leaders, concerned about the formal training of native children, experimented with alternative solutions.

II

Noteworthy was the North American Indian Association of Detroit. During the fifties it created an education fund and revised its constitution to reflect a primary commitment to native American history, culture, and education.[16] To aid needy students the NAIA solicited scholarship money from churches, clubs, and schools; also it sponsored such fund-raising activities as powwows and public dances. A thousand dollars was raised within six months, enabling them to award the first grants in the fall of 1958. Over the next twenty-two years more than seventy Indian students from Detroit and elsewhere in Michigan were helped to attend colleges and trade schools. During the 1970–71 academic year, for example, the association dispensed six thousand dollars in scholarships to sixteen deserving students.[17] Yet, as President Dean George commented two years later, such financial aid had only a limited effect. "If we had a million dollars, we'd have no problems, but we don't. We only make a dent. And years slip by before you know it."[18]

A second approach for alleviating urban Indian education problems was informing the schools about the special needs of native students. Classroom troubles usually stemmed from ignorance about Indians rather than from blatant prejudice, as one Indian observed in 1970: "The other day a neighbor's kid got lost and came to us. While we were calling his parents, he found out we were Indians and got scared stiff. He thought we were going to scalp him. It made my own kids feel bad."[19]

Direct dealings with the Detroit school board about such matters yielded only moderate successes. Before 1972 Russ Wright, Judy and Esther Mays, Thurman Bear, and other advocates got a few books (which they believed degraded Indians) banned from the curriculum. More often school leaders said they would investigate difficulties and nothing was resolved. Wright contended that black history so dominated the classroom after the 1967 riot that Indian heroes continued to be villains or were totally ignored.[20]

Indians occasionally skirmished with schools whose actions were offensive or seemed discriminatory. Early in the seventies, the Dearborn Heights school district suspended William C. Schuyler, Jr., a sixteen-year-old Oneida Indian, because his long hair exceeded the dress code. Director Fred Boyd of Native American Strategic Services complained to the Michigan Civil Rights Commission, and a suit was instituted claiming the school rule violated Schuyler's rights. Assistant Attorney General Michael Lockman argued before the Wayne County Circuit Count that "The hair length is a religious symbol of the coming of age in the Oneida tribe and many others. When an Oneida turns 16, he no longer is a boy. He becomes a man. And he is recognized so in large measure by the length of his hair. It is a cultural thing, much of it with a religious

141

nature." Schuyler's long hair was essential to his planned participation in a series of summer powwows, Lockman added. Persuaded by these and other arguments, the judge ordered Schuyler's readmission.[21]

Six years later a controversy between school officials and natives erupted in the Wayne-Westland school district. The Adams Junior High School planned to stage Irving Berlin's *Annie Get Your Gun*; costume material had been ordered, sets designed, and a hundred students cast in different roles. Irate native parents led by Joseph Robinson circulated a petition to stop the play, claiming it presented a stereotyped and disparaging view of Indians. "It shows us as drunken savages, cutthroats, and killers," claimed Fred Boyd, who sought support again from the state Civil Rights Commission and from the American Civil Liberties Union. Reluctantly the school canceled the production. Westland City Council later lauded this decision and encouraged Adams to "continue to be sensitive to the concerns of all our residents." Councilmen commended their native neighbors "for awakening the community consciousness regarding all minority groups."[22] In 1979 a similar incident occurred in the Clarkston school district. Again *Annie Get Your Gun* was the cause célèbre. The conflict was resolved when the school superintendent assured the HEW's Office for Civil Rights that from then on plays would be screened so as not to offend any racial or ethnic group.[23]

Widespread public ignorance about Indian cultures and character nevertheless persisted in the metropolitan area and bedeviled native leaders more than outright prejudice. "People make jokes, like the Polish jokes, about wampum and pow-wows," Majel De Marsh explained to a reporter in 1970. "They don't mean anything, but it gets very tiresome."[24]

III

No school tried harder than Burton Elementary to dispel such unreasoned fears and stereotypes about Indian people. In the center of the Cass Corridor, its large brick building was converted by the board of education into an international school, which, by the late 1970s, attracted students from all over the city. Colorful flags from a dozen nations hung from staffs on the first-floor walls, high above clanging green lockers and the boisterous parade of 460 youngsters—Arabs, Appalachian whites, blacks, native Americans, Koreans, Chinese, Philippinos, Indians—scurrying off to classes or gym or lunch.

Before becoming Burton's principal in the mid-1970s, Tom Daly had neither taught nor lived with natives during more than twenty-five years as a professional educator. He was annoyed by their bland response to Burton's multicultural programs and the staff's special interest in non-Anglo students. Compared with Orientals, whom Daly believed he also viewed objectively because of limited prior contact, the thirty Indians and their parents acted downright disinterested. Low grades, irregular attendance, lack of self-discipline, minimum social interaction, no apparent goals in life: native students contrasted sharply to Oriental classmates who composed the same percentage of the student enrollment. Never had Daly dealt with an Indian family in a positive setting. Conferences invariably centered on behavioral problems or alleged harassment from other students. Parents, no more responsive than their children, rarely visited the building to meet with teachers, for open houses, or other social get-togethers. Too often they condoned truancy and alibied for their children with questionable excuses about illness or not liking a teacher.[25]

Several of Daly's teachers verified these observations. A twenty-eight-year veteran at Burton and a father of three teenagers, Cy Servetter saw no marked improvement in his Indian pupils since the school converted to a citywide, international emphasis and cultivated more understanding and a tolerant attitude toward minority students. Disharmony with the formal public schooling presented here continued to be the Indian's most striking characteristic. Charles Dobry, an experienced social studies teacher who incorporated native history into his curriculum, also remained confounded by their below-average performance together with their disinterested demeanor. He predicted that such behavior would ultimately doom them to destruction. People must adapt to urban life or perish.[26]

Of the staff, George McMahon, longtime community agent, had the clearest understanding of Indian family disinterest in Burton. His insights came from a lifetime of work among society's underdogs, from Mexican American migrant workers to needy Cass Corridor residents. George and his family lived near the school in a remodeled brick home on Brainard Street.

McMahon claimed that the school failed to meet American Indian academic needs. Granted, the elementary program was less threatening than those at other schools, for Burton was more sensitive to cultural differences; it introduced students to different life-styles and fostered a tolerant atmosphere. But this was a mere deferential bow. Burton simply could not incorporate native American values into the daily routine, given the school board's rigid requirements and the cultural diversity in the building. Consequently, Indians still regarded Burton, more international in makeup than in curriculum, as the enemy. Its special promise was at heart a false one. The better a child did at Burton, the less Indian he became. For many inner-city Indian families, Burton Elementary School and the rest of the establishment's educational network remained a necessary evil, tolerated by native children who believed, fatalistically, that their academic performance did not make much difference. Chronic failure in Detroit classrooms, rooted in this sort of disinterest and defeatism, thus continued through the 1970s.[27]

IV

Parochial schools offered yet another alternative for downtown parents disenchanted with public education's deteriorating buildings, racial tension, insensitivity toward cultural differences, lack of classroom discipline, and other shortcomings. Most Holy Trinity's elementary school was among the most popular and influential during the postwar years. Near Michigan Avenue in Detroit's Corktown district, it served the families of Mohawk ironworkers and many other Great Lakes Indians who settled into the neighborhood and often intermarried with Mexican Americans. Family counseling, a health clinic, emergency food and shelter, financial help: all were provided by loving priests like Fr. Clement Kern. In turn, low-income Indian newcomers struggling to survive in an alien environment sent their children to Most Holy Trinity for an education, for discipline, and for religion. Many youngsters subsequently converted to Catholicism.[28]

Most Holy Trinity, Father Kern, and Catholic schools touched the lives of many inner-city native Americans: nurturing their families, ministering to physical needs, encouraging personal development. Yet for all its good work, the church's resources were too restricted to offer a practical panacea for Indian educational problems.

V

Aspiration for their own educational institutions emanated from native communities across North America, including Detroit. By the late 1960s many alternative schools, often dubbed free schools or survival schools, had been founded.[29] Detroit Indians launched no alternative schools. Nevertheless, leaders like Dean George strongly desired this type of educational setting where their school-age children could gather regularly to socialize, to share their heritage and culture and history, to nurture their sense of pride in being Indian.

Federal Indian education acts of the 1970s finally helped Detroit Indians and other tribesmen to launch the special education programs that they had desired for so long. New Indian-controlled schools, which operated with federal grants and within the HEW guidelines, could not enjoy the independence of private survival schools. Yet Washington helped create a cultural setting much like the one dreamed of by Dean George.

Indian self-determination legislation of the seventies was Washington's response to growing public anxiety over the human problems—poor health, low incomes, substandard housing, illiteracy—afflicting native communities. Focusing on education as the best remedy, the 1969 Kennedy Report first revealed the extent of our "national tragedy": the long, upsetting history of how both federal and public schools failed to serve Indian students. The Special Subcommittee then presented a "national challenge." "The costs of improving the education of Indian children are bound to be high," it wrote, but they "will be more than offset by the reduction in unemployment and welfare rates and the increases in personal incomes certain to follow as a result of effective educational programs." And effectiveness would be forthcoming only if Congress committed itself to "a national policy of educational excellence for Indian children, maximum participation and control by Indian adults and communities, and the development of new legislation and substantial increases in appropriations to achieve these goals."[30]

National leaders responded aptly. In his July 1970 message to Congress, Richard Nixon noted that "it is long past time that the Indian policies of the Federal government began to recognize and build upon the capacities and insights of the Indian people." Two years later he signed into law the Indian Education Act. From then on the United States would "provide financial assistance to local educational agencies [LEAs] to develop and carry out elementary and secondary school programs specially designed

145

to meet these special educational needs."[31]

The Commissioner of Education was directed to pay for LEA demonstration projects to test the effectiveness of different types of educational programs for Indians of all ages. Washington also authorized support for school enrichment services: remedial and compensatory instruction, school health, physical education, psychological, and other services designed to assist and encourage Indian children to enter, remain in, or reenter elementary or secondary school; comprehensive academic and vocational instruction; instructional materials; guidance and counseling; and preschool programs.[32]

Two other concepts were central to the act. The amount of money for LEAs would be based on how many Indian children were enrolled in their schools; furthermore, local policies and procedures would be determined by Indian parents in consultation with (1) teachers, (2) representatives of the LEAs, and (3) the native community. Only by deliberating in this way and by using "the best available talents and resources (including persons from the Indian community)," could the Indian Education Act expand the educational opportunities of Indian children and simultaneously help preserve the heritage and cultural integrity of native communities.[33]

To aid the commissioner in administering the Indian Education Act and to supply technical assistance to LEAs and Indian organizations, Congress created a Bureau of Indian Education within the Office of Education. A National Advisory Council on Indian Education, consisting of fifteen Indian and Alaska native members appointed by the president of the United States, was also established.[34]

Noteworthy successors, the Indian Education Assistance Act (1975) and the Education Amendments Act (1978), supplemented the grants for Indian students and schools. Increased, too, was the responsibility of native parent committees for planning local educational programs. Thus by the end of the 1970s Washington's innovative plan was in place: "It shall be the policy of the [Indian] Bureau ... to facilitate Indian control of Indian affairs in all matters relating to education."[35]

VI

The Detroit Indian Community won its first Title IV grant (Part A, Title IV of the Indian Education Act) by following the grass-roots procedures prescribed by Congress. In mid-February 1974 native leaders arranged an open meeting at the Stevenson Building to discuss financial opportunities under the act. Only nine persons attended, including Dean and Shirley George, Winona Arriaga, Carol Kawegoma and her son, John, plus Esther Mays and three of her children.[36] Determination to create an Indian educational and cultural center eventually overcame modest numbers. The new Parent Advisory Board promptly obtained information about eligibility requirements from the Detroit Board of Education; Indian parents and students simultaneously identified specific educational needs of their community. Then, with help from Harry Beusterien (LEA contact person and federal projects officer for the Board of Education) the Parent Committee launched a citywide campaign to register Indian youngsters for the proposed program. Beusterien dispersed certification forms to school principals. Dean George, Esther Mays, and others acquainted the Indian community with Title IV through the mass media and encouraged parents in the district to enroll their school-age children. In this hasty manner 223 American Indian children were located. (During the next two years, thanks to increased publicity, the total climbed to 1,028, a critical figure on which federal per capita money was based.) On March 11 the completed application was endorsed by the Detroit Public Schools and forwarded to the United States Office of Education.[37]

The requested $31,267 would establish an Indian Educational and Cultural Center to make a "concerted attack upon these problems ... unique to the Indian children whose lives have been difficult with only marginal identification and assimilation into the urban society." Through "improved academic achievement, motivation and self-image," it was hoped that Indian students "will be provided the wherewithal to function adequately in urban society." The proposal focused on five pressing needs: (1) reducing the high dropout rate, especially among Indian secondary school students; (2) sharing native educational experiences in the schools; (3) increasing teacher awareness of their Indian students' cultural backgrounds; (4) providing physical examinations for Indian pupils from low-income families; and (5) developing a positive self-image and pride in their native cultures.[38]

The best way to meet these needs, the proposal asserted, was to establish an education and cultural center "designed to gather, maintain, and disseminate information about Indian culture and also to provide active programs for Indian students."

> A cultural center for Indians will include an atmosphere of "Indian-ness" unique to the people it is designed to serve. The overall model must lend itself to involvement, learning, and participation styles to which Indians are historically and currently oriented. The programs and facilities of the center will combine the best of Indian traditions and the best from modern technical society. The project will supplement the existing school programs for Indian students who are currently enrolled in Detroit Public Schools. The cultural center will be in operation one day a week for approximately 40 Saturdays starting September, 1974. Each session will consist of approximately 6 hours each day of operation. Since this is a citywide program and the distance to the center is quite excessive, travel expenses will be provided for some of the target students, secondary tutors and paraprofessionals of the program. Also, emergency complete physical examinations and follow-up medical and dental service will be provided for target students from low income families.[39]

Washington granted this as well as subsequent requests, thereby creating the Detroit Indian Educational and Cultural Center (DIECC), and during the seventies and eighties Judy Mays was its project coordinator. A cheerful, bespectacled mixed-blood, Judy had grown up in the city. Her Indian mother, Esther Mays ("a very spiritual person" and an influential community elder) transmitted native culture to her many children and taught them the joy and responsibility of sharing goods and living quarters with a large, extended family. Judy earned a bachelor's degree in education at Michigan State University in the early seventies. She was committed to the education of fellow native Americans, but not just in the mainstream sense. Granted, Indian youngsters must complete public schooling as she did; they would be tomorrow's community leaders, and to care properly for their younger brothers and sisters and cousins they must obtain the white and black men's tools of knowledge. To "drop out is to give in." Young people had an important choice to make: doggedly resist the dominant society or compromise by going along and getting a degree and thus being in a position to help other Indians. Judy advocated the latter.[40]

Indian education had still another dimension for her. If mainstream, public school instruction were necessary for economic survival, Indian youngsters' education for life, with its many other facets, must be provided by their own people: primarily parents, but supplemented and enriched by a Title IV project like the DIECC. It supplied a critical cultural component. It could encourage self-awareness and positive Indian self-views as well as acceptance of the responsibility to pass on native ways of life to future generations. For Judy, Indian drumming, the "heartbeat" of her people, was just as important for children to learn as mathematics. To neglect these native traditions, to learn only the white and black men's ways, was tantamount to cultural suicide. Judy Mays' DIECC was avowedly dedicated to nourishing and transmitting Indianness.[41]

The Indian community annually refined the education center's programs, which basically were aimed at improving self-awareness and assisting students with their cultural and educational achievement. At first Judy Mays simply expected target pupils to demonstrate knowledge and understanding of their Indian heritage (arts, crafts, history, customs, folklore, music, dancing, languages); then her staff started remedial classes in reading and mathematics. They also provided personal and academic counseling. An "Indian youngster must see himself and his life, as it relates to the past and the wider society, so that he will have a full appreciation of man's diversity and ingenuity. While it is desirable for an Indian youngster to be aware of his Indianness," these Detroiters reasoned, "it is also necessary that he sees his position positively in the society of man."[42] Even more objectives were added at the close of the seventies: employment assistance for secondary students, reduction of their dropout rate, involvement of Indian parents in at least five center functions, Indian adult education, and dissemination of drug abuse information to students and parents. Furthermore, public school teachers were to be informed about the special educational needs of native American students.[43]

The DIECC budget reflected the native community's ambitions, rising from $60,790 for the 1975–76 school year to $126,453 in 1980. Personnel, including the project coordinator (Judy Mays), two to five certified teachers, two "life advisors," office staff, and between seven and fifteen student aids, annually consumed half these amounts. Staff travel and fringe benefits, office supplies, together with equipment, used up another 20 percent. Other costs included the Saturday lunch program, comprehensive student health services, paid Indian heritage and culture consultants, in-service teacher training, field trips, social activities (ceremonies, feasts, powwows), and student transportation to and from the center each Saturday (allotted $6,000 in 1977–78).[44] During its start-up

149

year, offices and classrooms were located at AIS on West Baltimore;[45] later, Judy's expanding program had to rent space in inner-city elementary schools, including Burton Elementary.

Besides budgetary matters, yearly grant proposals outlined strategies for reaching each educational objective. For example, in the 1976–77 request, Indian authors promised, under the heading "Product Performance Objective":

1. Individual(s): Approximately 100 potential dropouts in the Detroit Public Schools will comprise the target group.
2. Time ... September, 1976 through June 30, 1977.
3. Behavior and Object of Behavior: The dropout rate of target students in grades 9–12 will be reduced.
4. Conditions for Performance: The life advisor, teachers, home-school coordinator and consultants will use counseling techniques, small group discussions, tutoring, etc. The above persons will also implement the activities of the supportive services component.
5. Measurement Methodology: Data will be obtained from records kept by the Detroit Public Schools.
6. Criterion for Success: At least 90% of the target pupils will remain in school; in addition, target pupils will show improvement in attitude toward education.[46]

The proposal also elaborated on how the supportive services component would help potential dropouts:

The Home-School Coordinator will attempt to work with the staff in the schools to accurately identify those Indian students who are experiencing academic and/or self-concept problems in the classroom. Once identified, the Home-School Coordinator, the Life-Advisor and all other staff members relevant to each special case will encourage the pupil to participate in the Indian Education Program. A variety of methods and techniques will be used to encourage the student to participate in the program, and once in the program, used to encourage the pupil to remain in school. Some of these methods and techniques would be individual counseling sessions, group discussions, specialized instructional activities designed and taught by one or more of the five professional staff members, employment as a student aide, teaching arts by one of the ten consultants, or developing a more positive self-concept that develops as an active participant as a singer, dancer, or drummer.[47]

Native American students certified for Detroit's Title IV program numbered 785 during 1979–80, a typical academic year. Half lived downtown or in southwest Detroit; the rest lived around the outskirts of the district. Affiliated with forty different tribes, most prominently the Cherokees (38.8 percent), Chippewas (16.5), Ottawas (5.9), and Mohawks (5.2), their grade levels were evenly distributed (with fifty-five to eighty Indian youngsters in most elementary and junior high school classes) until eleventh and twelfth grades. Then registrations dropped by half.[48]

The historical significance of this data, so assiduously gathered by Detroit and Washington administrators, was somewhat clouded. Native students certified for the Detroit Title IV program numbered 1,028 during the 1976–77 school year, a tribute to the recruitment efforts of community leaders and school officials, and a figure that sparked a hefty increase in entitlement allowance. Yet Judy Mays insisted that Indian youngsters were seriously undercounted throughout the seventies, primarily because the certification procedure depended excessively on school principals. Some claimed they never got the forms; others only distributed them to pupils who "looked" Indian, missing many mixed-bloods.[49] Also, there were Indian parents who understandably (given their historic experience with "treacherous" whites) shied away from signing these documents. Washington further blurred enrollment trends in 1979. It tightened eligibility requirements under the Indian Education Act. Only a child with at least one grandparent who was recognized as a tribal member, as defined by the new enrollment form, could be served by Title IV programs. By the time school started in the fall of 1981, Detroit's eligibility count dropped drastically, to 423, with the accompanying loss of $40,000 in federal support to the DIECC.[50] One Indian parent, a respected community leader, responded philosophically. Detroit Indians had always "played the white man's game" to boost certification for the DIECC, he confessed. The cutback would certainly hurt; but the Saturday school would continue for the sixty to one hundred students who attended regularly and really wanted an Indian enrichment program.[51] This placed the numbers issue in proper perspective: notwithstanding the rise and fall in certified students and debates over the accuracy of their count during the seventies, federal moneys appeared adequate for whatever Indian-designed programs the community offered each Saturday.

Sharing in Title IV activities was taken more seriously by Detroit natives than the "white man's numbers game." For example, each year, as required by federal regulations, the community was invited to an all-day public hearing to help plan DIECC services. Mays and her staff distributed informational material about Title IV and Indian education in general; then participants evaluated current programs and set goals for the next school year. Officers and members of the influential Indian Parent Committee were also elected.

Over the years Parent Committee activities personified the self-determination philosophy of the 1972 Indian Education Act. Judy Mays insisted that the solution to native children's school problems was parental involvement—fathers and mothers studying for GEDs, attending college classes, serving on the Parent Committee, working with the PTA, or as teachers at the Saturday school. Only then would youngsters comprehend the high value placed on education.[52]

Dedicated parents eventually performed many functions. They helped pay the costs of Saturday lunches, convinced local dairies to donate milk, and bought athletic equipment. They sponsored parties as well as educational field trips. Community participation in center programs was regularized in February 1977 with the adoption of Indian Parent Committee bylaws. Besides setting program priorities to meet the special needs of Indian children, the committee's formalized responsibilities included assisting school district staff with proposal writing as well as implementation of educational projects, participation in all aspects of personnel selection and evaluation, together with verifying the native youngsters to be served by the Title IV project.[53]

Furthermore, the Indian Parent Committee fostered community awareness and participation in center activities. The Detroit American Indian Center's *Native Sun* and Mays's printed brochures (distributed throughout the city) regularly informed Detroiters about educational matters. Title IV also published a newsletter. Occasional open houses and powwows drew large, appreciative audiences for whom Saturday school students displayed the artistic skills developed in culture classes: silversmithing, basketmaking, beading, dancing, drumming, singing. Games, awards, and generous helpings of Indian food favorites—venison and fry-bread and corn soup—made these colorful social events memorable for hundreds of attendees. Finally, from program coordinator Judy Mays to student aides, local natives received preference when filling staff positions at the DIECC or in its programs.

Prominent in the Detroit Indian Educational and Cultural Center's publications and also highlighted on a wall poster in its offices were the famous words attributed to Sitting Bull: "Let us put our minds together and see what lives we can make for our children." Unquestionably, the 1972 Indian Education Act encouraged Detroit natives to do just that.

VII

Harry Beusterien helped natives put their minds together. During the seventies he became the critical link between the Parent Committee and two supervising organizations: the local public school system and, in Washington, the United States Office of Education. Beusterien regularly attended Parent Committee meetings. He familiarized its members with Title IV regulations. And whenever appropriate, he provided technical assistance to Mays, her staff, as well as native parents on a range of topics, from grant applications procedures to the maintenance of adequate project and budgetary records.[54]

Ensconced in his Woodward Avenue office at the School's Center building, Beusterien reflected on the DIECC. The first operations were plagued with the inexperience of Mays and her staff, particularly handling federal moneys. Judy had been trained as a teacher, not an administrator; her assistants, though knowledgeable about native cultures, had little formal education as personal counselors or academic tutors. The school board, accommodating and supportive, therefore allowed Mays greater flexibility (for example, in buying hard-to-find craft supplies) than most project administrators enjoyed. At Parent Committee meetings Beusterien was disturbed that so little emphasis was placed on boosting the children's academic achievement. That was the school's responsibility, Indians claimed; Title IV existed primarily to promote their heritage. Beusterien responded that Indian youngsters' special educational needs extended beyond this narrow vision. Ultimately the center's program struck a lopsided compromise between the cultural classes demanded by the native spokespersons, which got primary consideration, and Beusterien's tutorial component covering reading and mathematics and history. The Indian parents, in essence, got what they wanted. But for Beusterien it also meant that Title IV could never be a panacea for educational difficulties.[55]

Then another, attendant problem surfaced: how to evaluate a native culture program paid for by the public. Certainly the Detroit school board, composed of outsiders (non-Indians), would be suspect. Realistically, only the parents could judge; it was their program and Judy Mays was primarily accountable to them. Yet objective assessments by professional educators were required. So the board began annual reviews, using as criteria the goals embodied in Parent Committee grant proposals.[56]

Detroit Public School project evaluators, who generally rated the DIECC highly, conducted interviews and mailed questionnaires to public school teachers, the center's consultants, Parent Committee members, parents, and many students. Indian target pupils in the Saturday program, it was learned, numbered between 120 and 150. They enjoyed "adequate enrichment and cultural activities"[57] and improved their knowledge and understanding of several aspects of Indian culture, which should "assist them in keeping their Native American traditions even though they live in a large metropolitan area."[58] Also, evaluators verified that mathematics and reading teachers tutored native youngsters weekly, although little data was available to document measurable improvement. The center's life advisers provided the promised vocational, academic, and job placement services for students; they also consulted with school counselors and other agencies about the guidance needs of target pupils. Special emphasis had been given to the personal adjustment of urban Indian youth. For example, Harry Command and other staff members from AIS came to speak several times and distributed literature about American Indian youth and substance abuse. Another notable finding was the extremely low public-school dropout rate for Title IV students in the late seventies (less than 5 percent) compared with other native young people in Detroit.[59]

Information and resource materials related to the project objectives were disseminated throughout the school system and the Indian community, as pledged in the grant proposals. Staff members attended regional school board meetings. They made presentations to community groups in suburban areas. They described Title IV programs to radio and television audiences. The center designed Indian exhibits for several Detroit elementary schools and offered in-service workshops to inform teachers about the special educational needs of their native American students. Saturday school powwows gave Indian students another chance to show the public what they had learned.[60]

VIII

The 1980–81 school year for the DIECC began ceremoniously in October with in-service staff training and a colorful open house at the George School, which included a bake sale, raffle, and minipowwow. Among the certified teachers was a non-Indian, John Jeter: well-trained, outspoken, deeply concerned about young people, and starting his fourth year on the center's Saturday staff.

John and his wife, Marge, who tutored Indian pupils in Title IV mathematics classes, lived with their five children in a suburban Dearborn bungalow. At Detroit's Wayne State University John had earned three advanced degrees during the 1970s. The state certified him to teach several academic subjects and, at age thirty-eight, he was also a trained guidance counselor and a licensed social worker.[61] Jeter taught weekdays in the Detroit schools; consequently, he understood the challenges faced by native students. Familiar with their traditional cultures and history, he appreciated, too, the conflicts between rural reservation and urban lifestyles.[62]

Jeter's Saturday Indian history classes were but one set of student options; others included reading, mathematics, dance, sewing, woodcraft, elementary crafts, beadwork, and Chippewa language. During the four class hours between 9:30 A.M. and 2:30 P.M., he worked with all age-groups, from rambunctious kindergartners to blasé high schoolers.

Notwithstanding the suitable curriculum and Jeter's creativity, student response was disheartening. Boys and girls registered in the Title IV program numbered more than a hundred; thus each of Jeter's graded classes should have had at least ten pupils. Yet attendance patterns averaged half that figure, or less. Students congregated elsewhere on the premises instead of going to classes. Frequently they stayed away from Saturday school altogether. Absenteeism, besides the frequent official cancellation of academic classes so that children could prepare for pow-wows and parties and open houses, created a dreadful environment for Jeter, his wife Marge, and for reading teacher Jackie Mingo. Of the students who were taught, irregularly, Indian history and culture, most were mixed-bloods with prominent white or black physical features. Equally striking was their ignorance about Indian history and its importance, about stereotypes that masked native people, about contemporary reservation conditions, about Title IV's mission beyond merely fostering arts and crafts. Jeter's Indian history and culture classes supposedly served the special educational needs of more than 750 native young people in the Detroit school district. Clearly this was not the case. He challenged students enormously; he opened their eyes, stretched their minds, stimulated their senses, cultivated ethnic pride, sent them out to evangelize others. But he lacked significant numbers. Jeter urged Detroit Indians to solve their problems "within the system" by making public schools work for them. Yet, spread so thinly across southeastern Michigan, native influence was slight in individual schools and classrooms. More basic, he lamented, was that not enough Indian children attended their neighborhood schools. As a group they were strikingly undereducated.[63]

Jeter's evaluation of the DIECC's administrators, Judy Mays and the Parent Committee, was mixed. He applauded Mays's support of teachers and respected her dedication to center programs. These qualities partly compensated for her limited administrative experience. Jeter understood that it was not her style to be aggressive or negative, and when criticized too harshly by the Parent Committee she more than once threatened to quit. Each time the group recanted.[64] Most harsh was Jeter's critique of the Parent Committee: inexperienced lay administrators who like adolescents insisted on independence yet constantly clamored for help. Internal bickering wasted too much committee energy. It worried constantly about what "Whitey" was plotting, when in fact, Jeter insisted, most Detroiters were unaware that Indian neighbors still existed.[65]

IX

Other Detroiters with firsthand knowledge of the DIECC confirmed many of Jeter's assessments and supplemented the reports of school board evaluators. Two professionals at Burton revealed, for example, that the center's misuse of the school buildings it occupied in the late seventies was notorious: evidence of alcohol consumed in their offices, soiled diapers and coffee grounds dumped in wastepaper baskets; classrooms left askew after Saturday classes. Jackie Mingo, a Burton teacher who also instructed in Title IV, testified to widespread Indian absenteeism.[66] Their ignorance about traditional cultures and apparent family disinterest in education were also disappointing.

Concern about parental apathy once dominated an entire Title IV annual public meeting held during a November evening in 1979 at the DAIC. Judy Mays presided. She deplored that only 800 native children had been identified within the public school system. Even worse, only 120 of these attended Saturday school. The presence of just a dozen adult Indians at this open forum was downright discouraging, for its purpose was to set future policies and elect 1980 Indian Parent Committee officers. The previous year, six parents cared enough to come. Without greater input, Judy feared, the DIECC was doomed to stagnation. She had offered to pay native parents a stipend to attend Saturday classes and learn how to become cultural educators; still support was minimal. Bruce Albert and Teofilo Lucero explained that some Indians had shied away from Title IV because it enrolled too many students who looked non-Indian and were not known to the community. Other Indian youngsters and their weekday teachers were as yet unaware of Title IV because principals refused to publicize the program vigorously. That city educators neglected Indians was obvious; Judy observed that not a single school representative attended this evening meeting even though she had invited the board as well as teachers. Participants, what few there were, agreed that the center must focus more staff energies on parent outreach. Sensible Judy Mays, who attended enough regional and national meetings to keep her dilemma in perspective, added that inadequate parental involvement plagued native schools across the country. Besides, Detroit's Indian education experiment was only five years old. She and Teofilo urged the Saturday school's supporters not to lose heart. Education was too critical for urban Indians if they were to understand themselves and their cultures, if they were to develop enough pride and confidence to strike suitable compromises with mainstream society and achieve their true potential.[67]

Granted, her cause was worthy, but Judy Mays's success was minimal and she felt thwarted continually by restrictive federal regulations, halfhearted school board support, and lack of enthusiasm from the native community. After several years Judy had only a half dozen families who were unabashedly committed to the center. They attended all functions and she could rely totally on them to get tasks done.

X

The effect of Title IV extended well beyond the city limits. Thanks to extensive publicity about these grants and prodding from Washington, Lansing, and Indian residents, 112 other Michigan school districts (each with ten or more American Indian students) sponsored native heritage programs by 1977 and tried to meet the special educational needs of more than 19,000 students. Their annual budgets totaled $2.5 million. In the suburban districts surrounding Detroit, Indian parent committees guided their centers so that enrichment programs would reflect the cultural diversity of their neighborhoods. Common to most centers were Saturday cultural classes supplemented by field trips to powwows, museums, and other native communities, both rural and urban. Fathers and mothers benefited in several ways, as they did at Judy Mays's Detroit Indian Educational and Cultural Center. Paul Hunt, chairman of the Dearborn Parent Committee, emphasized: "It's a total involvement, not only for the students but for the parents ... [who] are learning as much about their heritage as the kids, through assimilation and in meeting with other Indian groups." In the tricounty metropolitan area, 7,292 pupils of American Indian ancestry were eligible for these Title IV services—cultural heritage classes, special counseling, tutoring—in 1979.[68]

During the sixties and seventies the Wayne-Westland school district burgeoned from a pastoral setting to become one of the half dozen wealthiest school systems in Michigan. Middle-class Indian parents held good jobs. They were ambitious for their children and believed formal education was fundamental to maintaining their satisfying life-styles. School was not the enemy. Parents felt no alienation from teachers. Native American youngsters were punctual and attended classes regularly. To stimulate the children's pride in their Indian heritage, parents turned to Title IV; its programs taught "a basic and accurate understanding of Indian history, treaties, customs, lore and contemporary issues." The school district supported all these efforts, according to Director Rozlyn McCoy of the Indian Education Project. Even in the sixties when she was a Wayne-Westland student, one of three natives in the high school, she suffered no discrimination. The number of Indian families in the district subsequently ballooned; administrators and teachers still treated them fairly and encouraged academic achievement. Most Indians obtained secondary diplomas and many went on to vocational training and higher education.[69]

McCoy's attractively decorated Indian Education Center, at the Nankin Mills Junior High School, contained a multimedia library (with books, pamphlets, periodicals, pictures, cassettes, films, slides, filmstrips, videotapes, records), an arts and crafts display, expensive instructional equipment, classrooms, as well as ample office and storage space. Wayne-Westland's cultural goals echoed the DIECC; project teaching also took place primarily on the weekends. The Wayne-Westland Saturday School attendance averaged thirty-one in 1979–80, its fourth year of operations. Twenty-one adults constituted the active Parent Committee. They oversaw a budget of $91,518.83 and seven staff persons including Rozlyn. That year Chris Ziegler assessed (for the school board) Title IV activities at Wayne-Westland and judged that all project objectives "had been met or exceeded." Particularly notable were the staffs dissemination activities. Besides consulting regularly with community leaders and school-teachers to determine Indian student needs, McCoy and her coworkers contributed textbook evaluations to state officials, presented cultural curriculum sessions at state and national education conferences, were active in such local organizations as the Westland Human Relations Commission, and started a publication project of cultural-based reading material.[70]

Program coordination among southeastern Michigan's busy Tide IV directors was minimal. They occasionally chatted on the telephone or discussed mutual concerns at state or national Indian education meetings.[71]

XI

Educational programming to meet the special needs of Detroit native Americans was not confined to the centers of Mays and McCoy. Project Good Start was based at the DAIC for the benefit of preschoolers during the seventies. Furthermore, the center sponsored classes for older adults, which culminated in the GED. Michigan capped these opportunities beginning in 1976 with tuition grants to Indians who attended state institutions of higher learning.

During the late 1970s half the Indian center's first floor was occupied by the Project Good Start classroom. Its aim was to assist parents in creating a more supportive home environment for their children, "the ones who will perpetuate the heritage, culture and lifestyle of Native Americans." By mid-decade, when Detroit's first grant application was filed, the future of these needy youngsters looked bleak. Indians admitted that boys and girls were often not

> prepared for school, causing a disability to learn; and later they became drop-outs from an environment they never were properly prepared for.
>
> With no meaningful Indian pre-school programs, Indian parents tend to feel helpless, and the result is eventual apathy toward a situation they perceive as unchangeable. Most of our Indian children are starting school with limited home enrichment experiences because of the parents' lack of money and home skills to expand the child's world.[72]

159

Project Good Start offered much hope. Based on the concept of Indian training Indian, it brought together parents and children (from two and a half to five years old) to strengthen their special relationship. Working together, they might share in the joy of learning and achieve a better understanding of one another. Fathers and mothers could learn more about early childhood development and hence become more confident; preschoolers' basic learning skills, especially reading and number readiness, would be enhanced by positive, successful experiences. The DAIC daily bussed in a dozen or two dozen children. Their before and after testing, as reported by project evaluators, showed statistically significant growth in various skill areas.[73]

Besides aiding native children through Project Good Start and the DIECC, the Indian Education Act of 1972 committed Congress to assist in providing opportunities "to all Indian adults to qualify for a high school equivalency certificate in the shortest period of time feasible."[74] In accordance with the act's general spirit, Indians were to develop local programs to meet their most pressing needs. The urgency of adult education was evident. The Indian community was beset by much unemployment, housing and health problems, together with low educational achievement. Wider opportunities for job training as well as other benefits would surely open up if the number of high school graduates increased.

AIS, so often a catalyst, sponsored Michigan's first Indian-controlled GED program. Later in the seventies classes met at two other centers: the Indians of North America Foundation and the AID. The DAIC at 360 John R became the major sponsor for adult education programs after its establishment in 1974. It used Title IV money to hire a coordinator, Muriel Youngblood, buy student books, and assist needy pupils with bus fare and baby-sitting. Most importantly, the DAIC subcontracted actual instruction to Ross Learning, Incorporated. By June 9, 1975, thirty-six urban Indians had completed studies and passed the equivalency examination administered by the city. Only one student who regularly attended Ross classes failed the test.[75] There was a brief lapse in federal grants for a few years, but by September 1980 Youngblood reported that forty-three Indian students had earned GEDs. Twelve more graduated from Ross Learning's clerical classes.[76] Throughout the decade dozens of Indians enjoyed studying with other native persons. Some alumni like Dean George and Joe Mesheky held important leadership positions in the community.

The State of Michigan afforded supplementary assistance to Detroit Indians whose educational aspirations were heightened by GED and other Title IV programs. On July 22, 1976, in his State Capitol office, Governor William Milliken signed Public Act 174. It provided free college tuition for North American Indians who were (1) academically qualified, (2) Michigan residents for not less than eighteen consecutive months, (3) certified by the Indian Commission as having one-half quantum of Indian blood, and (4) planned to enroll as full-time students in state-supported colleges, universities, and community colleges.[77] State Representative Jackie Vaughn III was justifiably proud. He remarked to his friend Fred Boyd, the Indian rights advocate: 'This historical bill signing, during this Bicentennial Year, marks a noble beginning in meeting the educational needs of neglected North American Indians. I am delighted that Michigan is a leader in this effort and that children of our generation will be given the assistance which is needed."[78]

Only about a hundred Indians annually took advantage of these grants; Vaughn and Boyd thus sought to liberalize the act's rigid requirements. Several native leaders lobbied in Lansing on September 22, 1978, "Indian Day," to build support for Vaughn's amendment, House Bill 6247. Bill Memberto spoke on behalf of many Wayne County Indians: "The Indian nation must develop leaders with the skills to deal with this modern technological society. In developing these skills we will learn, we will adapt what we learn to assist us in overcoming the cultural genocide that we face in these modern times. House Bill [number] 6247 is a necessary stepping stone to the preservation of the Indian way of life."[79] Enacted by year's end, the amendment lowered the residency requirement to twelve months and the blood quantum to one-quarter. From then on part-time and summer school students would also have tuition waived.[80]

The number of urban and reservation Indians attending state colleges climbed dramatically after 1978. Those at the University of Michigan, for example, formed a native American student association to advance their cause. Valuable campus services were also provided by the Office of Minority Student Services, housed in the Michigan Union. Its Indian counselor in the late seventies was Dorothy Goeman (previously employed as head of the DAIC's Manpower Office).[81]

XII

Educational problems persisted among Detroit Indians despite the reform whirlwind of the 1970s. For example, Indians remained part of a school system that failed to retain and to teach pupils of all races at least through grade twelve. When administrators took their annual high school census during the fall of 1980, they discovered a student dropout rate of nearly two-thirds, surpassing the rates of New York and Chicago. Youngsters "who drop out of school in grades 10 and 11 do so because of what happened in grade nine," commented Deputy School Superintendent Melvin Chapman. "They've had a very unsuccessful beginning in high school."[82] Undereducated Detroit Indians obviously were not alone in their dissatisfaction with the public schools. Sharp criticism was likewise leveled against the DIECC as well as other Title IV programs. Nevertheless, in 1981 Congress reauthorized Public Law 92–318, the Indian Education Act of 1972, through fiscal year 1984.[83]

With Indian programming still in its adolescence, and self-determination for Detroit natives only ten years old, inexperienced Indian administrators like Judy Mays must be allowed to falter occasionally, without recrimination. Harry Command contended, furthermore, that educational problems were extremely complex and too deep-seated to be alleviated overnight. Perhaps an entire generation must pass before Indian-run programs could be fully evaluated. Meanwhile, it was essential that contemporary Detroit native leaders vigorously promote the interests of their community: withstanding the inevitable barrage of complaints and drawing strength as well as wisdom from supportive constituents.[84] Although future prospects for Detroit Indian education were unclear, consensus was that native leaders must not lose heart. The issue was too critical. During the 1980 Wayne County Indian health survey, in which respondents ranked community problems, education was the third most important, after "cost of living" and 'jobs," and judged more serious than "crime," "housing," "environment," and "health care."[85] Surely they understood, as did Health Director Bill Memberto, that formal education was the key to self-determination. Only education could reduce native reliance on high-priced, non-Indian consultants, technicians, and government bureaucrats. Among its other benefits, predicted Bobby Crooks, would be higher-paying jobs, more comfortable homes, and even better health.[86] Indian community recognition of education's importance, together with the general acceptance—in Detroit, Lansing, and Washington—of local Indian input into decision making, therefore give cause for some optimism about the future.

>>> CHAPTER 6 <<<

The Seventies:
A Social-Cultural Revival

For Detroit the 1970s was an exhilarating, tumultuous time. Currents of change swept across the American Indian community. Newly militant natives, keenly aware of the successes achieved by the black civil rights movement, demanded better treatment for their people. Enhanced self-awareness coupled with determination on behalf of urban Indians brought about major changes, a veritable revival, in their social and cultural lives. Native arts and crafts and language classes appeared, along with programs to safeguard the entire community's social welfare: from young victims of broken homes to equally vulnerable senior citizens. Indian counselors assisted clients with pressing problems including alcoholism, marital difficulties, and legal entanglements. Indian-sponsored athletic teams, holiday parties, public parades and powwows, as well as more private religious ceremonies brought together thousands of isolated urban Indians. Identities were reinforced. Pride was enhanced. They felt less passive, more knowledgeable about issues related to their people, and strengthened for the ongoing struggle to achieve their rightful place in metropolitan society. Regular media coverage together with the traditional "moccasin telegraph" ensured that most metropolitan-area natives were touched and enriched by this revival.

Reform agencies that sponsored these wide-ranging urban activities were native-run and native-staffed, drawing heavily upon the talents of a new generation of inspirational leaders. Federal grants provided critical money. Innovative services also rested to a degree upon Detroit practices and institutions established before 1970: Indian personal networks of family and close friends, the bar culture, native neighborhoods, close reservation ties, and the venerable NAIA. By the early 1980s, after a decade of heady revivalism, an extensive Indian social-cultural infrastructure had thus evolved.

I

In the course of her local research, *Detroit News* staff writer Lucille DeView was impressed by the many ambitious Indians "reaching for the brass ring of career satisfaction and a higher standard of living. It's their means of escape from the merry-go-round of poverty and defeat in what has long been an alien world to their people." In this pursuit natives displayed two remarkable characteristics. One was "an almost frantic drive for education ... [for] the credentials, the degrees, the job training necessary for survival and a good life." Second, the reporter observed "a hunger to retrieve Indian culture—the languages, dances, legends and religion of their forebears which few young people today know." In short, they sought a meaningful role in the Detroit community without losing their identity as American Indians.[1]

Before the establishment of the DAIC in 1974, its predecessors in the city introduced programs to satisfy cultural hunger and to meet urgent social needs. Urban Indian Affairs started serving natives in 1970. As director, Russ Wright focused most of the office's attention on urgent paralegal work. He and the outreach staff likewise assisted indigent natives and counseled clients about personal finance, family troubles, employment, and education.[2] AIS, whose programs were also a powerful force in the early seventies, tried to create for its clients a healthy social alternative to the Cass Corridor bar culture. Its cheerful drop-in center, group therapy sessions, weekly community lunches, sponsorship of educational and recreational programs, employment counseling: all stimulated urban Indians, though caught between two cultures, to be proud of their rich heritage. AIS demonstrated that alcoholics could succeed in

Detroit society if they stopped drinking.[3] Harry Command's work in the
Cass Corridor was supplemented by the AID. One member remarked
that "Indians are finally realizing who they are and getting themselves
together. I truly believe that this is only the beginning. Indian people
are going to fight."[4] The AID did fight: gathering food donations, clothing, bus tickets, and financial contributions to help Cass Corridor neighbors. Besides their constant struggle with poverty and health programs,
this "Indian for Indians organization" struggled to revive native traditions. Cultural classes (Chippewa language instruction, tribal singing,
dancing, Indian history) were featured along with Saturday minipowwows. For too long, claimed AID Director Carleen Pedrotti, Detroit Indians aspired to a big car and an expensive suburban home. For too
long, Indians "let it be beaten into their heads that to dance and sing in
thanksgiving is paganism. Is savage. There are young ones who think that
to smoke a peace pipe is a laughable idea. They forget THEY are the native Americans." By the early seventies attitudes were changing, Pedrotti
noted. Successful "members of the [Indian] community have ... begun
returning to their past, to the powwows and Indian conferences held in
Michigan and Canada several times a year." They spoke publicly with new
pride in their identity and about a determination to live a "full life as
Indians, for Indians."[5] A fourth agency provided social services to natives
still living along Michigan Avenue; this was the Indians of North America
Foundation, housed in Father Kern's Most Holy Trinity complex. Volunteer workers offered drop-in services (emergency food and clothing),
referral to city agencies, GED classes, and cultural workshops.[6]

II

The activities of the DAIC ministered to the accumulated needs of a large
constituency that, like other urban migrants, had spent years in shadowy
exile—neglected, subject to racial slurs, and lacking in confidence. By
the mid-seventies, native leaders, brimful of ethnic pride and a "can do"
spirit, launched a dozen social and cultural programs to assist their people. "Indianness is making a comeback," proclaimed one reporter.[7] And
well it should; if revived, native American traditions could be the keys
for relieving not only their own urban difficulties but many of their
neighbors' as well. With regard to loving thy neighbor, for example,

native peoples had much to teach an avowedly Christian society. "Before the explorers came, we didn't have any jails," declared Dean George, "or any old folks homes or any orphans' homes. And no locks. Nowadays, heck, you gotta lock the door every time you go out, and then lock the lock! Before, all an Indian had to do when he left his home was lean a stick across the doorway. He could be gone 20 years, and nobody would touch his stuff."[8] This pride in heritage, a willingness to share ancient philosophies with non-natives who would live in peace, the lack of cultural and social services for urban Indians: each spurred significant action at the DAIC.

Because youngsters benefited from Title IV cultural enrichment programs, the DAIC's board of directors reasoned that older Indians should have the same opportunities. Thus the Native Arts and Crafts Department was established in 1976 to foster Great Lakes crafts such as beadwork, basketmaking, woodcarving, and the construction of woodland dance outfits. Indian singing, drumming, and dancing were also taught. Staff members instructed interested persons at the DAIC and decorated the building's interior with colorful murals. Through minipowwows, slide presentations, and speeches they enlightened the general public about America's Indian heritage. Teofilo Lucero took charge of the new department, only to discover that he was also expected to finance its activities from outside sources. Inexperience with grant writing plagued Lucero at first as it did other center colleagues. After agonizing over his first proposal to the Lutheran Church ("the hardest thinking and hardest thing I ever had to do"), he came to work one Monday dejected and reckoned that Executive Director Hank Bonga would surely fire him, for Teofilo could not meet the impending deadline. Instead, Bonga encouraged him to call the agency and request an extension. Lucero got one month. Church officials furthermore coached him over the telephone, emphasizing that he should simply and clearly explain what supplies he required. Shortly thereafter the Lutherans awarded the Arts and Crafts Department two thousand dollars.[9]

The social and cultural well-being of Indian youth remained a prime concern of the DAIC during the seventies, even though metropolitan Title IV programs took responsibility for formal enrichment programs. Nationally, the stability and security of native families drew more attention. Legislators were appalled by the "high percentage of Indian families [that] are broken up by the removal, often unwarranted, of their children from them by nontribal public and private agencies and that an alarmingly high percentage of such children are placed in non-Indian

166

foster and adoptive homes and institutions." To counteract this trend Congress declared in its 1978 Indian Child Welfare Act (ICWA) that from now on it was "the policy of this Nation to protect the best interests of Indian children" by preventing the breakup of their families. Title II of the act authorized grants to Indian tribes and organizations so that they could provide Indian child and family services. The hope was that more children could remain with their families. Should child-custody proceedings result, state courts must adhere to new national standards requiring significant consultation with a youngster's tribe. If, as a last resort, a boy or girl were to be removed from parental control, the act required that the courts give preference to placement in a foster or adoptive home that "will reflect the unique values of Indian culture."[10] Congress at first appropriated $5.5 million to implement the ICWA in fiscal year 1980 and increased the level to $9.3 million the following year. The Interior Department distributed the money through a formula grant process to tribes, off-reservation groups, and programs operated in several urban areas.[11]

In 1972, before federal legislation, the Native American Child Protection Council (NACPC) was established in Detroit to stop the removal of Indian children from supposedly unfit homes. According to Bernice Appleton, NACPC vice president, state agencies frequently told parents

their homes were unfit because they have two children, or three children, sleeping in one bed. Now I've had three daughters sleeping together for years and I was never aware that I was an unfit mother.

The standards they have set up for Indian homes are the same standards as for white homes—or should I say they want to set non-Indian standards for Indian homes, and that can't possibly be.

Indians are different. It isn't necessary for Indian children to have one bed apiece. I don't even think it's good for children to sleep apart. Our children, you see, learn sharing right from the start.

Oftentimes the state claimed that native children were being neglected when in fact they were under the care of responsible relatives who, according to Indian custom as the NACPC explained it, were part of the youngsters' extended family. Not until passage of the ICWA were Detroit families given real protection against what they claimed was the "wholesale abduction and adoption of Indian children."[12]

Collette Schott had no difficulty grasping the significance of Washington's actions. Her Mohawk mother, like so many natives of an earlier era, was uprooted as a girl and sent to a government boarding school because some official judged her home unfit. In 1983 Schott provided ICWA services at the DAIC. She worked with a special diligence and sensitivity in hopes that this program would prevent the sort of cultural losses sustained by her family.[13]

By the early 1980s the Indian child welfare program at the DAIC was doing just that. Collette and her supervisor, Carol Coulon Kawegoma, assisted the courts in dealing with troubled families. They testified as expert witnesses about customs and social standards characteristic of native communities and families. The center's ICWA staff consulted with tribes ranging from Michigan and Wisconsin to North Carolina, Oklahoma, and Texas. Carol and Collette became intermediaries between these organizations and Michigan's Department of Social Services, assuring that Indian parental rights were asserted during judicial proceedings. When it became necessary to remove a child from its parents' custody, the DAIC worked with the state in placing the boy or girl in a licensed Indian foster home whenever feasible. A major frustration was that ICWA services could not be extended to Detroit Indians with Canadian citizenship, even though, as a border city, it attracted many such families. Nevertheless, the center's heavy caseload by March 1984 testified to the program's significance on a restricted basis. Kawegoma also contended that their efforts would be successful if "we can save one child from going off to a non-Indian family like I did" at the Thomas Boarding School. After such an experience, her family members became strangers. Her language was lost, a void created. She has carried these painful scars ever since.[14]

Nurturing native families demanded more than a child-welfare program. The DAIC also set a high priority on counseling low-income adults—hard-core Detroit unemployed, Indian transients from across North America, senior citizens—caught in a bewildering tangle of city troubles. The key to understanding these social difficulties, declared DAIC counselor Ron Giles, was their Indianness. Natives remained unique. Unlike Detroit's Polish, Italian, and German immigrants or its southern white and black newcomers, native Americans brought no traditional adherence to European values or the Protestant work ethic. Therefore, to be effective, counselors must take into account native passiveness and present-mindedness. Equally distinctive was the Indians' lack of education and their generosity (it was not uncommon for a hard-pressed client to give his rent money to a friend whom he judged to be more needy). Others, less altruistic, might be so addicted to generations of reservation welfare, that, like alcoholics, they merely sought to manipulate the new urban environment for their own benefit.[15]

The DAIC counselors and programs tried to help a variety of clients. Thus the board hired streetwise native American counselor-outreach workers, persons trusted by the community and familiar with its concerns. They were survivors, like Harry Command and his colleagues at AIS, of life's toughest tests: broken homes, poverty, race discrimination, alcoholism. In their offices, counselors cultivated an informal and non-judgmental Indian atmosphere. Outside, they were liaisons between the DAIC and the native community, frequently visiting the Cass Corridor to study its problems and to provide immediate help where needed.

Mona Stonefish Jacobs, a DAIC counselor, added general advocacy to her job description. No task was too great or group too formidable. The police, employers, courts, hospitals: each would be challenged if she felt it mistreated Indians. No task ranked too small. While going to her apartment in the Cass Corridor one August afternoon in 1977, she spied an Indian woman sprawled in the middle of Cass Park. Mona asked the driver to stop while she investigated. The intoxicated woman was known to Jacobs, who awakened her, identified herself, and warned her not to lie around; she could get killed. Mona then saw that the tipsy native was driven safely home.[16]

Besides spontaneous Good Samaritan gestures, DAIC counselors offered more formal social assistance to individuals and families. This included, first of all, assessment of their full range of needs. Emergency cash (often raised by DAIC staff through bake sales, raffles, and fifty-fifty drawings) helped clients in small ways: with overnight housing, food, bus fare to a new job, or travel expenses back to the reservation. When appropriate, personal encouragement and guidance were given to persons struggling to resolve their problems. Counselors referred clients to Indian and non-Indian agencies with special expertise or greater resources. Substance abusers, for example, were directed to AIS or to treatment centers like Harbor Light and Sacred Heart. Russ Wright at Urban Indian Affairs specialized in unsnarling legal troubles, whereas those needing employment counseling or training could be sent to the DAIC's Manpower Department.

Native counselors at times felt deep frustration. Those whom they served protested the filling out of forms and the DAIC's growing bureaucracy with its regular hours, staff dress code, and required appointments. Clients contributed to these difficulties. Some waited, complained counselor Linda La Roque, "until they have no place else to turn to before requesting services. What they don't realize is that a lot of times we can do more for the person if they contact us before the problem gets to [sic] serious." Conscientious counselors often felt thwarted by the center's board of directors. They abetted the escalation of "white tape" and, from their middle-class, suburban perspectives, seemed insensitive to the pressing needs of poor inner-city Indians. Mona Stonefish Jacobs, for instance, championed the transformation of the DAIC into a round-the-clock drop-in facility where natives would feel welcomed and safe and could find help during emergencies, which frequently occurred after business hours.[17] But the board had a different vision. Indian center counselors, though sometimes disappointed and harassed, nevertheless provided critical social services to adult urban Indians, which they could not or would not seek elsewhere.

Native elders also benefited from social services.[18] The Indian center senior's program, paid for by the Detroit Area Agency on Aging, was in cheery ground-floor facilities, which included a lounge, color television, tables, and games and magazines. Another fixture was Louise Morales, herself a senior and since May 1976 the jovial hostess for the hot lunches catered each weekday. Quiet seniors bussed in from isolated apartments and houses became exceedingly animated upon arrival at the center: joking, eating, playing bingo, reminiscing, sipping coffee, and as one termed it, engaged in "group therapy." A DAIC staff member coordinated their busy social calendar. It included special events at the center (movies, an exercise program, bookmobile visits, self-defense lectures), seasonal parties (at Valentine's Day, Easter, Halloween, Thanksgiving, and Christmas), and fund-raisers (sales of corn soup, fry-bread, tacos, baked goods). With the proceeds they traveled across Michigan and southwestern Ontario: to metropolitan-area recreation sites, to Lansing each May for Senior Power Days, and to powwows in the Upper Peninsula as well as on Walpole Island Reserve. In August 1980 they spent a week at Camp Wathana near Holly, Michigan, and reveled in the horseback riding, fishing, and square dancing. If one of their number became ill, Detroit seniors rallied with get-well cards and visits. They attended funerals as a group. Sometimes they sponsored receptions for out-of-town friends and relatives of the deceased. For needy elders the DAIC supplemented its social activities with counseling, grocery shopping, a shuttle service, and emergency food. Referrals were made for those requiring legal aid or medical assistance.

Indian seniors were survivors and thus models. Most had migrated to Detroit from home reserves and adapted satisfactorily to city life while retaining their sense of Indian identity. Not surprisingly, their social lives became a happy mixture of Indian and non-Indian ways: powwows and

Christmas parties, Indian dance steps followed by square dancing, a Santa Claus costume alongside native beads and buckskins, corn soup and frybread and pizza, traditional woodland prayers offered at an Easter banquet. During the Indian community's social-cultural revival beginning in the 1970s, elders were respected resource persons.

Besides the center's formal programs, from Indian child welfare to senior citizen activities, it sponsored easygoing social events that enriched the lives of urban natives. Tradition dictated that children should be a focus of attention. In conjunction with the NAIA, the center thus staged annual Halloween and Christmas parties. More than a hundred expectant youngsters arrived at 360 John R for one such gala in December 1980. After a hot dog lunch, a magician mystified the audience while Director Jim Hillman interrupted periodically to announce that Metro Airport radar had spotted a high-flying sleigh and reindeer headed toward the city. When Santa Claus (a costumed Indian center staff member) finally appeared, all restraint vanished. Only the promise of presents permitted Santa to line up the children. Each gift, donated by center friends or bought with money raised during the year, was beautifully wrapped and coded for suitability to boys and girls of different ages. Brown little faces marveling at a white magician's wizardry, an Indian center festooned with Christmas decorations, a native American Santa Claus: outsiders might think these incongruous, but the happy-go-lucky participants did not notice.

The social season also catered to adults. For those desiring physical activity, the DAIC sponsored annual basketball squads (the "Bucks"), baseball teams (the "Skins"), and participated in a mixed bowling league. Less demanding but equally popular were holiday dances and dinners. A Fall Feast in October 1980, held at Most Holy Trinity School, attracted several dozen families. Highlights included a buffet table heaped with tasty food, an Indian pipe ceremony, a prayer by Teofilo Lucero, plus joyous drumming and dancing and singing on into the night.

The social-cultural atmosphere at the DAIC was decidedly Pan-Indian, a gathering place for visitors, clients, and staff representing tribes across Canada and the United States. The influences they exerted on one another were subtle yet far-reaching. A GED teacher at the center observed, for example, that several of her Detroit students had grown up isolated from other natives. Parental teachings about their Indian heritage were minimal. So the class at the DAIC was their first experience with other Indians, and they were bursting with curiosity. Yet they did not openly ask questions at first. They seemed tentative, merely listening and making themselves available to others. Eventually their pressing concerns surfaced. What were reservations like? How was it to grow up there? Could you describe powwows and traditional ceremonies? At one point several attentive students from Great Lakes bands were instructed about Southwest ceremonies and native spiritual life by a Navajo DAIC staff member.[19] Pan-Indianism was thus promoted in a process reminiscent of when Teofilo Lucero had taught his fellow NAIA members, also largely from Midwestern tribes and the victims of cultural loss. Rather than the YWCA, the Detroit American Indian Center became the central gathering place by the 1970s and therefore a major social-cultural force.

The center's public-relations program assaulted urban-Indian social barriers and dispelled myths about contemporary native peoples held by the public. The *Native Sun*, a monthly newsletter edited and photocopied by DAIC staff, achieved a circulation of 1,550 by January 1978.[20] Original essays, reprints of articles from other Indian publications (both urban and reservation), current events announcements, editorials, poetry, art work: all kept Detroiters aware of center services and activities as well as national issues confronting native Americans.

Hard-hitting editorials sought to galvanize the community. John Shano, the newsletter's first editor, urged urban Indians to get an education and acquire the skills needed to survive in twentieth-century America. Too many were "saying 'gimme' for their needs instead of jumping up and going after the 'where with all' so important to living. The animals, fish and birds did not stand still to be hunted, neither will the modern jobs wait til you are ready." Equally earnest was Sandy Muse, also writing for the *Native Sun:*

> The question has been raised as to whether or not Detroit Native Americans should participate in the Detroit Bi-Centennial. Many Native Americans feel we should not because we have nothing to celebrate.... On the other side of the coin, a lot of Native Americans believe that attention can be brought to the problems of Native American people if we take part. If we don't take part, the Bi-Centennial committee will probably use Hong-Kong Indian crafts. ... All the stereotype images will continue, just like in the John Wayne movies.... Our newsletter staff urges Indians to get involved in Detroit's Bi-Centennial.... Otherwise, many non-Indians will never know that we even exist. So come on, Native People!!![21]

Indian Center staff used two other methods to increase Indian awareness. First, they hosted the "Indian to Indian" radio program heard weekly in the metropolitan area on WDET-FM. It featured powwow music, interviews and, like the *Native Sun*, urban Indian viewpoints on current events. Second, the center employed a public relations officer. During the late 1970s this was Cary Severt, a Vietnam veteran and construction worker whose Walpole Island mother raised him in Detroit. Severt spoke regularly to school groups and churches. He gave interviews to newspaper reporters and prepared public-service announcements for radio and television. Always the message was the same: Detroit's many native Americans, struggling to exist in two worlds, had been neglected for too long. The new Indian center's programs were designed to help, but native people must take advantage of its services. The support of non-Indians also was sorely needed; annually the center had to collect thousands of dollars in cash and in-kind gifts, the community matching funds required by federal agencies subsidizing the center.

Also effective in transmitting urban Indian viewpoints to the public were powwows, clearly the most popular social-cultural functions sponsored by the DAIC. By the early eighties almost every Great Lakes reservation and urban community staged a powwow on alternating weekends between May and September. Crowds were large and appreciative. Costumed native dancers who followed this summer circuit competed each Saturday and Sunday for prize money and became addicted to the exhilarating social experience. "If I couldn't dance with my people, I couldn't live," remarked one Detroiter.[22]

A 1970s powwow combined the excitement and significance of a county fair, ethnic festival, and religious ceremonial. Its center was the drum, the heartbeat of native people and a sacred tie to their traditional past. During outdoor gatherings it lay sheltered beneath a leafy arbor. Around the drum sat singers. They observed a strict protocol while their songs and drum beating set the tempo for male and female dancers. These agile Indians, faces agleam with pride, were costumed in striking traditional outfits or fancier ones replete with hair roaches, bells, bustles, and elaborate beadwork. Participants came from different age-groups and tribes. They also represented different religious persuasions, levels of formal education, and income. Judges scrutinized as competitors whirled their way through social dance interpretations during the two days. Farther out from the drum and circling the dance arena sat Indian traders, some of whom traveled great distances to sell tasty native food, pottery, hand made rugs, wood carvings, woven baskets, silver and turquoise jewelry. Behind the artisans and spectators sprawled a bustling campground for weekend guests. An eagle eye view of the dynamic powwow thus revealed a series of concentric circles radiating like pulse beats from the rhythmic, pounding drum. Truly this was a social-cultural extravaganza, a two-day glimpse into the Indians' proud and colorful heritage. Divisiveness was replaced by unity, the powwow circle, and by brotherhood: the hospitality of the host community, the renewing of old friendships, and the creation of new ones.

The Detroit American Indian Center staged its first big powwow in June 1977 at the State Fair Coliseum on Woodward Avenue near Eight Mile Road. Teofilo Lucero coordinated the affair with ample help from center colleagues who hawked raffle tickets (prizes included a 1977 Dodge Colt, a color television set, and Indian artwork) and publicized the event widely in the media. The DAIC also assumed logistical responsibilities during the two day spectacular. Thousands of observers were thrilled by the grand entry and subsequent contest dancing. Amid the pounding drums and the kaleidoscope of dancers, at least one spectator reflected on how fortunate it was for American culture that these rich native traditions had survived. As the hosts, Detroiters worked diligently throughout the festivities and enjoyed themselves immensely. They grossed sixteen thousand dollars, with expenses totaling a little more than twelve thousand dollars.[23]

For the next six years DAIC powwows became routinized. In 1978 it was moved to the air-conditioned Yack Recreational Center in Wyandotte. Gary Severt joined Lucero as joint coordinator. Many contestants and spectators were lured by seven thousand dollars in prize money plus a Las Vegas trip for two and five hundred dollars in cash for the winning ticket number. To offset expenses, the center counted on admission fees, trader table rentals, plus sales of Indian food (cooked by DAIC senior citizens), soft drinks, powwow buttons, and raffle tickets. Once again the audience was enthusiastic. Once again Indian center staff sold tickets, prepared food, hosted visitors, and afterward cleaned up the arena. Their powwow moved out-of-doors in subsequent years to the suburban campus of Oakland Community College at Highland Lakes. Attendance dropped but the pastoral setting seemed more appropriate.[24]

Talk of attendance, profit and loss calculations, dancers vying for prize money, and the commercialization of the Great Lakes powwows troubled some participants. Still, for most, its setting was supercharged with meaning. When a half dozen men sat around a drum, Lance White felt a sense of kinship and goodwill as their beating and singing became perfectly synchronized. Not only did the vibrations travel up his drumming arm; White sensed them radiating through the dancers and into the crowd. For him powwows had power: to unite Indians and to produce personal satisfaction. When Ben Bearskin, Jr., emceed a powwow at

Keweenaw Bay in the Upper Peninsula, he challenged all participants to leave differences and concerns outside the sacred circle and become one as Indians. In such a way could the powwow circle heal and strengthen all within.[25] For another Detroiter, Majel De Marsh, powwows were akin to a spiritual experience. Most non-Indians did not understand; native dances seemed like "forms of entertainment, colorful ceremonies. But to Indians they have a deeper meaning." Thurman Bear agreed:

> It's a communal thing.... It's a way to express your inner self. When I dance, I'm speaking for my mother and father, for my grandparents, and to other Indians....
>
> I'm with my people when I dance.
>
> Once, in Oklahoma, an old Cheyenne man came up to me after a dance. He spoke to me in Cheyenne and his little grandson translated for me.
>
> "You dance well," he told me, "you made me happy." He shook my hand and a ten dollar bill was in it. There were tears in his eyes.
>
> People you haven't seen in six months turn up at a dance and you feel closer to them than to the white people you work with all week.[26]

III

Because the social and cultural well-being of urban Indians was intimately connected to other facets of their lives, native organizations that ministered to special needs, education and health, for example, also contributed to the 1970s revival. One was the DIECC. Central to its program was the belief that through "knowledge and respect for Native American cultural values and traditions the Native American student will be more effective in his ability to understand himself and better equipped to cope in a public school system that has not geared itself to meet his individual needs."[27] On Saturdays during the school year, scattered youngsters were bussed to the DIECC. "It's the only chance for my kids to see other Indian kids," reported one young mother.[28] Here was an educational support group for children and their parents. The DIECC's cultural awareness program offered Indian heritage classes and simultaneously fostered a sense of community among native people. By seeking to combine the best of Indian traditions with the best of modern, technical society, the center helped many young people bridge the gap between reservation and urban life. To do otherwise, to neglect native traditions, was tantamount to cultural suicide, according to Director Judy Mays.[29]

No one was more cognizant of native social-cultural attitudes than the DAIC's Health Clinic staff. Ben Bearskin, Jr., spoke forcefully about the importance of the clinic. One key was a greater awareness of the needs of clients, many of whom were trying to preserve native heritage in the metropolis. (If these cultural remnants were a treasure worth guarding, the clinic should adapt its services accordingly, rather than pressure patients to surrender totally to the dominant society's value system. Certainly there must be no disparagement of supposed inner-city Indian laziness or lack of motivation, which, Bearskin claimed, one heard too often at the DAIC.) Second, clinic staff nurtured Indian traditions outside their offices. For example, after an automobile accident killed one prominent community member and severely injured her husband, support was given to a ceremonial vigil. Mourners sat around the deceased's casket at a private home. They also lit a fire, voiced their prayers, and made offerings of cedar, tobacco, and sweet grass. Throughout the night friends comforted the family. Telephone calls came from around the country as the group huddled against the night and waited for news from the intensive care ward. Tragedy had brought them together and rekindled a time-honored method for handling misfortune.[30]

In a more lighthearted vein, the Health Clinic promoted native solidarity and traditions by sponsoring in 1981 a first annual spring feast. The site was Most Holy Trinity school. The entire native community was invited, with no admission charge, for "Good Food, Good People and [a] Good Time!" At least two hundred attended. City families were well represented—Martin Kiyoshk, Frank Alberts, a van load of senior citizens—as well as a cross section of suburbanites. Ben Bearskin, Jr., addressed the crowd about the Health Clinic's services. But mainly he thanked them for their support and asked that they accept this feast as a gift from the staff. Director Bill Memberto called for community unity. Teofilo Lucero gave a thanksgiving prayer in his Pueblo tongue; then they enjoyed a sumptuous meal. The evening culminated in a festive atmosphere of drumming, singing, the scamperings of rambunctious children, plus the inevitable fifty-fifty drawing. A point seemed well made: the Health Clinic wanted to serve all native people.[31]

IV

During the 1970s the population of Wayne County, Michigan (Detroit and its environs), declined by 12.5 percent. Many residents moved to northern suburbs. For instance, Macomb and St. Clair counties, which bordered Lakes St. Clair and Huron, gained 11.1 and 15.5 percent respectively. Indians joined these migrants. Macomb's native American population increased from 536 to 1,928 in the decade, and St. Clair's rose to 553 (from 214 in 1970).[32] Not all newcomers succeeded in their quest for better jobs; consequently, the need for economic assistance programs in the metropolitan area escalated. Even those who enjoyed financial success still craved the camaraderie of the inner city and their home reservations.

To serve this pyramiding population, South Eastern Michigan Indians (SEMI) was incorporated as a nonprofit organization, supported by state and federal grants as well as private donations. By 1984 its center, in the former Krammer Elementary School off Ten Mile Road in Centerline, had ten employees and boasted of more than a thousand active members. In May 1983 its programs served 510 clients, with a major emphasis on economic development initiatives.[33]

SEMI's social and cultural activities were equally popular. Feasts, holiday dances, fairs—even Las Vegas nights—provided pleasant opportunities for suburbanites to congregate. The center also sponsored classes in Indian beadwork, herbal medicines, and, until July 1983, Title IV adult education courses. The *Talking Peace Pipe*, a community newsletter like the *Native Sun* and the Walpole Island *Jibkenyan*, circulated widely to SEMI's service population, which stretched as far north as Algonac and Port Huron.

SEMI members and staff were not self-indulgent. They demonstrated great concern for the less fortunate in Macomb and St. Clair counties. Needy Indians included the recently unemployed, some elderly, and long-standing welfare recipients in rural areas and in cities like Mt. Clemens. These families were less transient than DAIC clients. But their requirements were similar: emergency food, clothing, housing, transportation. The Social Services Department, coordinated by jeanette Allison, became SEMI's busiest. Thanks to the efforts of neighboring senior citizen groups, the Young Women's Catholic Association, local city governments and merchants, teen clubs, and SEMI canvassers, Allison oversaw a room and freezer stocked with commodities for families in extreme

177

want. In December 1982 she distributed sixty-eight Christmas baskets to Indian clients.[34]

Allison's activities embraced more than emergency assistance. She negotiated an agreement with the state's Department of Social Services so that her office could aid clients with the formidable paperwork associated with Aid to Dependent Children, food stamps, and other public assistance. SEMI helped obtain the tribal certification required of Indian applicants seeking tuition and fee waivers at public colleges and universities. Moreover, in her suburban travels Allison fought to dispel negative stereotypes about her people. "It's not true that the Indian is loose, and that he is not goal-oriented. You can see the drive and the desire that we have for the betterment of our children. And the kids are becoming more education-oriented." Allison asserted, finally, that the center's mere presence served an important social function. Urban Indians rarely made a permanent decision to shun the native American community. Always some "closet" types wished to work their way back. SEMI provided an opportunity. Curious persons could loiter and perhaps attend a few social functions, as long as the staff remained open and friendly. If asked, newcomers might assume some volunteer work. These cautious natives would eventually get fully involved with center work and even feel comfortable about asking for needed services.[35]

The influence of SEMI radiated throughout the northern suburbs. Its programs were crucial, whether clients required financial assistance or simply a cheery center where they could stay in touch with their native heritage. The historic social-cultural revival of the seventies, in short, could not be divorced from the work of South Eastern Michigan Indians.

V

The seventies revival among native Americans, which clarified and intensified their sense of identity, also stepped up conflict with local authorities. No rioters erupted onto the streets. No buildings smoldered, and no frantic telephone call summoned the Michigan National Guard. The most notorious incidents were legal battles to determine whether Detroit Indians could safeguard their ancestors' remains, a sacred part of their rich heritage. Much was at stake despite the absence of bloodshed.

Historically, big-city legal systems perplexed most newcomers from minority groups. Their vulnerability led to exploitation as consumers, while local service agencies overlooked them. Particularly serious was the predicament of native Americans; they migrated from rural reservations, including Canadian ones, which were far removed from the mainstream practices of United States police and courts. By the 1970s Indians from Boston to San Francisco complained of police harassment, both verbal and physical, as well as mistreatment by judges. Authorities arrested native Americans six times more often than whites and twice as frequently as blacks. The accused, so ignorant of legal-aid services and so convinced that they would be punished by the courts despite the validity of the charges, made scant effort to defend themselves. Feelings of powerlessness and racial rejection thus became a self-fulfilling prophecy.[36]

Detroit was no exception. In August 1977 the *Native Sun* carried an alarming editorial by Arlene Shampine about police harassment in the Cass Corridor. The incidents "included physical abuse, threats, and verbal abuse of Native American men, women, and youngsters.... To sit back and say that it has not happened to you or it cannot happen to you is an 'ostrich' attitude," she admonished. "When a person cannot go to the store or walk down the street, without fear of being harassed, THERE IS A PROBLEM!!!" What recourse did they have? According to the state Indian Commission there were not enough attorneys available to serve native people. Moreover, Indians lacked knowledge of or distrusted legal services.[37]

Several special programs eventually sprang up. Most Holy Trinity opened the doors of its Legal Aid Clinic to disadvantaged native Americans. Volunteer attorneys and judges provided them with free advice or, in complex cases, referred Indians to lawyers who would counsel them for a low fee. Social workers assisted clients in resolving difficulties with government agencies. But the clinic, which was open one evening a week, could not handle all native troubles.[38]

Far more influential than generous volunteer efforts was the assistance offered by the full-time staff of a state agency: Urban Indian Affairs. Director Russ Wright and his coworkers, acting as paralegal representatives, sought to bridge "the gap between existing legal services and the Native American in need of such services." This meant intervening on behalf of Indians with the United States Department of Justice, United States and Canadian immigration officials, and the Detroit schools. Urban Indian Affairs also consulted with attorneys, referees, and judges from Michigan and other states in matters of Indian welfare. Another critical service was verification of native blood quantum, making clients eligible for special benefits such as the Indian tuition and fee waiver at state institutions of higher learning.[39]

As a Detroit Indian, Fred Boyd was equally concerned about the civil rights of native peoples. Yet his personal background, admiration for militant native leaders in other communities, plus the set of his personality ordained that Boyd's methods would be different from Wright's and far more controversial.

Boyd had been vigorous and combative since youth. Born in 1926 to Cree parents, both of whom died of tuberculosis, Fred was adopted at age three by James and Lula Boyd. While growing up on Detroit's near east side, a series of stepfathers neglected Fred. He turned to the Boy Scouts for male companionship. Knowledgeable about the inner city, he finally developed a sense of self-sufficiency but had no regular contact with other Indians. At age sixteen Fred quit school. Joining the military, he fought in the South Pacific island-hopping campaign, which culminated for him in the Philippines with a Bronze Star decoration. Boyd earned a livelihood soldiering and then sleuthing for several Detroit private detective agencies in the postwar years. Learning how to build a case with public records, commitment to a dogged pursuit of the facts, understanding the importance of a statewide network of contacts: each characteristic would serve Fred well during his civil-rights battles of the 1970s.[40]

Boyd became deeply involved in Detroit Indian affairs in the sixties after joining the NAIA. Within a few years he rose, like Dean George, to prominence in the association. He also was of major importance in establishing the Detroit American Indian Center.

The NAIA had a historic concern for native civil rights. In 1960, for instance, it championed the cause of George Nash, a World War I veteran and United Automobile Workers member, who was denied burial in the suburban White Chapel Memorial Cemetery even though the family owned a plot. Charging discrimination against Indians, the association campaigned energetically throughout the state and nation, but to no avail. A memorial service was held at the State Fairgrounds in August 1961; then a procession of Indian cars, with a police escort, wound its way to Perry Mount Park, in Pontiac, where Nash was interred.[41]

This sort of struggle would have appealed to Boyd. But by the 1970s the NAIA had been transformed into a nonprofit corporation, which contracted with the federal government and did not want to jeopardize receiving money by engaging in politics. According to Boyd, its suburban board members had become far too squeamish about criticizing Uncle Sam, not to mention state and local bureaucrats. Boyd also observed how ineffective Detroit's militant young Indians had become; they seized media attention but did not know where to go with it. Even when a goal was forged, they lacked the expertise to bring about change by working through the system. From Fred's perspective, the solution was to found a freewheeling, activist organization that better suited his confrontational style.[42]

What ultimately emerged was Native American Strategic Services (NASS): a civil-rights advocate for persecuted and oppressed Indians. Membership never reached more than about fifty Indians, and its money came from its members. (There were no charges for services to clients, either.) Committed to working within the confines of the law but with a tinge of insurgency, Boyd, NASS's leader, fashioned a formidable network of political clout. At its center were legislators, like Congressman John Conyers, with whom Boyd had been close since their postwar days in a local Democratic Club. By the 1970s this network included Boyd's friends in the Michigan legislature and on Detroit's Common Council as well as concerned persons in the governor's office, the state Civil Rights Commission, the Michigan Bar Association, the Michigan Indian Commission, the American Civil Liberties Union, the Detroit Police Department, plus mass media editors and reporters.[43] Fred Boyd—self-assured, courageous, impetuous, military in bearing and dress, with a small hard-hitting organization behind him—was an urban Indian warrior prepared to battle for the cause.

The most important social and cultural issue that Boyd and NASS tackled was the sanctity of Indian burial sites. Their first encounter was with Detroit's Fort Wayne Military Museum. During the summer of 1972 two native visitors to the site discovered that the skeleton of a twelve-hundred-year-old Indian was on display in a glass case. (An archaeologist had removed the prehistoric remains from a nearby burial mound in the 1940s and donated them to the University of Michigan. For twenty years they remained in storage. The university then loaned the skeleton to the museum, which put it on display in 1968.) The incensed native visitors asked curator James V. Ciaramitaro to dismantle the exhibit. He refused. Ciaramitaro claimed they represented no Indian organization. Yet he requested guidance from the NAIA about handling the issue and insisted that the four-year-old display was intended to educate the public about Indian culture.[44]

Once informed, association members voiced strong opinions. "When I heard about this thing, I couldn't believe that one of my people was on display," said Bernice Appleton. "I saw my father, grandfather and—if this sort of thing was condoned—I see my son there." Thurman Bear, a staff member at AIS, asserted that such an exhibit in a military museum, surrounded by "guns and tanks and weapons" was tantamount to a "symbol of conquest" over Indian people. The native plan for resolving the issue was summed up by Fred Boyd: "We're mainly concerned that the remains be returned to some sort of religious environment."[45]

A meeting was arranged for February 1973 (thanks in part to Boyd's political influence) with Ciaramitaro, members of the Detroit Historical Commission, which administered the museum, and native community representatives. The commission consented to remove the skeleton from its glass case. But much to the chagrin of Boyd, Appleton, Bear, and Dean and Shirley George, the remains would be returned to the university. If the skeleton were to be reburied with proper Indian ceremony, the University of Michigan must be convinced to surrender it.[46]

Dealings with the University of Michigan in February and March 1973 were fraught with frustration for Detroit Indians, culminating in a minor victory. At first they got a bureaucratic runaround from university officials. Each claimed he lacked authority to grant the Indians' request: release of the Fort Wayne skeleton and other prehistoric remains. Even the board of regents acted slowly. Native tempers flared. "I have controlled my anger for 29 years," Bear told the regents, "but it seems an Indian still can't be buried properly." Before the press they charged the University of Michigan with "debasing the dignity of our ancestors by performing research on bones robbed from a sacred burial place." About twenty-five to thirty Indians, including Boyd, regrouped in Detroit at the Cass Methodist Church to consider staging a sit-in. Instead, on one occasion, they sang at the university museum for their ancestors' remains and, on another, protested with beating drums and chants outside the administration building.[47]

The regents finally agreed to turn over some skeletons, despite objections by anthropology department faculty. Natives branded the concession mere tokenism and an insult to their intelligence. In early March Dean George nevertheless accepted two containers whose contents were subsequently buried on Indian land somewhere in the state. "May they rest in peace," he wrote.[48]

The next month George drafted a report to the Michigan Indian Commission. It summarized the importance of Detroit community leaders, like Fred Boyd, and concluded: "It is extremely difficult to put on paper the super-charged emotions that surfaced many times at the many meetings involved in this one incident. The Native Americans of Southeastern Michigan displayed a tremendous effort of unity in a peaceful demonstration that culminated in only a portion of what we set out to do. The rest of the work lies with the Commission to actively seek the necessary changes in the existing burial laws in the State of Michigan."[49]

To safeguard their burial sites against future desecration by the University of Michigan and members of the Michigan Archaeological Society, an Indian group (Detroiters Fred Boyd and John Muse plus the tribal chairmen of Michigan's four federally recognized reservations) filed a class-action suit in the United States District Court on December 3, 1973. Outside the Federal Building in Detroit that day native pickets conducted a ceremonial march. The plaintiffs charged that their religious rights, as guaranteed by the Fifth and Fourteenth amendments to the Constitution, had been violated by a Michigan statute, which, in a discriminatory manner, permitted archaeologists to dig up and remove for scientific study the remains of prehistoric persons and aboriginal inhabitants. The Indians' lawyer explained to the court the seriousness of the issue: their religion taught "that by digging in Indian burial grounds we disturb the natural cycle; that the Great Spirit allows the forefathers' spirits to remain with those presently living to guide them; that those spirits remain in the area of the burial grounds; and that those spirits influence Indian leaders in their councils; that disturbing the burial ground disturbs these spirits and so disturbs the Indians' communication with nature." The court was asked to (1) declare the Michigan law unconstitutional and (2) provide "a true and complete accounting of all remains of human bodies at any time taken from Indian burial grounds." Despite this, Judge Fred W. Kaess dismissed the case in April 1974.[50] Fred Boyd, undeterred by the judge's ruling, tried to alleviate Indian concerns by "going around through the back door." His friend, State Representative Jackie Vaughn III, sponsored an amendment to Michigan's archaeology law. House Bill No. 5847 restricting disinterment and scientific examination to prehistoric remains; no longer could aboriginal inhabitants only two hundred or three hundred years old be dug up and removed. A partial victory, the bill was not entirely to the Indians' liking. But Boyd and others attended the June 1974 ceremony in Lansing when the governor signed it into law.[51]

Smoldering issues surrounding native burial sites burst into flame again in November 1977. Neighborhood children discovered Indian bones while playing at a construction site along Paint Creek north of

Rochester. Prof. Richard Stamps, from nearby Oakland University, was called to the scene and soon removed from a shallow grave twelve skeletons estimated between seven hundred and a thousand years old. Stamps transported them to the university for scientific study. He promised that if the remains were indeed aboriginal, they would be released to the native community for proper reburial.[52]

This pledge proved unsatisfactory to many Detroit Indians. The combatants were soon engaged. On November 11, Fred Boyd gathered supporters at the DAIC (including Lucero and *Native Sun* editor Shampine). The group traveled by car north to Pontiac where they met Noreen See, director of the local Indian center. She directed them to the building site where Stamps awaited. The professor emphasized that he had at first informed the Michigan Indian Commission of his archaeological plans; he and his students also had shown proper respect for the remains during excavation. The skeletons were presently locked up at his university. Boyd's belligerent party nevertheless attacked the professor head on. They demanded that the remains be turned over to Noreen See within a week, even though Stamps's study was incomplete. If not, the Indian community would (1) bring down the wrath of many civil-rights organizations on Oakland, (2) seek suspension of federal grants to the university, and (3) place upon the institution a powerful curse. In rebuttal, Stamps explained that both Indians and non-Indians could learn more about their past from his proposed study of the skeletons.[53]

His accusers refused to listen. They were angry. How would whites react if natives exhumed their parents and grandparents? Boyd's smug delegation also claimed to know all about Indians and did not need information from Stamps. Because whites were so culturally confused, they should dig up their own dead, not the Indians'. Besides, as Boyd repeatedly pointed out, whites had historically broken too many promises to his people. Why should Stamps now be trusted?[54]

Negotiations continued as well as the battle for public opinion. Although the November 16 deadline passed without Oakland relinquishing the bones, no suit was filed against the university. Boyd met with the president, who made it clear that he wanted his institution out of the newspapers. On November 28 some Indian community members asked for United States Department of Justice intervention to prevent racial conflict, for Boyd warned that if Oakland officials did not return the remains soon "there may be a mass meeting of Indians on the university's campus."[55]

Two days later a breakthrough in the crisis occurred. William B. Connellan, assistant to the president, announced that within a week five boxes of materials would be released. The remaining six containers were to be handed over to the Indians the following June.[56]

On June 20, 1978, Fred Boyd orchestrated an elaborate and well-attended press conference at Oakland University campus to commemorate the occasion. Indian participants represented DAIC, NASS, Urban Indian Affairs, and the Pontiac Indian Center. Teofilo Lucero conducted a purification ceremony, scattering tobacco over the returned artifact boxes. Boyd's friend John Muse presented Oakland officials with a peace pipe. Noreen See broke an arrow and offered it to the university, symbolic of the return to peace and the hope that "we may continue to live as brothers, and respect each others religious beliefs." Boyd read what he believed was a victory statement. He praised the university for keeping its word and publicly thanked several persons and groups for their support. He also claimed to have educated Oakland University during the past eight months about the importance of Indian religious and cultural beliefs. A proud Fred Boyd closed with a warning: "no longer will our people allow the desecration of our graves and our cemeteries for we intend to defend our cultural and religious beliefs by whatever means necessary."[57]

In this affair, as well as in a dozen other cases, Fred Boyd was central to the restoration and revitalization of the native American community's sense of identity. Controversy surrounded his methods and motives. Some Indians labeled Boyd self-serving and high-handed. He called in the press too quickly; detractors claimed they were also angered and embarrassed by his public discussion of witchcraft, which violated a long-standing native code of silence about such matters. But Boyd had his supporters. When he retired from NASS early in 1979, both houses of the Michigan legislature praised his "vigor and wisdom" in fighting for Indian causes. Detroit Common Council likewise passed a testimonial resolution: "Working untiringly for native Americans, Frederick Boyd was instrumental in leading the group's efforts in civil rights, social services, legal, treaty, cultural and religious matters and in monitoring and spearheading legislation of concern to Indians." "To me," wrote Aaron Baker in the *Native Sun*, "Mr. Boyd personifies the modern day American Indian warrior."[58]

VI

Native organizations like NASS and the Detroit American Indian Center were not the sole agents of social-cultural change in the seventies. The revival was spurred on by individual Indians, suburban and inner city, whose blossoming touched the lives of other Detroiters.

For more than thirty years Rose Silvey's world was restricted to suburban Romulus.[59] Her parents separated when she was three. She sojourned in California, living with her father and in several foster homes; then she returned to Michigan and spent the rest of her childhood with her mother, an Ottawa Indian. Their home was modest: a converted horse stable with an outhouse. Rose lacked fashionable adolescent possessions of a class ring or a varsity sweater. But her mother kept her neat and clean. The woman also worked diligently as a domestic to keep the family off the welfare roles, and by her example exerted a profound influence. The remnants of an Ottawa cultural heritage, left after a boarding school's purge of her mother, were likewise imparted to Rose. She visited her ancestral community, near Harbor Springs, during the summer and was swayed by native elders. Nevertheless, home was Romulus. Upon high school graduation in 1956, with expensive colleges out of reach, she married a local man, Lee Silvey. For the next nineteen years Rose settled contentedly into the roles of wife, homemaker, and mother of three daughters.

By the time the 1970s social-cultural revival erupted, all her children attended school. Rose Silvey—comfortably middle class, a sheltered suburbanite—looked eagerly about for ways to help Indian people and to discover more about her native heritage. She applied for an editorial job at the downtown American Indian Center and was hired. New worlds unfolded.

One was a journey of self-discovery. Through associations with other Indians she gained knowledge of her lost Indian heritage. Rose was particularly struck by traditional Indian women whose reserve and quiet confidence she emulated. She also shared these new undertakings and new friends with the Silvey family. Her youngest daughter, Mary, became especially close to Teofilo Lucero. For the three girls and their mother, the seventies became a decade of personal revitalization when their Indian identities were clarified and intensified.

Equally significant was Rose's outer passage, beyond the safe harbor at Romulus. As she broadened personally, her responsibilities were increased by the center. At various times she held the titles of *Native Sun* editor, office manager, executive secretary, acting director, and CETA coordinator. Rose regularly met with Michigan native leaders and traveled with them to Indian conferences across the country. She learned federal regulations as well as how to pick up the telephone and fight for Detroit programs with Washington bureaucrats. Rose assertively enforced center rules. She hired and fired; she praised and cajoled and castigated fellow workers. In short, she became a worldly-wise and productive Indian administrator.

Through it all Rose admired her people and observed them astutely. At first she was extremely judgmental toward inner-city natives, the bulk of the center's clients. Later she accepted them for what they were and came to admire some of their traits. One was the generosity of friends like Frank Alberts, Winona Arriaga, and Teofilo Lucero. They assisted fellow Indians to the point that they never got ahead economically themselves. They opened their homes to needy Indians passing through Detroit without regard to tribe and with no expectation of receiving anything in return. Second, Rose noted that Indian men and women living downtown seemed content with their lot. Unambitious materially, they were quick to splurge and seemed unable to save for the future. They were self-protective, too. They looked out for one another, alibied for one another, and refused to call the police about another native. Finally, Silvey noted the unfortunate conflict between inner-city and suburban Indians. Both had much to offer one another. Instead, they resorted to stereotypes; downtown dwellers were classed as lazy and those living outside the city as sellouts to the dominant society.

Rose Silvey changed during the seventies. Her inner and outer worlds expanded. She became an Indian woman, proud and knowledgeable, who altered the lives of her Romulus family as well as native colleagues and clients at the DAIC. Her story was an illuminating facet of the Detroit Indian community's social-cultural revitalization.

VII

Anthropologist Sox Tax wrote that "Indian people from time immemorial have explored and found ways to live in new environments without losing their identities and values." After more than a century of domination by the United States, natives thus remained "peaceful conscientious resisters." They certainly were not assimilated en masse into the American mainstream; instead, they accepted some features of "modern life" while retaining what they most valued of the traditional ways.[60]

Selectivity characterized urban Indians as much as it did their reservation counterparts. To be sure, the cities presented a wider range of attractive alternatives, from jobs and churches to schools and recreational facilities, then rural home communities. Pressure to conform to non-Indian ways intensified off the reservations. Social anonymity beckoned. Urban migrants were also isolated from the taproots of their cultures. Nevertheless, migration to the cities did not submerge all natives in the mainstream. Indian identity in Detroit was often enhanced through urban experiences, as natives responded the way they had always done: patiently and skillfully adapting to new environments and technologies, while maintaining their individuality and even developing bonds of unity with Indians from different tribes.[61]

>>> CHAPTER 7 <<<

The Urban Indian Experience

I

Postwar Detroit was not an idyllic Promised Land for Indians. Like wilderness pioneers they had to adjust to a threatening new environment and they had to fight to survive: first for subsistence, then for decent housing and control of their lives. The struggle was painful and lengthy. They suffered discrimination by the dominant society. Yet Indians organized to promote self-interests and went on to achieve economic self-sufficiency. Hardship also strengthened their sense of identity; Detroit's native peoples fought courageously to safeguard their ethnic heritage and group solidarity amid the centrifugal forces of urban-industrial life. In the seventies came national recognition of their plight, a massive outpouring of assistance, and quantum leaps forward. Detroit's historic promise to its minority citizens was being fulfilled.

Diverse woodland cultural traditions dictated that Indian bonds would be informal compared with Detroit's orderly Polish neighborhoods, for example, which were characterized by the strict discipline of tidy homes and closely knit Catholic parish organizations. The metropolitan Indian population drew its members from reservations throughout the United States and Canada. Not surprisingly the dominant tribes in the Great Lakes area and neighboring southern Ontario were the most prominent:

the Chippewas with 950 persons in 1970 and the Iroquois with 822. Of the more than forty other tribal groups that year, especially notable were the Cherokees—568, Ottawas—208, Sioux—173, and Delawares and Stockbridges—99.[1] By decade's end sixty-seven tribes were represented in Wayne County with the Chippewas, Iroquois, and Cherokees composing 73 percent of the native population.[2] Variety was further exhibited in the blood quanta of these Detroiters. Upon examining 5,745 cases, the 1978 distribution was as follows:

Table 15
Distribution of Detroit Indian Blood Quantum (1978)

Blood Quantum	Percent
Full	16(928)
3/4	5(290)
1/2	21(1,221)
1/4	27(1,555)
Less than 1/4	22(1,263)
Do Not Know	9(488)
Totals	100(5,745)

Source: Bashshur et al, *Native Americans in Wayne County*, 38.
Note: Figures in parentheses are the numbers of respondents.

Detroit's working-class Indians, again unlike the Poles, were much more scattered throughout the metropolitan area and looked to no religion or local congregation for spiritual direction. Maps 1 and 2[3] display the 1978 distribution of Indian families living in each municipal subdivision of Wayne County. The Cass Corridor was included because it contained a heavy concentration of Indians. The rest of West Detroit, Taylor, and Westland were the homes of many native families. Far fewer lived in the affluent northeastern suburbs (Harper Woods, Grosse Pointe Woods, Grosse Pointe Shores, Grosse Pointe Farms, Grosse Pointe, Grosse Pointe Park), the downriver areas (Flat Rock, Gibraltar, Rockwood, Brownstone), and in the thinly populated western townships. Also prominent has been Indian dispersion beyond Wayne County, into Detroit suburbs and southeastern Michigan towns and cities.

Despite this dispersion and the diverse cultural traditions of its members, the native community served well the needs of its members. It helped socialize newcomers to urban life and provided social controls and opportunities for social mixing. Should misfortune occur, mutual support was provided.

Historically, the Motor City thus provided an environment where lives could be refashioned, phoenixlike, amid abundant opportunities. Indians were not totally assimilated, nor did they forsake Detroit en masse for their former homelands. Instead, they forged vibrant lives for themselves as Indian-Detroiters. They were not as numerous or politically powerful as their black neighbors, but the story of these native peoples left no doubt about their importance to Detroit and of the city's effect on them.

II

Before 1970, and during the heyday of federal reform legislation, the historical experience of Detroit's native Americans paralleled that of other urban Indians who migrated to metropolitan areas because of the substantial economic advantages compared with home reservations. Their numbers also skyrocketed in the sixties (table 16).

Table 16
Increases in Indian Population

City	1960	1970	Increase (%)
New York	3,262	9,984	261
Chicago	3,394	8,203	141
Minneapolis	2,007	9,911	377
Denver	1,133	4,104	278
Los Angeles– Long Beach	4,130	23,908	479
San Francisco– Oakland	2,234	12,041	439
Seattle	1,729	8,814	409

Source: Sorkin, *Urban American Indian*, table 2–2, p. 11.

During the decade the proportion of off-reservation Indians throughout the United States rose dramatically from 27.9 (in 1960) to 44.5 percent.[4]

191

The crisis caused by the shift in Indian population from rural to urban areas alarmed both the White House and Capitol Hill. Lyndon Johnson's "Special Message to Congress on the Problems of the American Indian: 'The Forgotten American,'" "emphasized the urgent needs of off-reservation natives. That three-quarters of these Indians lived in poverty by 1970 was equally disturbing to President Nixon. He remarked to Congress of their plight: "Lost in the anonymity of the city, often cut off from family and friends, many urban Indians are slow to establish new community ties. Many drift from neighborhood to neighborhood; many shuttle back and forth between reservations and urban areas. Language and cultural differences compound these problems." The upshot, observed the American Indian Policy Review Commission, was that urban Indians were "really at home nowhere."[5]

Adjustment by rural natives to urban-industrial life, a prominent part of Detroit Indian history, was equally stressful in other metropolitan areas across the country. Disoriented natives often lacked knowledge about social agencies that could help. These in turn were unaware of the needs of this most invisible minority. By the late 1960s Chicago's St. Augustine Center, a social agency of the Episcopal Church, provided emergency assistance (cash, food, clothing) for more than a thousand American Indians and in the process grasped the severity of economic and social dislocation caused by rural-urban migration. To the northwest, the Minnesota Indian Commission characterized the state's neophyte urban Indian as distrustful of non-Indians and inhibited by "strong attitudes of dependency."[6] Researchers also noted these features among Salt Lake City Indians, attributing them to reservation upbringings. Here government agents aggressively reached out with their services to needy natives. City offices worked differently; clients must take the initiative by walking in or obtaining a referral. Cut off from familiar surroundings and leery of new white neighbors, rural Indians often chose to do without assistance rather than ask non-Indians. Consequently, not all Salt Lake City newcomers triumphed over the first challenges of big-city life. Unable to find employment, suitable housing, or a new network of supportive friends, some became permanent residents of slum neighborhoods or dejectedly drifted back to rural home communities.[7]

Employment problems were linked to unsatisfactory adjustment. One analyst commented that many urban migrants merely continued the "aimless poverty that they experienced in their home communities." National census data from 1970 documented that 20 percent of off-reservation Indians had incomes below the poverty line. Although their unemployment rate was only one-quarter that of reservation counterparts (9.4 vs. 41.0), it was twice as large as whites' (4.0) and roughly comparable to blacks' (8.2). Moreover, the urban native labor force was concentrated in the lowest-paying occupations.[8]

Studies of individual cities highlighted these conditions. The St. Augustine staff in Chicago noted that the poverty of clients fresh from the reservation forced them to take the first jobs they could find. Frequently these were monotonous, unskilled, seasonal positions with minimum compensation. Because of the rapid influx of Indians into Minneapolis during the sixties, their percent of the city's relief rolls rose threefold. Moreover, a 1973 study of 498 of these families determined that 23 percent of the household heads were unemployed. The situation was no better in Spokane, Washington. Indians suffered from a standard of living only 56 percent as high as whites.[9] Explanations for all these difficulties were reminiscent of those offered for the Motor City's Indians: not enough education and skills, little information about how to obtain a well-paying position, and not enough ready cash to buy tools or to provide a reliable means of transportation back and forth to work. Natives also cited employer discrimination. Finally, in any city, it was difficult to exaggerate the seriousness of these problems. Economic adjustment conditioned other facets of urban living, as a Denver study concluded. A good job was the critical "way station to cultural integration."[10]

By the early 1970s urban Indian poverty and a reluctance to use (or unfamiliarity with) mainstream medical facilities had precipitated chronic health problems. In both Seattle and Chicago, for example, only a few of the native residents surveyed had health insurance. Financial barriers doubtless explained why only 40 percent of Dallas native Americans availed themselves of dental care during this period.[11] Alcoholism, which notoriously plagued reservations, debilitated urban Indians and also caused conflicts with law-enforcement officials. Of those Indians arrested by Salt Lake City police in 1971, 70 percent were charged with drunkenness. Very little was known about the specific health needs of urban Indians until a special board studied the Minneapolis community. Home visits by its outreach workers revealed that 89 percent of the native American households had health-care needs. One out of every nine persons ought to have been hospitalized immediately. Ninety-one percent of those more than fourteen years of age had periodontal disease. The board could only conclude that the city's health-delivery services were not properly organized to meet pressing Indian needs.[12]

Deficient housing likewise stemmed from inexperience with urban institutions plus limited economic resources. Living quarters were a marked improvement over reservation facilities but not as good as the general population's. In 1970, 44 percent of rural Indian housing was rated as crowded as against only 19 percent of their city dwellings. Impoverished families, clustered downtown, nevertheless experienced much hardship. For example, low incomes together with landlord discrimination forced Minnesota's off-reservation natives to settle for the worst housing: "Living 'all bunched up' in subdivided old houses on bar-studded inner-city streets devoid of safe places for children to play."[13]

Not enough formal education severely handicapped metropolitan Indians. Some suffered more than others. Compared with rural males twenty-five years and older, who averaged 8.7 years of schooling in 1970, big-city counterparts (with 11.2 years) were better prepared to compete in the job market.[14] In facing urban white rivals, most of whom were high school graduates, success naturally favored the better-educated Indian communities (table 17).

Table 17
Urban Indian Education and Family Income Levels

City	Indian High School Graduates in 1970 (%)	Indian Family Income Less than Poverty Level in 1970 (%)
Los Angeles– Long Beach	48.7	19.3
San Franscisco– Oakland	52.5	20.6
Tulsa	50.2	18.7
New York	44.7	17.9
Tucson	17.9	62.6
Phoenix	35.9	44.5
Buffalo	29.8	26.7
Seattle	40.6	23.8

Source: U.S. Bureau of the Census, *1970 Census of Population.*
Subject Reports: American Indians, tables 11 and 14.

THE URBAN INDIAN EXPERIENCE

Even the more prosperous populations, like Tulsa's, were still under-educated and economically disadvantaged when contrasted with whites. Furthermore, frustrated native parents across the United States complained that they lacked influence with urban schools, whose teachers ignored the unique heritage and special educational needs of Indian children.

III

In July 1970 Richard Nixon remarked to Congress: "We have concluded that the Indians will get better programs and that public monies will be more effectively expended if the people who are most affected by these programs are responsible for operating them." Native leaders clearly grasped the significance of subsequent federal reform legislation. We must act decisively now to develop Indian communities "in a manner beneficial to our people," urged Navajo Tribal Chairman Peter MacDonald, because self-determination opportunities could mean "a new beginning or our last hurrah."[15] Act they did, on and off the reservations. Urban Indians investigated local conditions and then set priorities for action; they sponsored millions of dollars in CETA programs and operated hospitals and health clinics through contractual arrangements with the Indian Health Service; they worked through parent committees to reaffirm a traditional role in Indian education and to better meet the needs of their children.

By 1977 the HEW's Office of Native American Programs (ONAP) granted "seed money" (ranging from forty thousand to two hundred thousand dollars) to sixty Indian centers, which, like the facility at 360 John R in Detroit, provided vital services tailored to urban natives. ONAP support also enabled Indian-run institutions to attract more money from other agencies. Indian centers assisted native peoples in many ways: counseling, referrals, financial and medical help for low-income families, as advocates, and as sponsors of educational programs and social events. Their psychological role was particularly important. "Having left the Indian community, and often their families," wrote Alan L. Sorkin, "migrant Indians are victims of isolation and loneliness. They have developed these centers to ameliorate such problems and to provide a place where they can join together in social gatherings that substitute for the personal security of the reservation."[16]

These institutions grappled with momentous challenges during the seventies. Local leaders had to overcome the same sort of start-up problems and administrative inexperience that plagued Dean George and his colleagues at the DAIC. Much of their limited resources was spent just documenting native community needs. Each year, too, they struggled with federal reporting guidelines and competitive grant-renewal procedures. High staff turnover rates, factionalism, infighting—often coupled with apathetic and distrustful constituents—further bedeviled Indian centers throughout the United States. Painful though this evolutionary process was, "[t]here can be no doubt," concluded the American Indian Policy Review Commission, "that the Indian centers are a firmly based and creative response to the Indian frustrations with their off-reservation and urban environments."[17]

Employment, health, and educational programs sponsored by urban Indian centers were wide-ranging like their Detroit counterparts. CETA, for example, involved twenty thousand urban Indians in its training and employment programs during 1976.[18] Even more impressive were accomplishments stemming from the Indian Health Care Improvement Act. Title V helped establish ten new urban Indian health programs and expand thirty-one others. In fiscal year 1979 they provided the following services to patients and clients: 108,645 medical; 33,893 dental; 154,987 outreach and referral; and 77,188 other services, which included mental health, nutrition, health education, and family planning.[19] Twenty-two organizations (including those in Boston, Albuquerque, and Denver) had completed needs assessments and focused their energies on outreach and referral in hopes of encouraging greater use of medical facilities. Limited direct health-care services were offered by fourteen programs, including Detroit's. Only the Seattle Indian Health Board and four other urban Indian institutions provided comprehensive care: primary medical, dental, nutrition, mental health, and optometric. Particularly impressive was the progress made by Seattle, which brought together the resources of federal, state, local, and private agencies. The board's emphasis "on primary care and sensitivity to cultural values," reported Assistant Director Don Aragon, "has encouraged patient acceptance and utilization." The major shortcoming of these centers, according to outraged urban tribesmen, was not enough money. Title V had authorized a total of $30 million to meet their needs for fiscal years 1978, 1979, and 1980. Instead, appropriations were only $11,200,000.[20]

196

HEW's Office of Education confessed that Indian cultural diversity prevented Washington from determining the best practices for native people.[21] Thus, legislation in the 1970s emphasized goal setting and program administration by community leaders. Federal grant procedures for Indian education were just as irksome as employment and health grants, yet they generated an innovative array of urban Indian projects like Detroit's Indian Educational and Cultural Center. The Dorothy LePage Indian Community School in Milwaukee, partly supported by grants from the Indian Education Act, provided an alternative education with an "Indianness core" to 102 pupils from kindergarten through twelfth grade. In 1978 the Chicago Indian Education Program received $110,582 to help it attain several objectives; one was a 10 percent improvement in the mathematics and reading scores of participating high school students. Year-end results showed that basic skill deficiencies were lessened significantly. Among others assisted by the Indian Education Act were Minneapolis natives. Grants totaling $250,000 during one fiscal year enabled them to employ fifty-three persons (administrators, social worker aides, Indian student advocates, tutors) and to serve about two thousand youngsters.[22]

Early in the 1980s when federal grant moneys were threatened, the Senate Select Committee on Indian Affairs asserted that Indian education legislation was

> one of the most efficient means of targeting funds for compensatory education to Indians.... With the program in place, Indian students show increases in test scores, increases in school attendance rates, and decreases in dropout rates....
>
> [E]ducation for Indian young people is of such importance, if the Indian population is ever going to move towards self-sufficiency, that these programs should not be reduced.[23]

The results of Indian reform legislation were mixed. Some urban natives defended their implementation record on the grounds that they simply contended with normal self-determination start-up difficulties like their counterparts on the reservations. Staunch critics, on the other hand, would have none of this. They vilified Congress for reneging on its financial commitments and Executive Branch agencies—the Department of Labor, Indian Health Service, the Office of Indian Education—for raising every conceivable roadblock to protect themselves and thwart grass roots Indian program control. Rose Silvey, CETA coordinator at the Detroit American Indian Center, concluded sadly that the 1970s reforms nationwide had provided native communities with "only a Band-Aid over a gaping wound." Why had Washington promised so much and delivered so little? Many city Indians she knew concluded that the new initiatives had been designed to fail; that Congress's special appropriations were merely "conscience money."[24]

Washington's self-determination initiative, by 1980 only beginning its assault on intractable native community problems in Detroit and elsewhere, was nevertheless a milestone on the twisting road of American Indian history. Certainly its comprehensiveness was remarkable. Legislation addressed even the special social and economic needs of urban Indians, who by the 1970s composed nearly half the native population in the United States. Equally noteworthy was the shift in Indian policy goals and administration. Previous social experimentation programs emanating from Washington had resulted in "decades of confusion, hopelessness, and poverty," according to the American Indian Policy Review Commission. Then came a resolute break with the past, and the commission could report in 1977: "It is the fortune of this generation to be the first in our long history to listen attentively to the Indians ... and to heed their voices for the righting of wrongs, the ending of frustrations and despair, and the attainment of their needs and aspirations as Indians and as free and proud Americans."[25]

If the seventies was a time for new direction in federal Indian policy, were the results of reform measurable beyond the Potomac, in native neighborhoods like those along the Detroit River? Writing in 1976, historian Donald L. Parman judged that the previous fifteen years constituted a revolution in Indian affairs that was "perhaps the most significant since the start of the reservation system in the nineteenth century." The University of Chicago's Robert J. Havighurst saw greater change and growth in the educational experiences of American Indians than in any other period.[26] Sioux writer Vine DeLoria, Jr., was equally sanguine. Notwithstanding the lack of strong leadership from Washington and the lack of unity in the Indian community about future goals, native people still "made substantial progress in a tangible sense with the plethora of new social programs.... One thing was certain: Indians had broken the back of the termination mentality and had emerged from the shadows of social neglect into a better day."[27]

IV

Walpole Island Indian Reserve leaders like Dean Jacobs also had much of which to be proud in the 1980s. Particularly important were achievements in four areas: reserve infrastructure, economic development, cultural revival, and leadership. Basic to the community's vitality—to its health, housing, and resource management—was a safer water supply and improved drainage. To this end a new $600,000 network of pumps and ditches was built to draw off excess water from the low lying reserve. By 1984, thanks to another $700,000 investment, 80 percent of the reserve's homes had access to treated water. Marked progress was also made toward Walpole's goal of self-sufficiency while maintaining an appropriate relationship with its cultural traditions. The largest project was Tahgahoning Enterprises. A highly-mechanized band farm, it cultivated four thousand acres, provided jobs for seven natives, and had gross sales of $1.5 million in 1983.[28] Even more labor-intensive was Walpole Industries, a mold and die-makers plant owned and operated by the band and employing twenty-two persons. Housed in a six thousand-square-foot, $750,000 facility, its sales totaled $348,000 in 1984. Dean's father, Charles Jacobs, was chairman of the board of directors and one of the first instructors for its machine shop course. Another capital improvement of the eighties was the Algonquin, an $880,000 senior citizens center with twenty low-rental efficiency apartments. Both Charles and Mavis Jacobs helped plan the complex, which, it was hoped, would improve living conditions for the elderly and at the same time acknowledge their contributions to the community.[29] Renewed interest in traditions, like the role of elders, found further expression in an expanded July powwow, the island's most impressive annual event, and a revival in 1981, after a lapse of thirty years, of the colorful fall fair. Parades, dances, souvenir sales, socializing with visitors, and forty-six competitions ranging from pie baking to creative writing: all represented to Chief Bill Tooshkenig a chance to rediscover the island's heritage and to remember "we are Indian people."[30] The catalyst for community development, which made Walpole one of the most progressive reserves in Canada, was local leadership from band members like Tooshkenig and Dean Jacobs, especially their commitment to grass-roots input as part of the Band Council's decision-making process.

Walpole and many other Canadian reserves unquestionably improved social and economic conditions during the 1970s and 1980s. Nevertheless, poverty was still the norm for native families, and growing numbers migrated to large metropolitan areas. Indian family income, for example, was only two-thirds of the national average in 1981. "Levels of native education and the size and condition of housing fall so far below the non-native population," observed the Toronto *Globe and Mail*, that "one has to look to census studies in 1951 and 1961 to find a time when the rest of Canada lived in similar circumstances." After a scholarly examination of socio-demographic statistics, Andrew J. Siggner concluded that "in many respects the plight of Indians is extreme ... [and those] living on economically impotent reserves find themselves in a classic state of 'welfare dependency.' "[31] Walpole was exemplary. In the mid-1980s its housing stock still fell far short of estimated needs. Because the school drop-out rate continued at a high level, young people denied their reserve the qualified Indian personnel needed to run its programs. Widespread unemployment further hampered Walpole's movement toward self-sufficiency (in 1982, out of a potential labor force of 936, there were 460 without jobs). The band remained the largest island employer and continued to be dependent on government sources for monetary grants.[32]

The push-pull of the Walpole-Detroit connection likewise persisted into the 1980s with community members surging in both directions. Band members moved to Detroit to improve living conditions; yet, once resettled, the spell of the island drew them back regularly for vacations, social functions, for welfare benefits during big-city economic slumps, retirement, or, like Dean Jacobs, to take up the awesome challenge of reserve development. This ongoing Detroit-Walpole Island affiliation was typical of influential relationships between Detroit and other rural native communities whose populations also channeled back and forth. Life in the Motor City thus continued to be an important option for Canadian Indians bent on self-sufficiency yet frustrated by rampant poverty and limited employment on the reserves.

The recent history of United States reservations paralleled Canada's. Thanks to Washington's self-determination policy for Indians and expanded federal programs, tribes were rejuvenated and, judged one historian, "were probably better off in the late 1970s than they had been for decades. Indians began to glimpse the possibility that they might not have to put up with high unemployment, bad housing, and poor sanitation forever." Uncle Sam's largess nevertheless had its drawbacks. Chief among them were the dangerous native dependence on subsidies and a lack of local resource development. Reservation vulnerability was highlighted in the early eighties when the Reagan administration slashed grants for native programs. By January 1982 Navajo per capita income slipped from twenty-two hundred dollars a year to seventeen hundred dollars, while the tribe's unemployment rate, after a reduction of federal support, shot up from 38 percent (in 1980) to 72 percent. Promising health, education, and housing projects had to be terminated. Nor was the tribe's plight unique. 'The impact of Reaganomics on the Navajos," the largest United States Indian community and one of the wealthiest, wrote Hazel Hertzberg, "has been duplicated on many other reservations."[33]

This setback in native community development meant, as in Canada, that out-migration would escalate. The percentage of urban Indians climbed even during the heyday of the seventies from 44.5 percent in 1970 to 49 in 1980. Compared with reservation relatives, city Indians continued to enjoy better housing, more educational achievement, and less unemployment.[34]

V

Early in the 1980s, with the Motor City crippled by recession, the Detroit American Indian Center staff realized that their Band-Aid programs were only partly successful in alleviating native suffering in Detroit. Furthermore, unless the center "began to do some serious long-term planning and taking some risky but necessary steps toward real economic development, we might not survive the next downswing of the economy."[35]

What extended difficulties faced their people, in the center's judgment? Besides alleviating long-standing structural problems like poverty and not enough formal education, the nearly eighteen thousand Indians scattered throughout Wayne County's 645 square miles must overcome their low visibility. This hampered their drawing benefits from the metropolitan economy and social services network. Indians were undercounted as well. Detroit, as a border city with seasonal work for the unskilled, historically attracted a large transient native American population, which fell "through the cracks of the census." Lacking geographic concentration and with many Indians so mobile, they were ineligible for neighborhood improvement grants and the cost of serving them (with transportation, mailing, outreach) was abnormally high. Disadvantages were apparent, too, whenever group effort was needed to obtain services, program grants, or exert political influence. Irregular physical contact even restrained the Indians' sense of community.[36]

Troubles, as identified by Indian center officers, produced pressing community needs for the eighties. High native unemployment, for example, prevented the DAIC from meeting all requests for emergency food relief or adequately counseling clients about their diets. Poor nutrition thus plagued the population. The creative talents of teenagers were further dissipated by a secondary school dropout rate reckoned at 50 percent and unemployment double that of Indian adult males. Supportive and recreational services also were lacking. The center claimed that 838 Indian families (24 percent of the total for the Detroit metropolitan area) were headed by females. Their median income was $7,807, compared with $14,927 for all the city's native households. Besides their low budgets, Indian women needed help with day care, substance abuse, and family violence—including suicide. Equally distressed were the elderly, 36 percent of whom had incomes either below or near the poverty level that year. Compared with similar white populations in the Midwest, more than twice the proportion of Detroit native senior citizens fell below the poverty line. Shocking, too, was the fact that many aged sixty-five and above suffered in isolation; they lived alone or with nonrelatives and lacked access to transportation.[37]

During the first half of the 1980s, the Detroit Indian Center submitted several proposals for decreasing these difficulties. Remedies reflected not only native goals and strategies but the insistence of Washington grant sources that urban Indian centers concentrate on community economic development. The Motor City byword became self-sufficiency for city Indians while retaining their cultural values. One DAIC grant, intended to stimulate perspective native entrepreneurs, enabled it to sponsor workshops, start a collection of resource materials, and offer a referral service. Local response was so disappointing that the center resolved to establish its own model.[38]

But what type of enterprise would be best? Advice was sought in several quarters including the Southeast Michigan Development Center, a federally supported group, which provided technical assistance to minorities wishing to start or expand a business. Indian administrators settled on a restaurant/catering service. The benefits would be several: employment and training opportunities for needy community members, income generation for DAIC service programs (reducing their dependency on federal grants), and promotion of Indian entrepreneurship.[39]

To house this project and the others for which the DAIC requested financial support—a native American arts and crafts shop, day care, youth program, services for isolated seniors and other shut-ins—the board of directors hoped to acquire a centrally located community building. No longer would precious money be siphoned off to pay high rents. No longer would agencies serving Indian people be scattered throughout the metropolitan area. Native unity would surely be increased.[40]

The DAIC believed it was capable of carrying out such important initiatives. In 1985 the center's thirty full-time staff managed six programs, which boasted an average annual budget of $700,000. Furthermore, it claimed, over the previous eleven years the DAIC's leadership was recognized by other Indians as well as non-Indian agencies in the area.[41]

VI

In April 1985 the Detroit American Indian Center hosted a dinner-dance in honor of Elmer Sebastian, Michigan's "American Indian of the Year." Dean George noted in his written nominating statement that Elmer had worked steadfastly for his people. "He helped NAIA of Det. Inc. and its many subsidiaries ... Along the way, he held many elected offices ... Elmer also served on the Michigan Commission on Indian Affairs in the early 1950s. Elmer has stuck in there through thick and thin, good times and bad times, giving of his time, money, efforts, and hours away from his family, for more than forty-four years." The gala was attended by friends and family from across the continent, who testified to Sebastian's many admirable qualities: his industry, sense of responsibility, and his confidence in formal education (when his own children became discouraged and wanted to drop out, it was recalled, he urged them on and instilled in them ambitions beyond his own). Extolled, too, were Elmer's commitment to preserving native cultures and championing Indian causes in an urban setting. Above all there was his intoxicating faith in the future; this enabled him so often to help disheartened community leaders. The effervescent crowd, proud and hopeful, celebrated Elmer Sebastian and those like him who achieved so much for themselves and their race.[42]

Other native community members had equally distinctive views about the future. Harry Command, observing nineteen years of sobriety, was gratified by the accomplishments of American Indian Services and optimistic about Detroit. Granted, the downtown would never be the same; but the city was still vibrant and brimful of opportunity for Indians and others willing to hustle. He hoped that determined local leaders would also be patient as they strived to serve the community. Native administrators faced such inveterate social and economic problems that their constituents and grant supervisors must be forbearing as well. After all, Indian-run federal programs in Detroit were only ten years old.[43]

Rose Silvey was just as sanguine. Supervision of DAIC manpower programs strengthened her conviction that employment training was the key to helping off-reservation Indians. A good job assisted native families in all aspects of their lives. For Detroit natives to improve the future condition of their community, they must continue to articulate, forcefully, both its needs and how they can best be met with aid from the dominant society.[44]

Based on his interpretation of history, Ben Bearskin, Jr.'s prescription for the future drew more heavily on initiative. It also veered sharply from the code of accommodation personified by Elmer Sebastian and other association members. Once the Europeans invaded idyllic North America, as Bearskin saw it, they became a disruptive and evil influence. Even in the 1980s, self-serving whites could not be trusted by native people, whose only hope for a proper balance in their physical, spiritual, and intellectual lives lay in retrieving pre-Columbian traditions. In coming years, Bearskin noted, Detroit Indians must look within, rather than to Washington, for their salvation.[45]

VII

Elmer Sebastian, Harry Command, Rose Silvey, Ben Bearskin, Jr.: each was highly respected. Each had a following in the local Indian community, as did other leaders. These networks showed how diffused the native population was—politically, geographically, and even in its view of the future.

What existed in Detroit by the 1980s was a marvelously diverse and spiritually rich conglomerate of Indian Americans. Their race had withstood confinement on woefully small reservations and cultural assaults by missionaries, schoolteachers, and Indian agents. Through it all they maintained a sense of identity. They preserved a critical core of traditional values and languages. Indians survived by exploiting many of the white men's gifts: domesticated animals, newfangled technologies, and, later, urban centers. Thus it was not so extraordinary that thousands of reservation Indians, driven by necessity as well as ambition, ventured to Detroit during the twentieth century. Many had found the resources they needed and, like the Charles Jacobs family, returned home. Those who stayed and those who contemplated migration to Detroit later in the eighties had reason to be hopeful. Opportunity abounded. Also, aboriginal people—whether acting alone or in groups, in consort with non-Indians or in defiance of them—seemed destined to survive in this region and to prosper at least modestly. This was the Indian way, and so it has been for centuries.

⟫⟫ NOTES ⟨⟨

NOTES TO PROLOGUE

1. Parade memorabilia in possession of author.
2. *Native Sun* (newsletter of the Detroit American Indian Center), October 1983.
3. United States Bureau of the Census, *1980 Census of Population and Housing: Census Tracts, Detroit, Mich., Standard Metropolitan Statistical Area* (Washington, 1983), table P–4: 153.
4. DAIC, Grant Proposal for Social and Economic Development, Submitted to Administration for Native Americans, Department of Health and Human Services, June 29, 1985 (on file at the DAIC).
5. Arriaga, PI, February 24, 1979, Detroit.
6. Most historical data for this paragraph are taken from Beatrice A. Bigony, "A Brief History of Native Americans in the Detroit Area," *Michigan History* 61 (summer 1977): 136–63.
7. Mark Nagler, *Natives without a Home*, Canadian Social Problems Series (Don Mills, Ontario, 1975), 4–5, 7, 35; Diamond Jenness, *The Indians of Canada*, National Museum of Canada Bulletin, 65 (6th ed., Ottawa, 1963): 249–59. For a brief history of Indian–government relations before 1972, see J. Rick Ponting and Roger Gibbins, *Out of Irrelevance: A Socio-Political Introduction to Indian Affairs in Canada* (Toronto, 1980), chap. 1.

8. John Ruggles and Associates, *Isabella Reservation Household Survey* (on file at Tribal Council Office, 1976), 5, 14–21.

9. Amy D. Chosa and H. James St. Arnold, *Overall Economic Development Plan for the Keweenaw Bay Indian Community* (on file at Tribal Council Office, 1974), 10–13.

10. Paul Huddleston, "Walpole Island Indian Reserve Number 46. Comprehensive Development Plan" (on file at WIRC, 1978), 7–14, 20–21, 25–28, 43, 45–46, 58; Carolyn Hogg Harrington, "An Economic Survey of the Walpole Island Indian Reserve. A Cooperative Venture: Walpole Island Band Council and St. Clair Regional Development Association" (on file at WIRC, 1965), 1.

11. Lewis L. Meriam et al., *The Problem of Indian Administration. Report of a Survey Made at the Request of Honorable Hubert Work, Secretary of the Interior, and Submitted to Him, February 21, 1928.* Institute for Government Research, Studies in Administration (Baltimore, 1928), 736.

12. O. D. and Marjorie Armstrong, "The Indians Are Going to Town," *Reader's Digest* 68 (January 1955): 40.

13. Task Force Eight: Urban and Rural Non-Reservation Indians, *Final Report to the American Indian Policy Review Commission* (Washington, 1976), 57. Current research substantiates the primacy of economic motivation, as noted in Russell Thornton, Gary D. Sandefur, and Harold G. Grasmick, *The Urbanization of American Indians: A Critical Bibliography* (Bloomington, Ind., 1982), 52–53.

14. National Indian Brotherhood, *A Strategy for the Socio-Economic Development of Indian People. Background Report Number 1* (on file at WIRC, 1977), 32–34, 36–38. In its report, *Indian Conditions: A Survey* (Ottawa, 1980), the Ministry of Indian and Northern Affairs concluded that "job–seeking appears to be the single most important factor spurring migration off reserves," 138. See also James F. Frieders, *Native People in Canada: Contemporary Conflicts* (Scarborough, Ont., 1983: 142–43, 187–89, 192–95), who concluded: "Migration away from the reserve is much more the result of push factors than of pull factors. The urban setting is attractive only to those who are qualified to actively participate in it; few Natives are able to do so. Most Natives 'decide' to leave the reserve only when they are forced to by an absence of housing and employment opportunities."

15. Harrington, "An Economic Survey of the Walpole Island Indian Reserve," 16; Huddleston, "Walpole Island Comprehensive Development Plan," 7–14.

16. Elaine M. Neils, *Reservation to City: Indian Migration and Federal Relocation* (Chicago, 1971), 17; Meriam et al., *The Problem of Indian Administration*, chap. 12; Task Force Eight, *Final Report*, 57.
17. For analyses of this program, see: La Verne Madigan, *The American Indian Relocation Program....* (New York, 1956); Neils, *Reservation to City;* S. Lyman Tyler, *A History of Indian Policy* (Washington, 1973), 153–60, 201–4; Task Force Eight, *Final Report*, 23–43; Alan L. Sorkin, *The Urban American Indian* (Lexington, Mass., 1978), 25–45.
18. Quoted in Task Force Eight, *Final Report*, 28.
19. Neils, *Reservation to City,* 57–67.
20. Task Force Eight, *Final Report*, 31–39. For a more positive evaluation, which emphasizes how Indians benefited from relocation, see Kenneth R. Philp, "Stride toward Freedom: the Relocation of Indians to Cities, 1952–1960," *Western Historical Quarterly* 16 (April 1985): 175–90.
21. Charles K. Hyde, *Detroit: An Industrial Guide* (Detroit, 1980), 11, 21; Steve Babson et al., *Working Detroit: The Making of a Union Town* (New York, 1984), 22–23; Paul Wrobel, *Our Way: Family, Parish, and Neighborhood in a Polish–American Community* (South Bend, Ind., 1979), 32.
22. Tony Lazewski, "American Indian, Puerto Rican, and Black Urbanization," *Journal of Cultural Geography* 2 (spring/summer, 1982): 119; Babson et al., *Working Detroit*, 23; Melvin G. Holli, ed., *Detroit* (New York, 1976), 271.
23. Holli, *Detroit*, 271.
24. Census summary cited in Beatrice Anne Bigony, "Migrants to the Cities: A Study of the Socioeconomic Status of Native Americans in Detroit and Michigan" (Ph.D. diss., University of Michigan, 1974), table 3.
25. F. Clever Bald, *Michigan in Four Centuries* (New York, 1954), 106–10n.

NOTES TO CHAPTER 1

1. The main source for this and the following three paragraphs is John David, PI, October 24 and November 11, 1979, Detroit; Mohawk Institute described by Jennie Blackbird, Oral History Project Interview, September 1978–March 1979 (WIRC).
2. Command, PI, November 7, 1979, Detroit.
3. Arriaga, PI, February 29, 1980, Detroit; Carol Coulon Kawegoma, PI, May 2, 1979, Detroit.

4. Charles F. Wilkinson, "Shall the Islands Be Preserved?" *American West* 16 (May/June, 1979): 69.

5. Tom Nugent, "Leave Us Alone: Detroit's Indian Population Caught between 2 Worlds," *Detroit Free Press*, February 20, 1972.

6. Burton Jacobs, "Walpole Island—Its Struggle for an Identity" (manuscript on file at WIRC [1969], 5–7). See also Burton Jacobs, "The Indian Agent System and Our Move to Self–Government," in Sheila M. Van Wyck, ed., *Walpole Island: The Struggle for Self-Sufficiency—A Panel Presentation* (Walpole Island, 1984), 20–33.

7. Ralph West, "The Adjustment of the American Indian in Detroit: A Descriptive Study" (M.A. thesis, Wayne State University, 1950), 48–49.

8. Morales, PI, November 3, 1978, Detroit; Kiyoshk, PI, April 9, 1980, Detroit.

9. Boyd, PI, December 19, 1978, Detroit.

10. Colwell, PI, April 23, 1980, Walpole Island.

11. La Pointe, PI, August 3, 1977, Detroit.

12. Staats, PI, July 20, 1977, Detroit; Kiser, PI, summer 1977, Detroit; Morales, PI, November 3, 1978.

13. Ibid.; Montour, PI, summer 1977, Detroit. For a discussion of the importance of family ties in "channelized migration," see Lazewski, "American Indian, Puerto Rican, and Black Urbanization," 124–25.

14. West, "The Adjustment of the American Indian in Detroit," 58–59.

15. Alan L. Sorkin, *Urban American Indian*, 107–9.

16. Edith Beaulieu, PI, October 20, 1978, Detroit; Morales, PI, November 3, 1978, Detroit; Arriaga, PI, February 29, 1980, Detroit; Carol Coulon Kawegoma, PI, June 27, 1980, Detroit.

17. Arriaga, PI, February 29, 1980, Detroit; Carol Coulon Kawegoma, PI, June 27, 1980, Detroit.

18. Iron Shell, PI, February 22, 1978, Detroit.

19. Lucero, PI, May 30, 1979, Detroit; NAIA, "Salute to Our Founder," in Program for 37th Anniversary Dinner Dance, May 21, 1977 (on file with the author); West, "The Adjustment of the American Indian to Detroit," 55–56. For a history of the NAIA, see Gordon Douglas Northrup, "Pan–Indianism in the Metropolis: A Case Study of An Emergent Ethno-Syncretic Revitalization Movement" (Ph.D. diss., Michigan State University, 1970).

20. West, "The Adjustment of the American Indian to Detroit," 56–57, 59; *Native Sun*, May 1980; Northrup, "Pan–Indianism in the Metropolis," 1, 21, 125ff. The *Native Sun* is the official DAIC newsletter.

21. Northrup, "Pan–Indianism in the Metropolis," 130–31; Hirneisen, "The Indians of Detroit."
22. Carol Coulon Kawegoma, PI, June 27, 1980, Detroit.
23. Alberts, PI, March 28, 1979, Detroit.
24. Ibid.; Morales, PI, November 3, 1978, Detroit; Pedrotti, PI, summer 1977, Detroit; Arriaga, PI, February 29, 1980, Detroit; Nugent, "Leave Us Alone," *Detroit News*, August 30, 1973.
25. Wright, PI, December 2, 1977, and October 10, 1980, Detroit; *Native Sun*, August 1977; Office of Urban Indian Affairs brochures (copies on file at Office of Urban Indian Affairs).
26. Tom Pawlick, "Abandonment of the Indian in Detroit's Red Ghetto," *Detroit News*, March 5, 1970; Luise Leismer, "Indian Group Desires Center in Detroit to Share Heritage," *Detroit News*, March 15, 1972.
27. George, PI, February 8 and 15, 1978, Detroit.
28. "The North American Indian Association: Some Plans for the Future," n.d., Fred Boyd Papers (photocopies on file with the author).
29. Boyd, PI, August 1 and 8, 1977, Detroit; George, PI, December 14, 1977, and February 15, 1978, Detroit; James Hillman, PI, December 12, 1979, Detroit. In January 1974 Congress amended the Equal Opportunity Act of 1964 and created the Office of Native American Programs within the HEW, U.S., *Statutes at Large* 88: 2324–27. Since then, Office of Native American Programs grants have been the keystone to the Detroit Indian Center's money, though the office's name was later changed to Administration for Native Americans (within the Department of Health and Human Services).
30. DAIC, "Program Progress Review Report," December, 1974 (on file at the DAIC); George, PI, February 15, 1978, Detroit.
31. George, PI, February 15, 1978, Detroit.
32. Ibid.
33. *Native Sun*, July and August, 1975; George, PI, February 15, 1978, Detroit; DAIC, "Program Progress Review," 8–9, Fred Boyd Papers.
34. Lowry, PI, April 12, 1978, Detroit.
35. DAIC, "Program Progress Review," 9–10; John E. English to George Holland, March 20, 1975, Fred Boyd Papers; George, PI, February 15, 1978, Detroit.
36. DAIC, *A Random Sample Survey of the Detroit Indian Population in the Cass Corridor* (report on file at the DAIC, July 1975).
37. Staff meeting minutes, February 3 and March 13, 1975, Fred Boyd Papers; George, PI, February 15, 1978, Detroit; DAIC, "Program Progress Review," 13.

38. DAIC, "Program Progress Review," 21–22; staff meeting minutes for January, February, and March, 1975, Fred Boyd Papers; George, PI, February 15, 1978, Detroit.
39. Donna Acquaviva, "Indians Losing Center," *Detroit News*, May 9, 1975; DAIC, "Program Progress Review," 16–20; *Native Sun*, June 1975.
40. George, PI, February 15, 1978, Detroit.
41. George, PI, December 14, 1977 and February 15, 1978, Detroit; Anthony F. C. Wallace, *The Death and Rebirth of the Seneca* (Vintage Book Edition, New York, 1972), 30–31.
42. *Detroit News*, January 1, 1976; Boyd to William Moran, December 5, 1975, Fred Boyd Papers.
43. HEW Regional Director Richard E. Friedman to Detroit Councilman Clyde Cleveland, January 16, 1976, Fred Boyd Papers; Moman to Boyd and John Muse, January 20, 1976, Fred Boyd Papers.
44. *Detroit News*, January 1, 1976.
45. Moman to Boyd and Muse, January 20, 1976, Fred Boyd Papers.
46. Center Director Hank Bonga to Boyd, September 2, 1976, Fred Boyd Papers; DAIC board of directors minutes, April 3, 1976 (on file at the DAIC).
47. Montour, PI, July 27, 1977, Detroit; Boyd, PI, August 8, 1977, Detroit.
48. Cary Severt, PI, September 23, 1977, Detroit; Montour, PI, August 17, Detroit.
49. *Native Sun*, November 1977; Lowry, PI, April 12, 1978, Detroit.
50. Severt, PI, October 21, 1977, Detroit; Shampine, PI, October 21 and November 4, 1977, Detroit; Montour, PI, October 21, 1977, Detroit; George, PI, October 28, 1977, Detroit; Lowry, PI, April 12, 1978, Detroit; DAIC, board of directors minutes, November 5, 1977.
51. Shampine, PI, November 11 and December 20, 1977, Detroit; Boyd, PI, December 11, 1977, Detroit; DAIC, board of directors minutes, December 10, 1977.
52. *Native Sun*, January–February and May 1978.
53. DAIC, board of directors minutes, May 6, 1981; Lowry, PI, April 12, 1978, Detroit.

NOTES TO CHAPTER 2

1. Arriaga, PI, February 29, 1980, Detroit, and February 6–7, 1981, Pigeon, Mich., are the sources for the next eight paragraphs.

2. Josephy, *Now That the Buffalo's Gone: A Study of Today's American Indians* (New York, 1982), 86–87.
3. Lurie, "The Contemporary American Indian Scene," in Eleanor Burke Leacock and Lurie, eds., *North American Indians in Historical Perspective* (New York, 1971), 444; Evon Z. Vogt, "The Acculturation of American Indians," *Annals of the American Academy of Political and Social Science* 311 (May 1957): 139, 145–46.
4. Jack Forbes, "Traditional Native American Philosophy and Multicultural Education," *Multicultural Education and the American Indian* (Los Angeles, 1979), 4–8; National Indian Brotherhood, *Indian Control of Indian Education. A Policy Paper Presented to the Minister of Indian Affairs and Northern Development* (on file at WIRC, 1972), 1–2; Wilkenson, "Shall the Islands Be Preserved?" 69.
5. J. Milton Yinger and George Eaton Simpson, "The Integration of Americans of Indian Descent," *Annals of the American Academy of Political and Social Science* 436 (March 1978): 147; Lurie, "The Contemporary American Indian Scene," 445–46; "Ethics of Indian People," *Moosetalk* (winter 1981), 6.
6. "Ethics of Indian People"; Yinger and Simpson, "The Integration of Americans of Indian Descent," 147; Lurie, "The Contemporary American Indian Scene," 446–47.
7. National Indian Brotherhood, *Indian Control of Indian Education,* 2; Forbes, "Traditional Native American Philosophy and Multicultural Education," 9–10; Lurie, "The Contemporary American Indian Scene," 444; Yinger and Simpson, "The Integration of Americans of Indian Descent," 147.
8. Poem by Starr Maxwell, in *Talking Peace Pipe* (September 1983), 7.
9. For a discussion of the Indian kinship system in an urban context, see Thornton, Sandefur, and Grasmick, *The Urbanization of American Indians,* 32–38.
10. The following five paragraphs are based on extensive PI with Kiyoshk and his niece in Detroit during 1980–81.
11. Charles and Mavis Jacobs, PI, October 18, 1983, Walpole Island.
12. Kern, PI, June 5, 1981, Plymouth.
13. Ibid.; Jerry Belleau, PI, October 30, 1980, Detroit.
14. Schott, PI, June 4, 1981; September 16 and October 19, 1982; December 13, 1983, Detroit.
15. Kern, PI, June 5, 1981, Plymouth.
16. Northrup, "Pan–Indianism in the Metropolis," 132–36, 146.
17. Wright, speech on occasion of the NAIA 41st anniversary dinner,

May 23, 1981 (copy in author's file); Northrup, "Pan–Indianism in the Metropolis," 178–80, 201–4.

18. Northrup, "Pan–Indianism in the Metropolis," 180–82.
19. Ibid., 184–96.
20. Ibid.
21. Ibid., 138–45, 150–51, 166.
22. Ibid., 129, 131–32.
23. Ibid., 127, 144–46, 150, 221–22. Preamble quoted in NAIA 40th anniversary program.
24. Nugent, "Leave Us Alone: Detroit's Indian Population Caught between 2 Worlds"; Northrup, "Pan–Indianism in the Metropolis," 146, 148.
25. Wright, PI, December 5, 1980, Detroit; Jeanne May, "Russ Wright: Dedicated to the Indian," *Detroit Free Press*, February 3, 1984; Northrup, "Pan–Indianism in the Metropolis," 187–90.
26. Rodd, PI, December 4, 1980, Romulus. Rodd recently regained band membership on the Sarnia Reserve.
27. Charles and Mavis Jacobs, PI, May 21, 1981 and October 18, 1983, Walpole Island.
28. Lucero, PI, June 1977, and May 30 and November 5, 1979, Detroit.
29. Lucero, PI, December 5, 1979 and May 15, 1981, Detroit; May 17, 1982, Bowling Green, Ohio.
30. George, PI, May 28, 1981, Detroit.
31. Bigony, "Migrants to the Cities," 217–19.
32. Jane Johnson, PI, October 10, 1980, February 27 and March 27, 1981, December 13, 1983, Detroit.
33. Bigony, "Migrants to the Cities," 109–12, 149.
34. Kern, PI, June 5, 1981, Plymouth.
35. Bigony, "Migrants to the Cities," 138.

NOTES TO CHAPTER 3

1. Jacobs, PI, February 9, 1980, Walpole Island; Fisher, PI, March 23, 1980, Walpole Island.
2. Jacobs, PI.
3. Charles and Mavis Jacobs, PI, March 23 and October 2, 1980, Walpole Island.

4. Beaulieu, PI, October 20, 1978, Detroit.
5. Lucero, PI, May 30, 1979, Detroit.
6. West, "Adjustment of the American Indian to Detroit," 10–24.
7. United States Bureau of the Census, *Census of Population: 1970...
American Indians,* table 14:168–77; Sorkin, *Urban American Indian,* 17.
8. Rashid Bashshur et al., *Native Americans in Wayne County, Michigan:
Cultural, Demographic, and Housing Characteristics* (Ann Arbor, 1979),
102.
9. Wright, PI, October 10, 1980, Detroit; Julie Morris and Edward Shanahan, "City Poverty Awaits Many Indians Leaving Reservations,"
Detroit Free Press, April 28, 1970; United States Bureau of the Census,
Census of Population: 1970 ... American Indians, table 13:158–67.
10. Sorkin, *Urban American Indian,* 21.
11. Bashshur et al., *Native Americans in Wayne County,* 99.
12. Ibid., 104–10.
13. Ibid., 111–17.
14. Kiser, PI, October 17, 1980, Detroit.
15. Pawlick, "Abandonment of the Indian in Detroit's Red Ghetto."
16. Nugent, "Leave Us Alone."
17. Bashshur et al., *Native Americans in Wayne County,* 103. Gail Chakur,
who owned an employment agency in the late seventies and worked
in the DAIC's Manpower office, likewise observed that most Indians
new to the city lacked training and were inexperienced in jobs requiring close supervision (Chakur, PI, February 20, 1981, Detroit).
18. Pawlick, "Abandonment of the Indian in Detroit's Red Ghetto."
These Detroit Indian employment difficulties were confirmed by
Thomas E. Glass, "A Descriptive and Comparative Study of American
Indian Children in Detroit Public Schools" (Ed.D. diss., Wayne State
University, 1972), 97–100.
19. Bigony, "Migrants to the Cities," 128–30.
20. Lucero, PI, May 30, 1979, Detroit; Northrup, "Pan–Indianism in the
Metropolis," 124–25; West, "Adjustment of the American Indian in
Detroit," 11–12.
21. Staats, PI, July 20, 1977, Detroit; Lucero, PI, May 30, 1979, Detroit;
Kiyoshk, PI, April 9, 1980, Detroit.
22. Kiser, PI, October 17, 1980, Detroit; Beaulieu, PI, October 20, 1978,
Detroit; David, PI, June 20, 1979, Detroit; Boyd, PI, October 24, 1980,
Detroit.
23. Wright, PI, October 10, 1980, Detroit. Gail Chakur concurred. Most

employment agencies and probably 80 percent of the employers in the metropolitan area never had experience with natives. Historically, Indians usually worked for companies that hired other Indians; thus they clustered in the automobile factories and construction unions (Chakur, PI, February 20, 1981, Detroit). Ron DeLeary, the first Indian to hold elected office in Detroit's ironworkers union, for example, observed no overt company discrimination. Trouble came only from a few isolated individuals (DeLeary, PI, May 21, 1981, Detroit). Director of the DAIC's Manpower department Rose Silvey also agreed with Wright's assessment, adding that some of the Indian workers who claimed they were discriminated against had, it was discovered upon investigation, just misinterpreted the legitimate stern demands of teachers or employers (Silvey, PI, December 12, 1980, Detroit).

24. Lucille DeView, "Urban Indians: A 'New Wave' with Old Roots," *Detroit Sunday News*. November 20, 1977; Command, PI, March 1, 1979, Bowling Green, Ohio.

25. Elmer Sebastian, PI, October 30, 1980, Detroit. Gail Chakur also noted that urban Indians recently arrived from reservations in the United States and Canada were at first fearful of interacting with large numbers of non–natives. Others simply did not want to compete in the marketplace. Frequently, too, Indians were mistreated by blacks (Chakur, PI, February 20, 1981, Detroit).

26. Arriaga, PI, February 29, 1980, Detroit; Nugent, "Leave Us Alone"; Pawlick, "Abandonment of the Indian in Detroit's Red Ghetto."

27. Mesheky, PI, October 23, 1980, Detroit.

28. Ibid.

29. Ibid.

30. Ibid.

31. Ibid.

32. U.S., *Statutes at Large* 87:839, 858–59.

33. NAIA, "Detroit American Indian Center" (on file at the DAIC).

34. DAIC, "Quarterly Summary of Participant Characteristics," October 5, 1980 (on file at the DAIC).

35. Silvey, PI, October 23, 1980, Detroit; Goeman, PI, May 9, 1978, Ann Arbor; Gail Chakur, PI, July 14, 1978, Detroit.

36. Goeman, PI, May 9, 1978, Ann Arbor; Mesheky, PI, October 30, 1980, Detroit.

37. Rolando Garcia, PI, August 31, 1977, Detroit; Mike Dashner, PI, October 28, 1977, Detroit; Goeman, PI, May 9, 1978, Ann Arbor.

38. *Native Sun*, May 1980.
39. Mesheky, PI, October 23, 1980, Detroit.
40. *Native Sun*, May 1980.
41. Silvey, PI, October 23, 1980, Detroit; Mesheky, PI, October 23, 1980, Detroit; *Native Sun*, May 1980.
42. Mesheky, PI, October 23 and 30, November 21, December 12, 1980, Detroit; *Native Sun*, January 1980.
43. Silvey, PI, December 12, 1980, Detroit; Arlene Shampine, PI, October 27, 1978, and March 28, 1979; Chakur, PI, August 9, 1978, January 31, 1979, and February 20, 1981, Detroit; DAIC, board of directors minutes, September 9, 1978.
44. Silvey, PI, October 23, 1980, Detroit; Mesheky, PI, October 23, 1980, Detroit.
45. Mesheky, PI, October 23 and 30, 1980, Detroit. Linda, for example, counseled a hundred clients in November 1980 (Linda Isaac–Halfday, PI, December 5, 1980, Detroit).
46. Dashner, PI, October 28, 1977, Detroit; Garcia, PI, August 31, 1977, Detroit.
47. Hillman, PI, August 9, 1978 and September 13, 1978, Detroit; DAIC, board of directors minutes, August 10, 1978.
48. Silvey, PI, July 20, 1977 and October 23, 1980, Detroit; *Native Sun*, November 1977.
49. *Native Sun*, December 1979, and January 1980. Rose Silvey nevertheless voiced some serious complaints about the Department of Labor. It not only failed to provide all the money promised to the DAIC but fell woefully short with its technical assistance. Across the nation, in fact, centers like the DAIC often felt frustrated and threatened in their dealings with Washington. A major source of confusion was the rapid turnover in "federal reps" who supervised local programs. In one seven–year period, the DAIC's CETA office had fourteen different supervisors (Silvey, PI, August 5, 1983, Detroit).
50. Wright, PI, October 10, 1980, Detroit.
51. Hillman, PI, October 9, 1980, Detroit. The DAIC's CETA contract for fiscal year October 1, 1980–September 30, 1981, was $544,764 (DAIC, board of directors minutes, April 4, 1981).
52. United States Bureau of the Census, *1980 Census of Population and Housing: Census Tracts, Detroit, Mich., Standard Metropolitan Statistical Area*, table P–4: 553; P–12: 553; P–14: 599; P–16: 667, 670; P–17: 673–76. See also Bashshur et al., *Health Care of Urban Indians in Michigan. Volume One: Assessment of Health Needs among Indians in Wayne County*

(Ann Arbor, 1981), 15–17, 108–9. In line with the Reagan administration's strategy of shifting more power from Washington to the state governments, Congress supplanted CETA in 1982 with the Jobs Training Partnership Act. Title IV, Part A, of this legislation focused on native American training and employment programs. Congress found that "serious unemployment and economic disadvantages exist among members of Indian, Alaskan Native, and Hawaiian Native communities" and that "such programs are essential to the reduction of economic disadvantages among individual members of those communities and the advancement of economic and social development in the communities consistent with their goals and lifestyles." Thus the Manpower office at the DAIC continued operations with Jobs Training Partnership Act grants. In 1985 it offered many services, including employment and vocational counseling, assistance with transportation and baby–sitting, GED and other classes, as well as job placement (U.S., *Statutes at Large* 96: 1324, 1368–69; NAIA, "1985 Services Available at the Detroit American Indian Center" [on file at the DAIC]; Joe Hallett, "More Than New Name Involved as CETA Leaves, JTPA Arrives," Toledo *Blade*, October 1, 1983). The office served about two hundred clients per month, mainly young males who were seasonal laborers with no clear occupational goals (Sharon George, PI, April 26, 1985, Detroit).

53. John Coleman, "He's Serious about the Walpole Claim," *Windsor Star*, April 23, 1977.
54. Dean Jacobs, PI, July 19–20, 1979, Walpole Island; *Windsor Star*, May 10, 1980.
55. Charles and Mavis Jacobs, PI, October 2, 1980, Walpole Island.

NOTES TO CHAPTER 4

1. Iron Shell, PI, December 20, 1977, January 4, February 22, and March 8, 1978, Detroit.
2. Ibid., January 4 and March 29, 1978, Detroit.
3. Ibid.
4. National Council on Alcoholism—Greater Detroit Area, Statement to Substance Abuse Advisory Commission for Wayne County, June 8, 1978 (on file at AIS); National Council on Alcoholism—Greater Detroit Area, Educational Flier (on file at AIS).

5. Iron Shell, PI, February 22, 1978, Detroit; Native American Alcoholism Therapist Training Program brochure (on file at AIS); AIS brochure (on file at AIS). Bashshur's 1981 assessment of the health needs of Wayne County Indians challenged these high figures. Based on a sample of 205 families (820 individuals), the study concluded that only 36 percent of the population more than seventeen years of age were heavy drinkers. Beer was the preferred Indian alcoholic beverage and the "total amount of drinking (a function of frequency and volume of drinking) did not vary substantially among the Indian population by sex, age, or marital status." Nevertheless, survey data indicated "a positive association between Indian blood quantum and problem drinking, that is, the 'more' Indian and *sic*] individual, the more likely he or she is to drink excessively and to encounter drinking problems. This problem may be related to recency of migration and social isolation of the Indians with higher blood quantum levels" (Bashshur et al., *Health Care of Urban Indians*, 185, 198, 239–40).
6. West, "Adjustment of the American Indian to Detroit," 8–9, 25–35.
7. United States Bureau of the Census, *Census of Population: 1970... American Indians*, table 15: 178–87.
8. Bashshur et al., *Native Americans in Wayne County*, 126, 132, 136, 141.
9. According to the 1980 census, the metropolitan Indian population occupied 4,739 housing units, roughly half of which they owned. The rate of ownership was greatest in suburban counties like Oakland, where 690 were owned and 385 rented, and lowest in the city where Indians rented 767 housing units and owned only 592. Likewise the median value of Indian-owned homes was highest in the outlying counties—$41,700 in Oakland, for example, as against $19,200 in Detroit (United States Bureau of the Census, *Census Tracts: Detroit. Mich., Standard Metropolitan Statistical Area*, tables H–4: 125–26 and H–13: 439–42).
10. Alberts, PI, January 9, 16, 29, 1981, Detroit.
11. Tom Pawlick, "Abandonment of the Indian in Detroit's Red Ghetto"; Don Tschirhart, "A Blighted Area Still Hopes," *Detroit News*, September 6, 1972; Lee Winfrey, "Cass Corridor: Where the Action Is," *Detroit Free Press*, February 3, 1973; Bigony, "Migrants to the Cities," 92–93, 120–28, 148–49.
12. Ibid.
13. Arlene Shampine, PI, March I, 1980, and January 29, 1981, Detroit.
14. Command, PI, January 15, 1981, Detroit.

15. Martin Dockstader, PI, July 30, 1977, Detroit.
16. "Remember When" Alcohol Awareness Group Open Meeting, April 23, 1980, Detroit (author's field notes).
17. Grant Application for Native American Alcoholism Therapist Training (on file at AIS).
18. Iron Shell, PI, February 22, March 29, and May 29, 1978, Detroit; Iron Shell quoted in Donna Acquaviva, "American Indian Study to Fight Their Worst Disease: Alcoholism," *Detroit News*, August 27, 1977.
19. Wulff, PI, October 24, 1979, Detroit; Kiyoshk, PI, January 15–16, 1981, Detroit.
20. Jane Johnson, PI, October 10, 1980, Detroit.
21. Grant Application for Native American Alcoholism Therapist Training.
22. Bashshur et al., *Native Americans in Wayne County*, 46–55.
23. Ibid.; Ruth Davis, PI, January 15, 1981, Detroit.
24. Neighborhood Services Department, *'76 Annual Report* (in author's files).
25. Bureau of Substance Abuse, "Drug and Alcoholism Treatment Centers" brochure (in author's files).
26. Vivian Akiwenzie, PI, February 27, 1981, Detroit; "The Place of New Beginnings" brochure (in author's files).
27. Gene Iron Shell, PI, January 4, February 22, and March 29, 1978; "Sacred Heart Center" brochure (in author's files).
28. Pawlick, "Abandonment of the Indian in Detroit's Red Ghetto."
29. Bigony, "Migrants to the Cities," 146–48.
30. Arrell M. Gibson, *The American Indian: Prehistory to the Present* (Lexington, Mass., 1980), 556–59.
31. U.S., *Statutes at Large* 84: 1848–55; Task Force Eleven: Alcohol and Drug Abuse, *Final Report to the American Indian Policy Review Commission* (Washington, 1976), 5.
32. U.S., *Statutes at Large* 90: 1400–1402, 1410–12.
33. Command, PI, December 7 and 12, 1977, and March 1 and November 7, 1979, Detroit; Hirneisen, "Indians of Detroit."
34. Command, PI, December 7 and 12, 1977, and September 13, 1978, Detroit; Hirneisen, "Indians of Detroit."
35. Walker obituary, *Kalamazoo Gazette*, August 12, 1963; Command, PI, September 13, 1978, Detroit.
36. Command, PI, December 7, 1977, and June 28 and September 13, 1978, Detroit; Hirneisen, "Indians of Detroit."
37. Command, PI, September 13, 1978, Detroit; Hirneisen, "Indians of Detroit."

38. Application for grant, June 1, 1976, to May 31, 1977 (on file at AIS).
39. Command, PI, December 7 and 14, 1977, Detroit; Lucille DeView, "Urban Indians: A 'New Wave' with Old Roots."
40. Command, PI, December 17, 1977, and May 17, 1978, Detroit.
41. Wulff, PI, December 20, 1977, Detroit.
42. Command, PI, May 17, 1978, Detroit; Wulff, PI, April 5, 1978, Detroit.
43. Wulff, PI, February 22, May 17, and July 26, 1978, Detroit; Gene Iron Shell, PI, February 22 and May 29, 1978, Detroit.
44. Gene Iron Shell, PI, March 29, 1978, Detroit.
45. Command, PI, May 17, 1978, Detroit.
46. Details about these and other successful programs can be found in the organizational files at AIS.
47. Native American Alcoholism Therapist Training Program file (AIS).
48. Quoted in Acquaviva, "American Indian Study to Fight Their Worst Disease: Alcoholism."
49. Native American Alcoholism Therapist Training Program file (AIS).
50. Gene Iron Shell, PI, March 29, 1978, Detroit.
51. Memberto, PI, May 14, 1980, Detroit.
52. Andrea Smith, PI, October 28, 1977, and January 15, 1981, Detroit; Annual Report, Detroit Indian Health Planning Contract Number 241–76–0463, June 16, 1976, through July 15, 1977 (on file at the DAIC); *Native Sun,* December 1975 and October 1976.
53. *Native Sun,* October 1975 and October 1976.
54. Annual Report, Detroit Indian Health Planning Contract, 1976–77.
55. Ibid.; Crooks, PI, July 18, 1977, Detroit.
56. Annual Report, Detroit Indian Health Center, June 16, 1977, through May 31, 1978 (on file at the DAIC).
57. Memberto, PI, August 2, 1978, Detroit.
58. Bashshur et al., *Health Care of Urban Indians,* 1–5, 63–85.
59. Ibid., 130–35.
60. Ibid., 142–46, 174–77.
61. Ibid., 247–60.
62. Ibid., 343, 347, 350, 353, 355, 359, 364.
63. *Native Sum* March 1979; May 1979; May 1980; October 1980.
64. Bearskin, PI, February 5, 1981, Detroit. The Detroit American Indian Health Center continued its significant role in the eighties. For example, during fiscal year 1980 it offered the following services: outreach and referral, 15,201; medical, 2,398; dental, 336; other, 2,683 (total of 20,618). In July of that year the Health Center also separated from the NAIA and incorporated as the Michigan Urban Indian

Health Council. The next year offices were moved to the Detroit Medical Center Complex on Woodward Avenue. By 1984 the outpatient clinic, whose financing sources totaled $231,000, provided a comprehensive health program for the Indian community. This included medical, dental, pharmacy, mental health, optometric, and social services (Project Overview [on file at Michigan Urban Indian Health Council] and Program Background and History, enclosed in Ellie Webster [of the American Indian Health Care Association] to Program Directors, Urban Indian Health Programs, August 15, 1984 [on file at Michigan Urban Indian Health Council]).

65. Jane Johnson, PI, February 27, 1981, Detroit; George McMahon, PI, February 26, 1981, Detroit.

66. Alberts, PI, July 23 and 27, August 3 and 29, 1977; June 20, 1978; March 28, 1979; January 29 and February 26, 1981, Detroit. See also *Native Sun:* November 1975, February 1976, March 1976.

67. Thomas Hobbes, *Leviathan,* part I, chapter 13, quoted in John Bartlett, *Familiar Quotations,* ed. Emily Morison Beck (14th ed., Boston, 1968), 318.

68. Severt, PI, April 3 and 16, May 21, 1980, Detroit; *Native Sun,* May 1980.

69. Johnson, PI, March 27, 1981, Detroit.

70. Ibid.

71. Ibid.

72. Ibid.; Mona Stonefish Jacobs, PI, March 1, 1980, Detroit; Lance White, PI, January 29, 1981, Detroit.

73. Johnson, PI, March 27, 1981, Detroit.

74. Hirneisen, "Indians of Detroit."

75. Fred Boyd, PI, December 11, 1977, Detroit; Wulff, PI, February 22, 1978, Detroit.

NOTES TO CHAPTER 5

1. "Indian Education: A National Tragedy—A National Challenge. 1969 Report of the Committee on Labor and Public Welfare, United States Senate, Made by Its Special Subcommittee on Indian Education...." *Senate Report* no. 501, 91st Cong., Ist Sess. (serial 12836–1), 9, 21.

2. Estelle Fuchs and Robert J. Havighurst, *To Live on This Earth: American Indian Education* (Garden City, N.Y., 1973), 125, 134.

3. Governor's Commission on Indian Affairs, *A Study of the Socio–Economic Status of Michigan Indians,* 1971, p.10, quoted in Michigan Department of Education, *A Position Statement on Indian Education in Michigan, with Recommendations and Guidelines* (1973) (copy on file in State of Michigan Library, Lansing).

4. United States Bureau of the Census, *Census of Population: 1970 Volume I, Characteristics of the Population: Part 24, Michigan* (Washington, 1973), table 83: 307; United States Bureau of the Census, *Census of Population: 1970 ... American Indians,* table 11: 138.

5. Bashshur et al., *Native Americans in Wayne County,* 111, 114–17.

6. CETA Project, "Quarterly Summary of Participant Characteristics, October 1, 1979, to September 30, 1980" (copy on file at the DAIC).

7. Tom Daly, PI, March 12, 1981, Detroit; Charles Dobry, PI, March 12, 1981, Detroit; Cy Servetter, PI, March 26, 1981, Detroit.

8. Alberts, PI, February 5 and March 12, 1981, Detroit; West, "Adjustment of the American Indian in Detroit," 51; Bigony, "Migrants to the Cities," 135–36.

9. United States Bureau of the Census, *Census of Population: 1970 ... American Indians,* table 11: 138; United States Bureau of the Census, *Census of Population: 1970 ... Part 24. Michigan,* table 83: 307; Michigan Department of Education, *Indian Education in Michigan* (Lansing, 1973), 40, 54.

10. Sands, PI, April 23, 1980, Walpole Island; Left Hand quoted in Richard Hirneisen, "The Indians of Detroit," *Detroit Free Press,* June 3, 1973; Harry Command, PI, March 1, 1979, Bowling Green, Ohio.

11. For example, see Bigony, "Migrants to the Cities," 103–5.

12. Quoted in Pawlick, "Abandonment of the Indians in Detroit's Red Ghetto."

13. Dobry, PI, March 12, 1981, Detroit; Cy Servetter, PI, March 26, 1981, Detroit.

14. Glass, "A Descriptive and Comparative Study of American Indian Children in Detroit Public Schools," 237–38.

15. Quoted in Pawlick, "Abandonment of the Indian in Detroit's Red Ghetto."

16. Quoted in Northrup, "Pan–Indianism in the Metropolis," 146.

17. Ibid., 163–64; Luise Leismer, "Indians Plan Scholarship Fundraiser," *Detroit* News, June 10, 1972; *Native Sun,* May 1980.

18. Quoted in Hirneisen, "The Indians of Detroit."

19. Quoted in Pawlick, "Abandonment of the Indians in Detroit's Red Ghetto."

20. Wright, PI, June 4, 1981, Detroit.
21. Don Lenhausen, "Indian Wins Bid to Keep Hair Long," *Detroit Free Press*, April 15, 1972; William Schuyler Case, Fred Boyd Papers.
22. Cathy Trost, "'Annie Get Your Gun' is No Hit with Indians," *Detroit Free Press*, February 8, 1978; Cathy Trost, "Indians Win Fight: 'Annie' Is Cancelled," *Detroit Free Press*, February 11, 1978; Westland City Council resolution, in Wayne–Westland Case, Fred Boyd Papers.
23. *Detroit Free Press, May 4, 1979.*
24. Quoted in Pawlick, "Abandonment of the Indian in Detroit's Red Ghetto."
25. Daly, PI, March 12, 1981, Detroit.
26. Servetter, PI, March 26, 1981, Detroit; Charles Dobry, PI, March 12, 1981, Detroit.
27. McMahon, PI, March 26 and May 7, 1981, Detroit.
28. Kern, PI, June 5, 1981, Plymouth, Mich.; Collette Schott, PI, June 4, 1981, Detroit; Maria Rodriques, PI, December 5, 1980, and May 14 and June 4, 1981, Detroit.
29. Sorkin, *Urban American Indian,* 97–98.
30. "Indian Education: A National Tragedy—A National Challenge," 105–6.
31. "Special Message to Congress on Indian Affairs, July 8, 1970," *Public Papers of the Presidents of the United States, Richard Nixon. Containing the Public Messages, Speeches, and Statements of the President, 1970* (Washington, 1971), 565; U.S., *Statutes at Large,* 86:335.
32. U.S., *Statutes at Large,* 86: 340.
33. Ibid., 335, 337.
34. Ibid., 343–44.
35. U.S., *Statutes at Large,* 88: 2203–17; 92: 2313–33.
36. Detroit Public Schools' Office of Federal, State and Special Programs, Program Development Department, grant proposal for Detroit Indian Educational and Cultural Center (March 11, 1974), appendix B (on file with Detroit Public Schools, Program Development Department).
37. Ibid.; Beusterien, PI, May 7, 1981, Detroit; Dean and Shirley George, PI, May 28, 1981, Detroit.
38. Detroit Public Schools, grant proposal (March 11, 1974), 5–6.
39. Ibid., 10.
40. Mays, PI, January 10 and March 14, 1979, Detroit.
41. Mays, PI, January 10, 1979, Detroit.
42. Detroit Public School's Office of Federal, State and Special Programs,

Program Development Department, grant proposal for the DIECC (February 20, 1976), 25 (on file with Detroit Public Schools, Program Development Department).

43. These grant applications, which contained program goals, are on file with Detroit Public Schools, Office of Federal, State and Special Programs, Program Development Department.
44. Ibid.
45. Addendum to 1977–78 grant proposal for the DIECC, ibid., 1; Command, PI, October 7, 1981, Detroit.
46. Grant proposal for the DIECC, 1976–77, ibid., 14.
47. Ibid., 28–29.
48. Student demographic data, from which the author made these calculations, is on file with Detroit Public Schools.
49. Mays, PI, March 14, 1979, Detroit.
50. Beusterien, PI, May 7, 1981, Detroit; Mays, PI, December 16, 1981, Detroit.
51. Dean George, PI, May 28, 1981, Detroit.
52. Mays, PI, January 10, 1979, Detroit.
53. Detroit Public School's Office of Federal, State and Special Programs, Program Development Department, grant proposal for the DIECC (February 15, 1979), addendum and appendix D (on file with Detroit Public Schools, Program Development Department).
54. Beusterien, PI, May 7, 1981, Detroit.
55. Ibid.
56. Ibid.
57. Charles Green, "Evaluation of DIECC, 1975–76" (on file with Detroit Public Schools, Program Development Department), 42.
58. "Indian Education Grant Performance Report, 1976–1977," ibid., 9.
59. Annual evaluations are on file with the Detroit Public Schools, Program Development Department.
60. Ibid.
61. Curriculum vitae of John Douglas Jeter, December 11, 1980 (on file with the author).
62. General information for this and following paragraphs was drawn from the field notes of the author, who was a participant–observer in Jeter's classes between October 18, 1980, and May 30, 1981.
63. Jeter, PI, December 6 and 13, 1980, Detroit.
64. Ibid.
65. Jeter, PI, December 13, 1980, and March 14, 1981, Detroit.
66. Mingo, PI, January 31, 1981, Dearborn.

67. Author's field notes, November 28, 1979.
68. Ron Ishoy, "U.S. Helps Kids Learn Indian Heritage," *Detroit Free Press,* October 16, 1977; Southeast Michigan Indian Population (on file at American Indian Heritage Center, Central Middle School, Plymouth).
69. Roslyn McCoy, PI, May 14, 1981, Wayne–Westland; Chris M. Ziegler, "1979–1980 Final Evaluation Report, Wayne-Westland Community Schools, Indian Education Project, Title IV—Part A," 2 (on file at Indian Education Center, Nankin Mills Junior High School).
70. Ziegler, "1979–1980 Final Evaluation Report," 16, 19, 122.
71. Smith, PI, May 15, 1981, Plymouth-Canton; Mays, PI, October 3, 1979, Detroit.
72. DAIC brochure (on file at the DAIC); Patrick Bingham, "Final Report, Project Good Start, an Indian Education Act, Title IV, Part B Grant, June, 1976" (on file at the DAIC), 1.
73. Bingham, "Final Report," 1.
74. U.S., *Statutes at Large* 86: 342.
75. DAIC *Newsletter,* June 1975; Muriel Youngblood Report on Title IV–Part C of the Indian Education Act (May 1975), Fred Boyd Papers.
76. *Native Sun,* September 1980, 6.
77. State Representative Jackie Vaughn III to friends and supporters, July 16, 1976, Fred Boyd Papers; *Michigan State News* (East Lansing), July 2, 1976; DAIC *Newsletter,* October 1976; *Michigan Compiled Laws Annotated* 18 (supp. 1982–1983): 128–29.
78. Vaughn to friends, July 16, 1976.
79. Quoted in *Native Sun,* November 1978.
80. Public Act 1978, no. 505, *Michigan Compiled Laws Annotated* 18 (supp. 1982–1983): 128–29. Between 1976 and 1983, the Michigan Commission on Indian Affairs certified 2, 522 natives for college tuition waivers. The state's appropriation for this program in 1983 was $692,000 (Director of Michigan Commission on Indian Affairs William A. LeBlanc to author, October 12, 1983; in author's files).
81. Goeman, PI, May 9, 1978, Ann Arbor.
82. UPI, "Dropouts Total 2/3 of Students," Bowling Green, Ohio, *Daily Sentinel–Tribune,* December 26, 1981.
83. Omnibus Education Reconciliation Act of 1981 (Public Law 97–35), August 13, 1981; U.S., *Statutes at Large* 95: 448.
84. Command, PI, April 3, 1981, Detroit.
85. Bashshur et al., *Health Care of Urban Indians,* table 9–1: 343–44.
86. Memberto, PI, August 2, 1978, Detroit; Crooks, PI, July 18, 1977, Detroit.

NOTES TO CHAPTER 6

1. DeView, "Urban Indians."
2. Urban Indian Affairs brochures (on file at Urban Indian Affairs).
3. For more on AIS, see chap. 4.
4. Quoted in Bigony, "Migrants to the Cities," 150.
5. Lucille DeView, "Indian Women Carry Bittersweet Burdens," *Detroit News*, October 21, 1973; Tom Nugent, "Leave Us Alone."
6. See chap. 2 for more on the Indians of North America Foundation.
7. DeView, "Urban Indians."
8. Nugent, "Leave Us Alone."
9. Lucero, PI, November 18, 1977, and December 5, 1979, Detroit.
10. U.S., *Statutes at Large*, 92: 3069–78.
11. Select Committee on Indian Affairs, U.S. Senate, *Budget Views and Estimates for Fiscal Year 1983: A Report Submitted to the Budget Committee*, 87th Cong., 2d Sess., 1982, 28.
12. Hirneisen, "The Indians of Detroit."
13. Schott, PI, November 8, 1983, Detroit.
14. Kawegoma, PI, April 10, 1984, Detroit.
15. Giles, PI, January 8, 1981, Detroit.
16. Jacobs, PI, July 30 and August 29, 1977, Detroit.
17. La Roque, "Letter to the Editor," *Native Sun*, January–February 1981; Stonefish, PI, July 30, 1977, Detroit.
18. Facts for the following four paragraphs were drawn from the field notes of the author who, between 1977 and 1988, was a participant-observer at the DAIC.
19. Carman Garcia, PI, November 15, 1983, Detroit.
20. *Native Sun*, January–February 1978.
21. Ibid., April and August, 1975.
22. Thurman Bear quoted in Pawlick, "Abandonment of the Indian in Detroit's Red Ghetto."
23. Lucero, PI, July 27, 1977, Detroit; 1977 powwow memorabilia in possession of author.
24. Powwow memorabilia in possession of author.
25. White, PI, October 16, 1980, Detroit; Bearskin, PI, December 14, 1982, Detroit.
26. Quoted in Pawlick, "Abandonment of the Indian in Detroit's Red Ghetto."
27. DIECC, Honor Our Children Powwow Souvenir Program, June 12 and 13, 1982 (on file with author).

28. Rick Smith, "Strangers to the City," in Susan C. Farkas, ed., *Changes and Challenges: City Schools in America* (Washington, 1983), 54.
29. For more on the DIECC, see chap. 5.
30. Bearskin, PI, December 12, 1980; January 9 and February 5, 1981, Detroit.
31. Drawn from the author's field notes.
32. U.S. Bureau of the Census, *1980: Census of Population, Volume I. Characteristics of the Population, Chapter A: Number of Inhabitants, Part 24, Michigan* (Washington, 1982), table 2:8 and table 15:31; U.S. Bureau of the Census, *Census of Population: 1970, Volume I: Characteristics of the Population; Part 24. Michigan,* table 34:178–79.
33. Sandy Tomilenko, "Center Gives Food, Funds, Advice, and Hope to Indians," *Detroit Free Press,* January 12, 1984; *Talking Peace Pipe,* July 1983.
34. Allison, PI, December 13, 1983, Detroit; *Talking Peace Pipe,* January 1983; Tomilenko, "Center Gives Food."
35. Allison, PI, December 13, 1983, Detroit; Tomilenko, "Center Gives Food."
36. Joseph H. Strauss, Bruce Chadwick, Howard M. Bahr, Lowell K. Halverson, "An Experimental Outreach Legal Aid Program for an Urban Native Population Utilizing Legal Paraprofessionals," *Human Organization* 38 (winter 1979): 386–87.
37. *Native Sun,* August 1977; Urban Indian Affairs brochure (on file at Urban Indian Affairs).
38. *Native Sun,* November 1977 and January–February 1978.
39. Urban Indian Affairs brochure (on file at Urban Indian Affairs).
40. Boyd, PI, July 23, August 1 and 8, 1977; December 19, 1978; May 15, 1981, Detroit; *Native Sun,* March 1979; Frank Angelo, "Champion of Native American Rights," *Detroit Free Press,* May 2, 1979.
41. Northrup, "Pan–Indianism in the Metropolis," 169–71.
42. Boyd, PI, August 1, 1977; November 3, 1978; January 10, 1979, Detroit.
43. NASS brochures, Boyd Papers; Boyd, PI, August 1, 1977, and January 1, 1979, Detroit.
44. Ciarmitaro to Dean George, December 12, 1972, Boyd Papers; "Museum Ruling: Indians Win, Skeleton Goes," *Detroit Free Press,* February 2, 1973; Chronological Order of Events Concerning U of M, enclosed in Dean George to George Bennett (March 1973), Boyd Papers.
45. "Museum Ruling: Indians Win, Skeleton Goes."

46. Ibid. Boyd, PI, November 3, 1978, and January 10, 1979, Detroit; Detroit Historical Museum Director Solon Weeks to Detroit Common Council, February 5, 1973, Boyd Papers; Chronological Order of Events Concerning U of M.

47. "Indians Want U–M to Return Ancient Skeleton," *Detroit Free Press,* February 16, 1973; *Detroit News,* February 27, 1973; "Militants' Protests Succeed: U-M Yields Indians Remains," *Detroit News,* March 3, 1973; Chronological Order of Events Concerning U of M; Boyd, PI, January 10, 1979, Detroit.

48. Boyd, PI, January 10, 1979, Detroit; "Militants' Protests Succeed"; Chronological Order of Events Concerning U of M.

49. George to Bennett [March, 1973], Boyd Papers.

50. Clark Hallas, "Indians File Suit to Halt Digging of Burial Grounds," *Detroit News,* December 5, 1973; Donald Parish, Fred Dakota, Jake McCullough, Willis Jackson, Jr., Fred Boyd, and John Muse vs. The University of Michigan and The Michigan Archeological Society, Boyd Papers; Boyd, PI, January 10, 1979, Detroit. The law that the Indians claimed to be discriminatory was Act No. 328, *Public Acts of Michigan, 1931,* Section 160 (MCLA 750.160). The case was dismissed because the plaintiffs based their suit on 42 USC 1983, which applied only to legal action against persons, not state universities or an organization like the Michigan Archaeological Society (Case No. 4–70757, U. S. District Court for the Eastern District of Michigan, Southern Region).

51. Boyd, PI, January 10, 1979, Detroit; Vaughn to Boyd, April 26, 1974, Boyd Papers; James R. Hillman to Boyd and Muse, May 2, 1974, Boyd Papers; Boyd to PMS Michigan ICEP, June 19, 1974, Boyd Papers; Public Act 168, approved June 23, 1974, in Legislative Service Bureau, comp., *Public and Local Acts of the Legislature of the State of Michigan Passed at the Regular Session of 1974....* (Lansing, 1974), 378.

52. Jane Briggs–Bunting, "Oakland Township Bones Could be 1,000 Years Old," *Detroit Free Press,* November 10, 1977.

53. Drawn from author's field notes.

54. Ibid.

55. Boyd, telephone PI, November 28, 1977; Barbara Doerr, "U.S. Asked to Mediate Indian Row with University on Burial Site," *Detroit News,* November 29, 1977.

56. Barbara Doerr, "Oakland University Will Release Bones to Indians," *Detroit News,* November 30, 1977.

57. Based on author's field notes; copy of Boyd speech, Boyd Papers.

NOTES TO CHAPTER 6

58. Michigan Legislature, Senate Concurrent Resolution No. 91 ... of Tribute for Mr. Frederick Boyd, March 1979, Boyd Papers; Detroit City Council, Testimonial Resolution, June 11, 1979, Boyd Papers; *Native Sun,* June 1979.
59. Following six paragraphs are based on Silvey, PI, June and July 20, 1977; October 23, 1980; May 28, 1981; December 14, 1982; January 4, 1983, Detroit.
60. Tax, "The Impact of Urbanization on American Indians," *Annals of the American Academy of Political and Social Science* 436 (March 1978): 134–35; Yinger and Simpson, "The Integration of Americans of Indian Descent," 145.
61. Howard M. Bahr, "An End of Invisibility," in Bahr, Bruce A. Chadwick, Robert C. Day, eds., *Native Americans Today: Sociological Perspectives* (New York, 1972), 410.

NOTES TO CHAPTER 7

1. Cited in Bigony, "Migrants to the Cities," table 6: 108.
2. Bashshur et al., *Native Americans in Wayne County,* 30–32.
3. Ibid., photocopied from pp. 73 and 74.
4. Based on table 2–1: Indian Population, Selected Cities, 1960, 1970, and 1976, in Sorkin, *Urban American Indian,* 11.
5. Lyndon B. Johnson, "Special Message to Congress on the Problems of the American Indian: 'The Forgotten American,'" *Public Papers of the Presidents of the United States. Lyndon B. Johnson. Containing Public Messages, Speeches, and Statements of the President, 1968–69* (Washington, 1970), 335–44; Nixon, "Special Message to Congress on Indian Affairs," 572–73; Task Force Eight, *Final Report,* 7.
6. Prafulla Neog, Richard G. Woods, and Arthur M. Harkins, *Chicago Indians: The Effects of Urban Migration,* Training Center for Community Programs, University of Minnesota (Minneapolis, 1970), 1–2, 6; League of Women Voters of Minnesota, *Indians in Minnesota* (St. Paul, 1974), 40.
7. Mary Ellen Sloan, *Indians in an Urban Setting: Salt Lake County, Utah* (1972), American West Center Occasional Paper No. 2, University of Utah (Salt Lake City, 1973), 8–10.
8. Joann Westerman, "The Urban Indian," *Current History* 67 (December 1974): 261; Sorkin, *Urban American Indian,* 13, 16–18, 20–22.

230

9. Neog, et al., *Chicago Indians*, 2, 42; League of Women Voters, *Indians in Minnesota*, 33, 96; Prodipto Roy, "The Measurement of Assimilation: The Spokane Indians," in Bahr et al., *Native Americans Today*, 236.

10. Theodore D. Graves, "The Personal Adjustment of Navajo Indian Migrants to Denver, Colorado," *American Anthropologist* 72 (1970): 52; Robert S. Weppner, "Urban Economic Opportunities: The Example of Denver," in Jack O. Waddell and O. Michael Watson, eds., *The American Indian in Urban Society* (Boston, 1971), 246.

11. Sorkin, *Urban American Indian*, 49–50, 52.

12. Sloan, *Indians in an Urban Setting*, 37; League of Women Voters, *Indians in Minnesota*, 39.

13. Sorkin, *Urban American Indian*, 23; League of Women Voters, *Indians in Minnesota*, 39.

14. Sorkin, *Urban American Indian*, 18.

15. "Special Message to Congress on Indian Affairs," 576; Kate Winslow, "The Last Stand?" *American Indian Journal* 6 (September 1980): 11.

16. Sorkin, *Urban American Indian*, 110–11.

17. Task Force Eight, *Final Report*, 41.

18. Sorkin, *Urban American Indian*, 39.

19. Testimony of George I. Lythcott, M.D., of the Public Health Service, in *Hearing before Select Committee on Indian Affairs*, U.S. Senate, 96th Cong., 2d Sess., 1980, on Reauthorization of the Indian Health Care Improvement Act (Public Law 94–437), 256.

20. Statement of John James of the American Indian Health Care Association, Minneapolis, Minn., ibid., 31–35; statement of Don Aragon, in *Hearing before the Select Committee on Indian Affairs*, U.S. Senate, 96th Cong., 2d Sess., 1980, on Oversight of Indian Health Services, Appendix—part 2, 1980, 792; statement of John James, ibid., part 1, 502.

21. Office of Planning, Budgeting, and Evaluation, U.S. Department of Health, Education and Welfare—Office of Education, *Annual Evaluation Report on Programs Administered by the U.S. Office of Education: FY 1975*, 471.

22. Sorkin, *Urban American Indian*, 98–99, 103; statement of the Commissioner of Education on Indian Education, *Hearings before a Subcommittee of the Committee on Appropriations*, U.S. House of Representatives, 96th Cong., 1st Sess., part 7 on Department of the Interior and Related Agencies Appropriations for 1980, 1077.

23. Select Committee on Indian Affairs, U.S. Senate, *Budget Views and*

Estimates for Fiscal Year 1983, 48–49.

24. Rose Silvey, PI, August 5, 1983, Detroit.

25. American Indian Policy Review Commission, *Final Report Submitted to Congress May 17, 1977* (Washington, 1977), 1–2.

26. Parman, "American Indians and the Bicentennial," 262; Havighurst, "Indian Education Since 1960," *Annals of the American Academy of Political and Social Science* 436 (March 1978): 14.

27. De Loria, "Legislation and Litigation Concerning American Indians," ibid., 96.

28. Onciota, "Draft Report on the Walpole Island Band" (on file at WIRC, June 1985); "Band Farm to Increase Acreage," *Chatham Daily News,* March 24, 1983; Chief William Tooshkenig, "Development on Walpole Island, Now and in the Future," in Van Wyck, ed., *Walpole Island,* 36.

29. Charles and Mavis Jacobs, PI, October 12, 1982, Walpole Island; *Jibkenyan* (December 17, 1982; August 26, 1983; October 14, 1983; March 14, 1984; October 19, 1984); "Walpole Industries: An Indian Band Owned Mould and Die Makers Plant" (brochure on file with author); Dean M. Jacobs and Chief William Tooshkenig, "Environmental Assessment on the Walpole Island Indian Reserve in Southwestern Ontario, Canada, prepared for Workshop on Environmental Impact Assessment Procedures, March 27–29, Wellington, New Zealand" (on file at WIRC), 12; "Walpole Island Home of Area's Most Progressive Indian Band," Wallaceburg *Courier Press,* February 6, 1985.

30. *Jibkenyan:* October 31, 1981; October 14, 1983; September 21, 1984; September 20 and October 18, 1985.

31. "Natives' Living Standard Back in '50s: Census," *Globe and Mail,* December 13, 1983; Siggner, "A Socio-Demographic Profile of Indians in Canada," in J. Rick Ponting and Roger Gibbins, *Out of Irrelevance: A Socio-Political Introduction to Indian Affairs in Canada* (Toronto, 1980), 62.

32. Onciota, "Draft Report on the Walpole Island Band." A 1984 survey revealed that 850 families occupied 359 dwellings, an average of 2.3 families per household (*Jibkenyan,* August 3, 1984).

33. Hazel W. Hertzberg, "Reaganomics on the Reservation," *The New Republic,* November 22, 1982, 16–18.

34. Francis Paul Prucha, *The Great Father: The United States Government and the American Indians* II (Lincoln, 1984): 1192–93.

35. DAIC, Grant Proposal for Social and Economic Development,

Submitted to Administration for Native Americans, Department of Health and Human Services, June 29, 1985 (on file at the DAIC).

36. Ibid.; DAIC, Grant Proposal to Archdiocese of Detroit's Campaign for Human Development, Submitted March 31, 1981 (DAIC, board of directors minutes, April 4, 1981).

37. NAIA, Grant Proposal for Social and Economic Development, June 29, 1985.

38. Tom Marzejon (DAIC economic development coordinator), PI, March 22, 1985, Detroit.

39. NAIA, Grant Proposal for Social and Economic Development, June 29, 1985.

40. Ibid.

41. Ibid.

42. George to editor, *Talking Peace Pipe*, March 1985; author's field notes for April 27, 1985.

43. Command, PI, April 3 and May 28, 1981; March 22, 1985, Detroit.

44. Silvey, PI, August 5, 1983, Detroit.

45. Bearskin, PI, August 5, 1983, Detroit.

>>> BIBLIOGRAPHY <<<

I. PRIMARY SOURCES

Personal Interviews (in Detroit unless otherwise indicated)
Akiwenzie, Vivian: February 27, 1981.
Alberts, Frank: 1977 (July 23, July 27, August 3, August 29); 1978 (June 20); 1979 (March 28); 1981 (January 9, January 16, January 29, February 5, February 26, March 12).
Allison, Jeanette: December 13, 1983.
Arriaga, Winona: 1979 (February 24); 1980 (February 29); 1981 (February 6–7, Pigeon, Michigan).
Bearkskin, Ben, Jr.: 1980 (December 12); 1981 (January 9, February 5); 1982 (December 14); 1983 (August 5).
Beaulieu, Edith: October 20, 1978.
Belleau, Jerry: October 30, 1980.
Beusterien, Harry: May 7, 1981.
Blackbird, Jennie: Oral History Project Interview (September, 1978–March, 1979), WIRC.
Boyd, Fred: 1977 (July 23, August 1, August 8, November 28, December 11); 1978 (November 3, December 19); 1979 (January 1, January 10); 1980 (October 24); 1981 (May 15).

Chakur, Gail: 1978 (July 14, August 9); 1979 (January 31); 1981 (February 20).

Colwell, Bill: April 23, 1980, Walpole Island Indian Reserve.

Command, Harry: 1977 (December 7, December 12, December 14, December 17); 1978 (May 17, June 28, September 13); 1979 (March 1, Bowling Green, Ohio, and November 7); 1981 (January 15, April 3, May 28, October 7); 1985 (March 22).

Crooks, Bobby: July 18, 1977.

Daly, Tom: March 12, 1981.

Dashner, Mike: October 28, 1977.

David, John: 1979 (October 24, November 11).

David, Leona Bailey: June 20, 1979.

Davis, Ruth: January 15, 1981.

DeLeary, Ron: May 21, 1981.

Dobry, Charles: March 12, 1981.

Dockstader, Martin: July 30, 1977.

Fisher, Roseline: March 23, 1980, Walpole Island Indian Reserve.

Garcia, Carman: November 15, 1983.

Garcia, Rolando: August 31, 1977.

George, Dean: 1977 (Spring, October 28, December 14); 1978 (February 8, February 15); 1981 (May 28).

George, Sharon: April 26, 1985.

Giles, Ron: January 8, 1981.

Goeman, Dorothy: May 9, 1978, Ann Arbor, Michigan.

Hillman, James: 1978 (August 9, September 13); 1979 (December 12); 1980 (October 9).

Iron Shell, Gene: 1977 (December 20); 1978 (January 4, February 22, March 8, March 29, May 29).

Iron Shell, Shirley: 1978 (September 13, September 22, September 29).

Isaac-Halfday, Linda: December 5, 1980.

Jacobs, Burton: February 9, 1980, Walpole Island Indian Reserve.

Jacobs, Charles and Mavis: 1980 (March 23, October 2); 1981 (May 21); 1982 (October 12); 1983 (October 18), all on Walpole Island Indian Reserve.

Jacobs, Dean M.: July 19–20, 1979, Walpole Island Indian Reserve.

Jacobs, Mona Stonefish: 1977 (July 30, August 29); 1980 (March 1).

Jeter, John: 1980 (December 6, December 13); 1981 (March 14).

Johnson, Jane: 1980 (October 10); 1981 (February 27, March 27, December 13).

Kawegoma, Carol Coulon: 1979 (May 2); 1980 (June 27); 1984 (April 10).

Kern, Father Clement: June 5, 1981, Plymouth, Michigan.

Kiser, Myrtle: 1977 (summer); 1980 (October 17).

Kiyoshk, Martin: 1980 (April 9); 1981 (January 15–16).

La Pointe, John: August 3, 1977.

Lowry, Irene: April 12, 1978.

Lucero, Teofilo: 1977 (June, July 27, November 18); 1979 (May 30, November 5, December 5); 1981 (May 15); 1982 (May 17, Bowling Green, Ohio).

Marzejon, Tom: March 22, 1985.

Mays, Judy: 1979 (January 10, March 14, October 3); 1981 (December 16).

McCoy, Roslyn: May 14, 1981.

McMahon, George: 1981 (February 26, March 26, May 7).

Memberto, William: 1978 (August 2); 1980 (May 14).

Mesheky, Joe: 1980 (October 23, October 30, November 21, December 12).

Mingo, Jackie: January 31, 1981, Dearborn, Michigan.

Montour, Frank: 1977 (summer, July 27, August 17, October 21).

Montour, Jerry: November 21, 1980.

Morales, Louise: November 3, 1978.

Pedrotti, Carleen: summer, 1977.

Rodd, Cecil: December 4, 1980, Romulus, Michigan.

Rodriquez, Maria: 1980 (December 5); 1981 (May 14, June 4).

Sands, Clayton: Oral History Project Interview (September, 1978–March, 1979), WIRC.

Sands, Priscilla: April 23, 1980, Walpole Island Indian Reserve.

Schott, Collette: 1981 (June 4); 1982 (September 16, October 19); 1983 (November 8, December 13).

Sebastian, Elmer: October 30, 1980.

Servetter, Cy: March 26, 1981.

Severt, Cary: 1977 (September 23, October 21); 1980 (April 3, April 16, May 21).

Shampine, Arlene: 1977 (October 21, November 4, November 11, December 20); 1978 (October 27); 1979 (March 28); 1980 (March 1); 1981 (January 29).

Silvey, Rose: 1977 (June, July 20); 1980 (October 23, December 12); 1981 (May 28); 1982 (December 14); 1983 (January 4, August 5).

Smith, Andrea: 1977 (October 28); 1981 (January 15).

Smith, Rick: May 15, 1981, Plymouth, Michigan.

Staats, Elsie: July 20, 1977.

White, Lance: 1980 (October 16); 1981 (January 29).

Wright, Russ: 1977 (December 2); 1980 (October 10, December 5); 1981 (June 4).

Wulff, Rod: 1977 (December 20); 1978 (February 22, April 5, May 17, July 26); 1979 (April 18, October 24).

Private Papers; Records of Organizations, Tribes, and Bands

AIS. Native American Alcoholism Therapist Training Program File. On file at AIS.

Bashshur, Rashid et al. *Health Care of Urban Indians in Michigan. Volume One: Assessment of Health Needs among Indians in Wayne County.* Ann Arbor: Produced for NAIA by Department of Medical Care Organization, School of Public Health, University of Michigan, 1981.

———. *Native Americans in Wayne County, Michigan: Cultural, Demographic, and Housing Characteristics.* Ann Arbor: Produced for NAIA by Department of Medical Care Organization, School of Public Health, University of Michigan, 1979.

Boyd, Fred. Papers. Photocopies in the author's files.

Brigham, Patrick. *Final Report, Project Good Start, an Indian Education Act.* Title IV, Part B Grant, June, 1976. On file at the DAIC.

Chosa, Amy D., and H. James St. Arnold. *Overall Economic Development Plan for the Keweenaw Bay Indian Community.* On file at Tribal Community Center, Baraga, Michigan, 1974.

DAIC Board of Directors. Minutes, 1973–1985. On file at the DAIC.

DAIC, CETA Program. Quarterly Summary of Participant Characteristics. On file at the DAIC.

DAIC. Grant Proposal to Archdiocese of Detroit's Campaign for Human Development, Submitted March 31, 1981. On file with board of directors minutes, April 14, 1981, DAIC.

———. Grant Proposal for Social and Economic Development, Submitted to Administration for Native Americans, Department of Health and Human Services, June 29, 1985. On file at the DAIC.

———. *Program Progress Review Report.* On file at the DAIC, December 1974.

———. *A Random Sample Survey of the Detroit Indian population in the Cass Corridor.* On file at the DAIC, July 1975.

Danziger, Edmund J., Jr. Detroit and Walpole Island Indian Reserve field notes, 1977–1988.

Detroit Indian Health Center. Annual Report: June 16, 1977, through May 31, 1978. On file at the DAIC.

———. Annual Report for Planning Contract Number 241-76-0463, June 16, 1976, through July 15, 1977. On file at the DAIC.

Harrington, Carolyn Hogg. "An Economic Survey of the Walpole Island Indian Reserve. A Cooperative Venture: Walpole Island Band Council and St. Clair Regional Development Association." On file at WIRC, 1965.

Huddleston, Paul. "Walpole Island Indian Reserve Number 46. Comprehensive Development Plan." On file at WIRC, 1978.

Jacobs, Dean M., and Chief William Tooshkenig. "Environmental Assessment on the Walpole Island Indian Reserve in Southwestern Ontario, Canada, prepared for Workshop on Environmental Impact Assessment Procedures, March 27–29, 1985, Wellington, New Zealand." On file at WIRC.

Jeter, John Douglas. "Curriculum Vitae of, December 11, 1980." On file with author.

Michigan Urban Indian Health Council. "Program Background and History," enclosed in Ellie Webster (of American Indian Health Care Association) to Program Directors, Urban Indian Health Programs, August 15, 1984. On file at Michigan Urban Indian Health Council.

———. "Project Overview." On file at Michigan Urban Indian Health Council.

National Council on Alcoholism—Greater Detroit Area. "Statement to Substance Advisory Commission for Wayne County, June 8, 1978." On file at AIS.

National Indian Brotherhood. *Indian Control of Indian Education. A Policy Paper Presented to the Minister of Indian Affairs and Northern Development.* On file at WIRC, 1972.

———. *A Strategy for the Socio–Economic Development of Indian People. Background Report Number 1.* On file at WIRC, 1977.

Onciota. "Draft Report on the Walpole Island Band." On file at WIRC, June 1985.

Ruggles, John, and Associates. *Isabella Reservation Household Survey.* Photocopy in author's files, August 1976.

"Southeast Michigan Indian Populations." On file at American Indian Heritage Center, Central Middle School, Plymouth, Michigan.

Wright, Russ. Speech on Occasion of NAIA 41st Anniversary Dinner, May 23, 1981. Copy in author's files.

Ziegler, Chris M. *1979–1980 Final Evaluation Report, Wayne-Westland Community School, Indian Education Project, Title IV—Part A.* On file at Indian Education Center, Nankin Mills Junior High School, Wayne-Westland, Michigan.

Public Documents: Federal, State, Local

American Indian Policy Review Commission. *Final Report Submitted to Congress May 17, 1977.* Washington: Government Printing Office, 1977.

Aragon, Don. Statement. U.S. Congress. Senate. Select Committee on Indian Affairs, *Oversight of Indian Health Services Appendix—Part 2,* 96th Cong., 2nd Sess., 1980, 780–93.

Detroit Neighborhood Services Department. '76 *Annual Report.* On file with author.

Detroit Public Schools, Office of Federal, State, and Special Programs, Program Development Department, DIECC File.

Education, United States Commissioner of. Statement. U.S. Congress House Committee on Appropriations. Part 7. *Department of the Interior and Related Agencies Appropriations for 1980,* 96th Cong., 1st Sess., 1980, 1068–1154.

HEW, Office of Education: Planning, Budgeting, and Evaluation Office. *Annual Evaluation Report on Programs Administered by the U.S. Office of Education: FY 1975.* Washington: Government Printing Office, 1975.

Indian Affairs, Governor's Commission on. *A Study of the Socio–Economic Status of Michigan Indians,* 1971, quoted in Michigan Department of Education, *Indian Education in Michigan.* Lansing, 1973.

Indian Affairs and Northern Development, Ministry of. *Indian Conditions: A Survey.* Ottawa: Ministry of Indian Affairs and Northern Development, 1980.

James, John. Statement. U.S. Congress. Senate. Select Committee on Indian Affairs. *Reauthorization of the Indian Health Care Improvement Act (Public Law 94–437),* 96th Cong., 2nd Sess., 1980, 17–118.

———. Statement. U.S. Congress. Senate. Select Committee on Indian Affairs. *Oversight of Indian Health Services, Appendix—Part 1,* 96th Cong., 2nd Sess., 1980, 501–5.

Johnson, Lyndon B. "Special Message to Congress on the Problems of the American Indian: 'The Forgotten American.'" *Public Papers of the Presidents of the United States. Lyndon B. Johnson. Containing the Public Messages, Speeches, and Statements of the President,* 1968–69. Washington: Government Printing Office, 1970, 335–44.

Legislative Service Bureau, comp. *Public and Local Acts of the Legislature of the State of Michigan Passed at the Regular Session of 1974....* Public Act 168, approved June 23, 1974. Lansing: Department of Management and Budget, 378.

Lythcott, George I., M.D. Statement. U.S. Congress. Senate. Select Committee on Indian Affairs. *Reauthorization of the Indian Health Care Improvement Act (Public Law 94–437)*, 96th Cong., 2nd Sess., 1980, 253–57.

Michigan Compiled Laws Annotated. Volume 18. Supplement 1982–1983. Public Act 1978, No. 505, 128–29.

Nixon, Richard M. "Special Message to the Congress on Indian Affairs. July 8, 1970." *Public Papers of the Presidents of the United States. Richard Nixon. Containing the Public Messages, Speeches, and Statements of the President.* 1970. Washington: Government Printing Office, 1971, 564–76.

Public Acts of Michigan, 1931. Section 160. (MCLA 750.160).

Task Force Eight: Urban and Rural Non-Reservation Indians. *Final Report to the American Indian Policy Review Commission.* Washington: Government Printing Office, 1976.

Task Force Eleven: Alcohol and Drug Abuse. *Final Report to the American Indian Policy Review Commission.* Washington: Government Printing Office, 1976.

U.S. Bureau of the Census. *Historical Statistics of the United States. Colonial Times to 1970.* Bicentennial Edition. Washington: Government Printing Office, 1970.

———. *Census of Population: 1970. Volume I. Characteristics of the Population: Part 24, Michigan.* Washington: Government Printing Office, 1973.

———. *Census of Population: 1970 Subject Reports, American Indians.* Washington: Government Printing Office, 1973.

———. *1980 Census of Population and Housing: Census Tracts, Detroit, Mich., Standard Metropolitan Statistical Area.* Washington: Government Printing Office, 1983.

———. *1980: Census of Population, Volume I. Characteristics of the Population. Chapter A: Number of Inhabitants, Part 24: Michigan.* Washington: Government Printing Office, 1982.

U.S. District Court, Eastern District of Michigan, Southern Region, Case No. 4-70757.

U.S. *Statutes at Large*, 84, 86, 87, 88, 90, 92, 95.

U.S. Congress. "Indian Education: A National Tragedy—A National Challenge. 1969 Report of the Committee on Labor and Public Welfare United States Senate. Made by Its Special Subcommittee on Indian Education. ..." *Senate Report* No. 501, 91st Cong., 1st Sess. (Serial 12836-1).

U.S. Congress. Senate. Select Committee on Indian Affairs. *Budget Views and Estimates for Fiscal Year 1983. A Report Submitted to the Budget Committee,* 87th Cong., 2d Sess., 1982.

Newsletters
Jibkenyan, 1978–85.
Native Sun, 1975–85.
Talking Peace Pipe, 1983–85.

Books
Meriam, Lewis et al. *The Problem of Indian Administration. Report of a Survey Made at the Request of Honorable Hubert Work, Secretary of the Interior, and Submitted to Him, February 21, 1928.* Institute for Government Research. Studies in Administration. Baltimore: Johns Hopkins Press, 1928.

Articles, Essays, and Poems
"Ethics of Indian People." *Moosetalk,* Winter 1961.
Jacobs, Burton. "The Indian Agent System and Our Move to Self-Government." Sheila M. Van Wyck, ed., *Walpole Island: The Struggle for Self-Sufficiency—A Panel Presentation.* Nin-Da-Waab-Jig Occasional Paper No. 3. Walpole Island Indian Reserve, 1984, 20–33.
———. "Walpole Island—Its Struggle for Identity." On file at WIRC (1969).
La Roque, Linda. "Letter to the Editor." *Native Sun,* January–February 1981.
Maxwell, Starr. Untitled poem. *Talking Peace Pipe,* September 1983.
Tooshkenig, Chief William. "Development on Walpole Island, Now and in the Future." Sheila M. Van Wyck, ed., *Walpole Island: The Struggle for Self-Sufficiency—A Panel Presentation.* Nin-Da-Waab-Jig Occasional Paper No. 3. Walpole Island Indian Reserve, 1984, 34–49.

Brochures (in the author's files)
"American Indian Services."
"Harry Command."
DAIC. "Detroit American Indian Center."
———. "1985 Services Available at the Detroit American Indian Center."
Detroit Bureau of Substance Abuse. "Drug and Alcoholism Treatment Centers."
DIECC. "Honor Our Children Powwow Souvenir Program, June 12 and 13, 1982."

"National Council on Alcoholism—Greater Detroit Area."
National Indian Brotherhood. "Full Circle: Health."
"Native American Alcoholism Therapist Training Program."
NAIA. "Salute to our Founder" in "Program for 37th Anniversary Dinner
    Dance, May 21, 1977."
"Sacred Heart Center."
Salvation Army Harbor Light Substance Abuse Treatment Center. "The
    Place of New Beginnings."
"Urban Indian Affairs."
"Walpole Industries: An Indian Band Owned Mold and Die Makers
    Plant."

Special
Le Blanc, William to author, October 12, 1983, in author's files.

II. SECONDARY WORKS

Books
Babson, Steve et al. *Working Detroit: The Making of a Union Town.* New
    York: Adama Books, 1984.
Bald, F. Clever. *Michigan in Four Centuries.* New York: Harper and Broth-
    ers, Publishers, 1954.
Frideres, James S. *Native People in Canada: Contemporary Conflicts.* Scarbor-
    ough, Ontario: Prentice-Hall of Canada Incorporated, 1983.
Fuchs, Estelle and Robert J. Havighurst. *To Live on This Earth: American
    Indian Education.* Garden City, N. Y.: Anchor Books, 1973.
Gibson, Arrell M. *The American Indian: Prehistory to the Present.* Lexington,
    Mass.: D. C. Heath and Company, 1980.
Holli, Melvin G., ed. *Detroit.* New York: New Viewpoints, 1976.
———. *Reform in Detroit: Hazen S. Pingree and Urban Politics.* New York:
    Oxford University Press, 1969.
Hyde, Charles K. *Detroit: An Industrial History Guide.* Detroit: Detroit His-
    torical Society, 1980.
Jenness, Diamond. *The Indians of Canada.* 6th ed. National Museum of
    Canada Bulletin 65, Anthropological Series No. 15. Ottawa: 1963.
Josephy, Alvin M., Jr. *Now That the Buffalo's Gone: A Study of Today's Ameri-
    can Indians.* New York: Alfred A. Knopf, 1982.

Madigan, La Verne. *The American Indian Relocation Program....* New York: Association of American Indian Affairs, Inc., 1956.

Nagler, Mark. *Indians in the City: A Study of the Urbanization of Indians in Toronto.* 2nd ed. Ottawa: Canadian Research Centre for Anthropology, Saint Paul University, 1973.

Neils, Elaine M. *Reservation to City: Indian Migration and Federal Relocation.* Chicago: University of Chicago Department of Geography, 1971.

Ponting, J. Rick, and Roger Gibbins. *Out of Irrelevance: A Socio-Political Introduction to Indian Affairs in Canada.* Toronto: Butterworth and Company Ltd., 1980.

Prucha, Francis Paul. *The Great Father: The United States Government and the American Indians.* 2 vols. Lincoln: University of Nebraska Press, 1984.

Sorkin, Alan L. *The Urban American Indian.* Lexington, Mass.: D. C. Heath and Company, 1978.

Thornton, Russell, Gary D. Sandefur, and Harold G. Grasmick. *The Urbanization of American Indians: A Critical Bibliography.* Bloomington: Indiana University Press, 1982.

Tyler, S. Lyman. *A History of Indian Policy.* Washington: United States Department of the Interior, Bureau of Indian Affairs, 1973.

Wallace, Anthony F. C. *The Death and Rebirth of the Seneca.* Vintage Book edition. New York: Vintage Books, Inc., 1972.

Women Voters of Minnesota, League of. *Indians in Minnesota.* St. Paul: North Central Publishing Company, 1974.

Wrobel, Paul. Our Way: Family, Parish, and Neighborhood in a Polish American Community. South Bend, Ind.: University of Notre Dame Press, 1979.

Articles

Acquaviva, Donna. "American Indian Study to Fight Their Worst Disease: Alcoholism." *Detroit News,* August 27, 1977.

———. "Indians Losing Center." *Detroit News,* May 9, 1975.

Angelo, Frank. "Champion of Native American Rights." *Detroit Free Press,* May 2, 1979.

Armstrong, O. D. and Marjorie. "The Indians Are Going to Town." *Reader's Digest* 68 (January 1955): 39–43.

Bahr, Howard M. "An End to Invisibility." In Bahr, Bruce A. Chadwick, and Robert C. Day, eds., *Native Americans Today: Sociological Perspectives.* New York: Harper and Row Publishers, 1972, 404–12.

"Band Farm to Increase Acreage." *Chatham Daily News,* March 24, 1983.

Bigony, Beatrice A. "A Brief History of Native Americans in the Detroit Area." *Michigan History* 61 (summer 1977): 13–63.

Briggs–Bunting, Jane. "Oakland Township Bones Could Be 1,000 Years Old." *Detroit Free Press,* November 10, 1977.

Coleman, John. "He's Serious about the Walpole Claim." *Windsor Star,* April 23, 1977.

De Loria, Vine, Jr. "Legislation and Litigation Concerning American Indians." *Annals of the American Academy of Political and Social Science* 436 (March 1978): 86–96.

Detroit Free Press, May 4, 1979.

Detroit News, January 1, 1976.

De View, Lucille. "Indian Women Carry Bittersweet Burdens." *Detroit News,* October 21, 1973.

———. "Urban Indians: A 'New Wave' with Old Roots." *Detroit Sunday News,* November 20, 1977.

Doerr, Barbara. "U.S. Asked to Mediate Indian Row with University at Burial Site." *Detroit News,* November 29, 1977.

Forbes, Jack. "Traditional Native American Philosophy and Multicultural Education." In *Multicultural Education and the American Indian.* Los Angeles: American Indian Studies Center, University of California at Los Angeles, 1979, 3–13.

Graves, Theodore. "The Personal Adjustment of Navajo Indian Migrants to Denver, Colorado." *American Anthropologist* 72 (February 1970): 35–54.

Hallas, Clark. "Indians File Suit to Halt Digging of Burial Grounds." *Detroit News,* December 5, 1973.

Hallett, Joe. "More Than New Name Involved as CETA Leaves, JTPA Arrives." Toledo *Blade,* October 1, 1983.

Havighurst, Robert J. "Indian Education Since 1960." *Annals of the American Academy of Political and Social Science* 436 (March 1978): 13–26.

Hertzberg, Hazel W. "Reaganomics on the Reservation." *New Republic,* November 22, 1982, 15–18.

Hirneisen, Richard. "The Indians of Detroit." *Detroit Free Press,* June 3, 1973.

"Indians Want U–M to Return Ancient Skeleton." *Detroit Free Press,* February 16, 1973.

Ishoy, Ron. "U.S. Helps Kids Learn Indian Heritage." *Detroit Free Press,* October 16, 1977.

Lazewski, Tony. "American Indian, Puerto Rican, and Black Urbanization . *Journal of Cultural Geography* 2 (spring/summer 1982): 119–34.

Leismer, Luise. "Indian Group Desires Center in Detroit to Share Heritage." *Detroit News,* March 15, 1972.

———. "Indians Plan Scholarship Fund-raiser." *Detroit News,* June 10, 1972.

Lenhausen, Don. "Indian Wins Bid to Keep Hair Long." *Detroit Free Press,* April 15, 1972.

Lurie, Nancy Oestreich. "The Contemporary American Indian Scene." In Eleanor Burke Leacock and Lurie, eds., *North American Indians in Historical Perspective.* New York: Random House, 1971, 418–80.

May, Jeanne. "Russ Wright: Dedicated to the Indian." *Detroit Free Press,* February 3, 1984.

Michigan State News (East Lansing), July 2, 1976.

"Militants' Protests Succeed: U-M Yields Indian Remains." *Detroit News,* March 3, 1973.

Morris, Julie, and Edward Shanahan. "City Poverty Awaits Many Indians Leaving Reservations." *Detroit Free Press,* April 28, 1970.

"Museum Ruling: Indians Win, Skeleton Goes." *Detroit Free Press,* February 2, 1973.

"Natives' Living Standard Back in '50s: Census." Toronto *Globe and Mail,* December 13, 1983.

New York Times, December 6, 1981.

Nugent, Tom. "Leave Us Alone: Detroit's Indian Population Caught between 2 Worlds." *Detroit Free Press,* February 20, 1972.

Parman, Donald L. "American Indians and the Bicentennial." In Roger L. Nichols, ed., *The American Indian: Past and Present.* 2nded. New York: John Wiley and Sons, 1980, 261–72.

Pawlick, Tom. 'The Abandonment of the Indian in Detroit's red ghetto." *Detroit News,* March 5, 1970.

Philp, Kenneth R. "Stride toward Freedom: the Relocation of Indians to the Cities, 1952–1960." *Western Historical Quarterly* 16 (April 1985): 175–90.

Roy, Prodipto. "'The Measurement of Assimilation: The Spokane Indians." In Howard M. Bahr, Bruce A. Chadwick, and Robert C. Day, eds., *Native Americans Today: Sociological Perspectives.* New York: Harper and Row Publishers, 1972, 225–39.

Siggner, Andrew J. "A Socio-Demographic Profile of Indians in Canada." In J. Rick Ponting and Roger Gibbins, *Out of Irrelevance: A Socio-Political Introduction to Indian Affairs in Canada.* Toronto: Butterworth and Company Ltd., 1980, 31–65.

Smith, Rick. "Strangers to the City?" In Susan C. Farkas, ed., *Changes and Challenges: City Schools in America*. Washington: Institute for Educational Leadership, 1983, 53–56.

Strauss, Joseph H., Bruce Chadwick, Howard M. Bahr, and Lowell K. Halverson. "An Experimental Outreach Legal Aid Program for an Urban Native Population Utilizing Legal Paraprofessionals." *Human Organization* 38 (winter 1979): 386–94.

Szasz, Margaret Connell. "Federal Boarding Schools and the Indian Child: 1920–1960." In Roger L. Nichols, ed., *The American Indian: Past and Present*. 2nd ed. New York: John Wiley and Sons, 1981, 214–23.

Tax, Sol. "The Impact of Urbanization on American Indians." *Annals of the American Academy of Political and Social Science* 436 (March 1978): 121–36.

Tomilenko, Sandy. "Center Gives Food, Funds, Advice, and Hope to Indians." *Detroit Free Press*, January 12, 1984.

Trost, Cathy. "'Annie Get Your Gun' Is No Hit with Indians." *Detroit Free Press*, February 8, 1978.

———. "Indians Win Fight; 'Annie' Is Canceled." *Detroit Free Press*, February 11, 1978.

Tschirhart, Don. "A Blighted Area Still Hopes." *Detroit News*, September 6, 1972.

United Press International, "Dropouts Total 2/3 of Students." Bowling Green, Ohio, *Sentinel-Tribune*, December 26, 1981.

Vogt, Evon Z. "The Acculturation of American Indians." *Annals of the American Academy of Political and Social Science* 311 (May 1957): 137–46.

Walker, George ("Chi"). Obituary. *Kalamazoo Gazette*, August 12, 1963.

"Walpole Island Home of Area's Most Progressive Band." *The Courier Press* (Wallaceburg, Ont.), February 6, 1985.

Weppner, Robert S. "Urban Economic Opportunities: The Example of Denver." In Jack W. Waddell and O. Michael Watson, eds., *The American Indian in Urban Society*. Boston: Little, Brown and Company, 1971, 244–73.

Westerman, Joann. "The Urban Indian." *Current History* 67 (December 1974): 259–62, 275.

Wilkenson, Charles F. "Shall the Islands Be Preserved?" *American West* 16 (May/June 1979): 33–37, 66–69.

Windsor Star, May 10, 1980.

Winfrey, Lee. "Cass Corridor: Where the Action Is." *Detroit Free Press*, February 3, 1973.

Winslow, Kate. "The Last Stand?" *American Indian Journal* 6 (September 1980): 2–11.

Yinger, J. Milton, and George E. Simpson. "The Integration of Americans of Indian Descent." *Annals of the American Academy of Political and Social Science* 436 (March 1978): 137–51.

Special

Hobbes, Thomas. *Leviathan,* part I, chap. 13. In John Bartlett, *Familiar Quotations...* ed. Emily Morison Beck. 14th ed. Boston: Little, Brown and Company, 1968, 317–18.

Neog, Prafulla, Richard G. Woods, and Arthur M. Harkins. *Chicago Indians: The Effects of Urban Migration.* Training Center for Community Programs, University of Minnesota. Minneapolis: 1970.

Oxenham, John. "The Ways." In Ted Malone, ed., *Pocket Book of Popular Verse.* New York: Pocket Books, Inc., 1945, 180.

Sloan, Mary Ellen. *Indians in an Urban Setting: Salt Lake County, Utah (1972).* American West Center Occasional Paper No. 2, University of Utah. Salt Lake City: 1973.

Unpublished

Bigony, Beatrice Anne. "Migrants to the Cities: A Study of the Socioeconomic Status of Native Americans in Detroit and Michigan." Ph.D. diss., University of Michigan, Ann Arbor, 1974.

Glass, Thomas E. "A Descriptive and Comparative Study of American Indian Children in the Detroit Public Schools." Ph.D. diss., Wayne State University, Detroit, 1972.

Northrup, Gordon Douglas. "Pan–Indianism in the Metropolis: A Case Study of an Emergent Ethno–syncretic Revitalization Movement." Ph.D. diss., Michigan State University, East Lansing, 1970.

West, Ralph L. "The Adjustment of the American Indian in Detroit: A Descriptive Study." Master's thesis, Wayne State University, Detroit, 1950.

$\gg\!\!\!\gg$ INDEX $\langle\!\langle\!\langle$

DeMarsh, Majel: on public ignorance about Indian, 142; on importance of powwows, 175
Detroit: Indian migration to, in twentieth century, 13–14, 22–23; general migration to, in twentieth century, 22–23, 208 n.14; Indian migration out of, by mid-nineteenth century, 17–18; rebuilding of, after 1805 fire, 24; 1970s downtown renaissance, 46; economic attractions of, 71–72; attractiveness of Walpole Island Indian reserve to tourists from, 71–72
Detroit American Indian Center (DAIC), 186; staff and budget of, 17, 203; founding of and early goals for, 39–41; offices of, 41–42, 43; directorship of Dean George, 41–43, personnel matters, 42, 45–46; assistance from HEW, 42, 44; federal funding for, 42; accounting procedures for, 42; Board of Directors activities, 42; 1975 survey of local Indian population, 42–43; education programs of, 43, 159–60; directorshp of Rose Silvey, 45, 187; directorship of James Hillman, 45; general services in 1980–81, 46; relations with Department of Labor, 95–96, 98, 217n. 49; housing program of, 129–31; social and cultural programs of, 165–75; directorship of Hank Bonga, 166; and Oakland University Indian rights controversy, 185; economic development plans of, 201–3; tribute to Elmer Sebastian, 203. *See also* Employment
Detroit American Indian Health

Center: founding of, 119; directorship of Bill Memberto, 125, 126–29; programs of, 125–29, 133; directorship of Bobby Crooks, 126; views of Ben Bearskin on, 129; services in 1980, 221–22 n.64
Detroit Board of Education, 147
Detroit Bureau of Substance Abuse, 116
Detroit Common Council: and Indian rights, 181
Detroit Department of Human Relations: and Indian rights, 44
Detroit Housing Commission, 130
Detroit Indian community: importance of, 12, 17, 191; problems by 1970, 13–14; progress by 1980, 14; population growth of, 23; survival and regeneration of, 24, 204–5; future of, 203–4. *See also* Adjustment to urban life; Employment; Health; Housing; Education; Social and cultural lives of Indians
Detroit Indian Educational and Cultural Center (DIECC): founding of, 147–48; goals of, 147–49; Judy Mays as Project Coorindator, 148–57, 162; curriculum of, 148–49, 153; budget of, 149, 151; educational strategies of, 150; students in its program, 151; Parent Committee role in, 152; assistance from Harry Beusterien, 153; evaluation of, 153–54; 156–57, 162; help from AIS, 154; experiences of teacher John Jeter, 155–56; problem of parental apathy toward, 156–57; and social-cultural regeneration, 175–76
Detroit Police Department: and Indian rights, 181

www.ingramcontent.com/pod-product-compliance
Lightning Source LLC
Chambersburg PA
CBHW050345270326
41926CB00016B/3601